Related Books o...

`D1647915`

Software Test Engineering with IBM Rational Functional Tester
The Definitive Resource

by Chip Davis et al
ISBN: 0-13-700066-9

"Finally, a manual for the Software Test Engineer! Many manuals on the market today are geared toward developers, and none exist for Rational Functional Tester. This is one of the first manuals geared toward the Automated Test Engineer acknowledging the depth of knowledge required for a very complex job. The manual will assist all levels of test engineering with very specific steps and hands-on advice. This manual is a reference book that no Automated Test Engineer using RFT should be without!"

—Penny Bowser, CTFL, CHE, QA Manager

Eight leading IBM testing experts thoroughly introduce this state-of-the-art product, covering issues ranging from building test environments through executing the most complex and powerful tests. Drawing on decades of experience with IBM Rational testing products, they address both technical and nontechnical challenges and present everything from best practices to reusable code.

Implementing the IBM Rational Unified Process and Solutions
A Guide to Improving Your Software Development Capability and Maturity

by Joshua Barnes
ISBN: 0-321-36945-9

This book delivers all the knowledge and insight you need to succeed with the IBM® Rational® Unified Process® and Solutions. Joshua Barnes presents a start-to-finish, best-practice roadmap to the complete implementation cycle of IBM RUP — from projecting ROI and making the business case through piloting, implementation, mentoring, and beyond.

Drawing on his extensive experience leading large-scale IBM RUP implementations and working with some of the industry's most recognized thought leaders in the Software Engineering Process world, Barnes brings together comprehensive "lessons learned" from both successful and failed projects. You'll learn from real-world case studies, including actual project artifacts.

Whether you're an executive, software professional, or consultant, this book will help you continuously improve the maturity of your development processes–and reap the benefits: better quality, faster delivery, and more business value.

Related Books of Interest

Requirements Management Using IBM Rational RequisitePro

by Peter Zielczynski Ph.D.

ISBN: 0-321-38300-1

Using IBM Rational RequisitePro®, you can systematically improve the way you create and maintain requirements — and use those requirements to build more effective, higher-quality software. Now, for the first time, there's a comprehensive, hands-on guide to optimally using RequisitePro in real-world development environments.

Utilizing a start-to-finish sample project, requirements expert Peter Zielczynski introduces an organized, best-practice approach to managing requirements and shows how to implement every step with RequisitePro. You'll walk through planning, eliciting, and clarifying stakeholder requirements; building use cases and other key project documents; managing changing requirements; transforming requirements into designs; and much more. Every stage of the process is illuminated with examples, realistic artifacts, and practical solutions.

This book is an invaluable resource for everyone who creates requirements, and everyone who relies on them: business analysts, systems analysts, project managers, architects, designers, developers, and testers alike.

IBM Rational Unified Process Reference and Certification Guide
Solution Designer (RUP)

by Ahmad K. Shuja and Jochen Krebs

ISBN: 0-13-156292-4

The IBM Rational Unified Process has become the de facto industry-standard process for large-scale enterprise software development. The IBM Certified Solution Designer — IBM Rational Unified Process V7.0 certification provides a powerful way for solutions developers to demonstrate their proficiency with RUP.

The first and only official RUP certification guide, this book fully reflects the latest versions of the Rational Unified Process and of the IBM RUP exam. Authored by two leading RUP implementers, it draws on extensive contributions and careful reviews by the IBM RUP process leader and RUP certification manager.

This book covers every facet of RUP usage. It has been carefully organized to help you prepare for your exam quickly and efficiently — and to provide a handy, compact reference you can rely on for years to come.

Related Books of Interest

IBM Rational ClearCase, Ant, and CruiseControl
The Java Developer's Guide to Accelerating and Automating the Build Process

by Kevin A. Lee
ISBN: 0-321-35699-3

Better builds mean better software. Effective, regular build processes accelerate development and improve quality, helping you identify small problems early, before they grow complex and costly to fix. Now, there's a step-by-step guide to creating Java™ build processes that are right for your organization. Leading build and release management expert Kevin Lee introduces best practices for integrating and using three exceptionally powerful and recognized industry standard tools: IBM Rational ClearCase software configuration management system, the open source Ant build tool, and CruiseControl for automating continuous builds.

No previous build experience is necessary: Lee thoroughly explains everything from configuring SCM environments and defining build scripts through to release packaging and deployment. He offers solutions and techniques for both Base ClearCase and Unified Change Management (UCM) — IBM Rational's best practice Software Configuration Management usage model. Key techniques are presented in real-world context, through a full-fledged three-tier application case study.

Implementing IBM Rational ClearQuest

Buckley, Pulsipher, Scott
ISBN: 0-321-33486-8

Visual Modeling with IBM Rational Software Architect and UML

Quatrani, Palistrant
ISBN: 0-321-23808-7

Project Management with the IBM Rational Unified Process

Gibbs
ISBN: 0-321-33639-9

Software Configuration Management Strategies and IBM Rational ClearCase

Bellagio, Milligan
ISBN: 0-321-20019-5

Developing Quality Technical Information

Hargis, Carey, Hernandez, Hughes, Longo, Rouiller, Wilde
ISBN: 0-13-147749-8

Service-Oriented Architecture (SOA) Compass

Bieberstein, Bose, Fiammante, Jones, Shah
ISBN: 0-13-187002-5

Outside-in Software Development

by Carl Kessler and John Sweitzer
ISBN: 0-13-157551-1

A Practical Guide to Distributed Scrum

A Practical Guide to Distributed Scrum

Elizabeth Woodward, Steffan Surdek, Matthew Ganis

IBM Press
Pearson plc
Upper Saddle River, NJ • Boston • Indianapolis • San Francisco
New York • Toronto • Montreal • London • Munich • Paris • Madrid
Cape Town • Sydney • Tokyo • Singapore • Mexico City
ibmpressbooks.com

IBM Press Program Managers: Steven M. Stansel, Ellice Uffer
Cover design: IBM Corporation

Editor-in-Chief: Karen Gettman
Marketing Manager: Kourtnaye Sturgeon
Publicist: Heather Fox
Executive Editor: Chris Guzikowski
Senior Development Editor: Chris Zahn
Managing Editor: Kristy Hart
Designer: Alan Clements
Senior Project Editor: Lori Lyons
Copy Editor: Water Crest Publishing, Inc.
Indexer: Lisa Stumpf
Compositor: Jake McFarland/Nonie Ratcliff
Proofreader: Kathy Ruiz
Manufacturing Buyer: Dan Uhrig

Published by Pearson plc
Publishing as IBM Press

IBM Press offers excellent discounts on this book when ordered in quantity for bulk purchases or special sales, which may include electronic versions and/or custom covers and content particular to your business, training goals, marketing focus, and branding interests. For more information, please contact:

U.S. Corporate and Government Sales
1-800-382-3419
corpsales@pearsontechgroup.com.

For sales outside the U.S., please contact:

International Sales
international@pearson.com.

Library of Congress Cataloging-in-Publication Data

Woodward, Elizabeth, 1965–
 A practical guide to distributed Scrum / Elizabeth Woodward, Steffan Surdek, Matt Ganis.
    p. cm.
 ISBN 978-0-13-704113-8 (pbk. : alk. paper) 1. Agile software development. 2. Scrum (Computer software development) 3. Electronic data processing—Distributed processing.
I. Surdek, Steffan, 1972- II. Ganis, Matt, 1963- III. Title.
 QA76.76.D47W66 2010
 005.1—dc22
                              2010014806

Text printed in the United States on recycled paper at R.R. Donnelley in Crawfordsville, Indiana.

First printing June 2010

ISBN-13: 978-0-13-704113-8
ISBN-10: 0-13-704113-6

Contents

Chapter 9   Retrospectives   163

Chapter 10   Closing Thoughts   179

Index   181

Foreword
by Ken Schwaber

Agility is the word of the new millennium. As the world around us grows more complex, we strive to build more complex products. These products often consist of many components that must interact precisely through sophisticated interfaces. At the same time, these products are being used in more sophisticated, critical applications, including life-critical products such as pacemakers and nano-robots, and society-critical applications such as an intelligent energy grid. In parallel with the growth of complexity, there has been a need for increased safety, predictability, risk management, and control—both of the development process itself and the resultant products. At the same time, our need to be nimble, flexible, and adaptable has increased. Enter the era of agility.

Agility first formally entered the product development arena with the publishing of the *Agile Manifesto* in 2001. As of 2008, more organizations are employing agile techniques and processes to develop and sustain complex products than those that continue to employ more traditional techniques. Of those using agile techniques, 84% of them employ an agile framework process, Scrum.

A complexity faced by almost all large organizations is distribution of teams (many teams working in different locations) and dispersed teams (team members within a team are dispersed to different locations). Among the compelling reasons for distribution and dispersion are scarcity of skills, flexibility of forming teams rapidly, and sustaining adequate workforces. One of the original reasons for distribution and dispersion that has proven to be elusive, however, was lowered costs. By the time the development infrastructure was in place, the teams and team members had familiarized themselves with each other, and integration issues were addressed, cost savings were no longer the compelling reason.

When organizations begin to use Scrum, they often run into the difficulties inherent to distributed and dispersed teams. Because Scrum uses frequent inspection and adaption of transparent artifacts to control risk and create predictability, distribution and dispersion make these techniques difficult. For instance, if I have never worked closely with someone on my team from Asia and I am in Boston, how do I interpret what he or she means in the Daily Scrum? If we have many teams scattered throughout the world, what techniques can we use to resolve our dependencies and frequently integrate our work, so that transparency is retained? There are no optimal solutions, only best possible solutions.

I have known Elizabeth since she and a small group within IBM took on the challenge of making the IBM culture agile, and doing this with Scrum as its framework. When IBM began its path to use Scrum and other agile techniques, it arose from a grass-roots initiative. As success occurred and became visible, senior management provided needed support and leadership to realize the benefits at an enterprise level.

This book is about how to use Scrum in a very large, heterogeneous, globally distributed organization, such as IBM. This book contains many of the best practices that have emerged during IBM's transition to agile. Each practice is well stated with tips and alternatives. These techniques are not ethereal, but have emerged from hard, empirical experiences that the teams in IBM have faced.

I have found that change only happens one person at a time. If a person doesn't understand what the benefits of the new way of doing things are, both to his or her organization and to him or her personally, passive and/or outright resistance will occur—singly, then in groups, and then in political action. The authors have carefully and subtly demonstrated the advantages of agile, not by selling, but by creating insight everywhere and in everyone, and by having the natural leaders within the organization lead the change.

I encourage you to read of the changes to agility that those contributing to this book have been able to initiate, support, and sustain. Read this book and gain insights that may assist you in your efforts to gain agility in your organization.

Elizabeth told me the community would be honored if I wrote this Foreword. I am honored to write this Foreword for them, and the cunningly thoughtful change they have caused.

Ken Schwaber
Co-creator of Scrum
www.scrum.org

Foreword
by Scott Ambler

If you're reading this foreword, you're probably trying to answer one or more of the following questions: "What will I learn?," "Should I spend my hard-earned money on this book?," "Will it be worth my valuable time to read it?," and "Is this a book that I'll refer to again and again?" To help you answer these questions, I thought I'd list a few user stories that I believe this book clearly fulfills.

As a reader, I want:

- A book that is well-written and understandable.
- Real-world examples that I can relate to.
- Quotes from actual people doing this in the field.
- To understand the challenges that I'll face with distributed agile development.

As someone new to agile, I want to:

- Learn the fundamentals of Scrum.
- Understand the fundamentals of agile delivery.
- Learn about what actually works in practice.
- Discover how to extend Scrum into an agile delivery process.

As an experienced agile practitioner, I want to learn:

- How to scale agile approaches for distributed teams.
- How to overcome the challenges faced by distributed teams.

- How to tailor existing agile practices to reflect the realities of distribution.
- About "new" agile practices that we might need to adopt.
- Techniques so that distributed team members can communicate effectively.
- How to extend Scrum with proven techniques from Extreme Programming, Agile Modeling, and other agile methods.
- How to address architectural issues on a distributed agile team.
- How agile teams address documentation.
- How agile teams can interact effectively with non-agile teams.

As a ScrumMaster, I want to learn how to:

- Lead a distributed agile team.
- Facilitate a distributed "Scrum of Scrums."
- Facilitate the successful initiation of a distributed agile project.
- Facilitate communication and collaboration between distributed team members.

As a product owner, I want to learn:

- How to manage a product backlog on a distributed team.
- About different categories of stakeholders whom I will need to represent.
- About techniques to understand and capture the goals of those stakeholders.
- How to manage requirements with other product owners on other sub-teams.
- What to do during an end-of-sprint review.
- How I can streamline things for the delivery team that I'm working with.

As an agile skeptic, I want to:

- See examples of how agile works in practice.
- Hear about the challenges faced by agile teams.
- Hear about where agile strategies don't work well and what to do about it.

I work with organizations around the world helping them to scale agile strategies to meet their real-world needs. Although this book is focused on providing strategies for dealing with geographical distribution, it also covers many of the issues that you'll run into with large teams: complex problem domains and complex technical domains. An important aspect of scaling agile techniques is to first recognize that there's more to scalability than dealing with large teams, something that this book clearly demonstrates.

At the risk of sounding a bit corny, I've eagerly awaited the publication of this book for some time. I've known two of the authors, Elizabeth and Matt, for several years and have had the pleasure of working with them and learning from them as a result. Along with hundreds of other IBMers, I watched this book get written and provided input where I could. The reason why I'm so excited about it is that I've wanted something to which I could refer the customers who I work with and honestly say, "yes, we know that this works because this is what we do in practice."

IBM is doing some very interesting work when it comes to scaling agile. We haven't published enough externally, in my opinion, due to a preference for actively sharing our experiences internally. This book collects many of our experiences into a coherent whole and more importantly shares them outside the IBM process ecosystem. The bottom line is that I think that you'll get a lot out of this book.

Scott W. Ambler
Chief Methodologist/Agile, IBM Rational
https://www.ibm.com/developerworks/mydeveloperworks/blogs/ambler/

Foreword
by Roman Pichler

My early experiences of distributed software development include attending conference calls without having access to the documents being discussed; hoping for an upgrade to get some sleep on a long-haul flight; and being surprised when I finally met the face to a voice I only knew from telephone conversations. Distributed software development is challenging, as Elizabeth Woodward, Matthew Ganis, and Steffan Surdek clearly point out in their book, *A Practical Guide to Distributed Scrum*. Things don't get easier when Scrum is applied. I remember one Scrum project I worked on where the build times grew longer and longer, as the number of teams and locations increased. On another project, we had to figure out how to run the sprint meetings with teams distributed across several times zones. And on a third project, an empowered chief product owner was missing, causing the distributed teams to follow their own goals and agendas.

I wish *A Practical Guide to Distributed Scrum* had been available then. It would have saved me plenty of time and provided invaluable help. The advice in Chapter 2 on telephone dynamics would have helped avoid the painful telephone calls; following the recommendation in Chapter 3 to organize for the lowest level of distribution could have made some of the flights unnecessary; using videoconferencing as suggested in Chapters 2 and 6 would have made communication more effective; employing continuous integration, as discussed in Chapter 7, would have mitigated the build time problem; Chapters 4, 5, 8, and 9 would have helped greatly to organize the distributed sprint meetings; and the advice in Chapter 3 would have avoided the chief product owner issue.

The book does an outstanding job at raising the reader's awareness of the problems that are likely to arise on a distributed Scrum project. It excels at providing practical tips to avoid and overcome these issues. Woodward, Ganis, and Surdek take the reader on journey through the lifecycle of a distributed Scrum project—from creating the product vision and setting up the right project organization to preparing the sprint planning meeting and running distributed sprint review and retrospective meetings. They point out the traps along the way and explain specific practices like lookahead planning, test automation, and being aware of culture and language differences.

If you are involved in distributed Scrum projects, then this book is for you.

Roman Pichler
Author of *Agile Product Management with Scrum*

Foreword
by Matthew Wang

Agile development has gained popularity in recent years. Software companies adopted agile to better respond to frequent requirement changes. When agile was introduced in the mid 90's, collocated development teams were common (that is, the whole project team was in one location). So the daily Scrum meetings could be conducted in the same place at the same time. Nowadays, a distributed development team is the norm as companies embrace global sourcing. A project even could have team members located in different continents. The challenge is how to apply the agile principles that were established in a collocated environment to a distributed development environment.

As a global integrated enterprise, IBM has been on Agile for years and has set up the agile community to drive this effort. The book *A Practical Guide to Distributed Scrum* is one of the major achievements of the community. It offers an unprecedented view on how distributed teams can also implement Scrum, the leading framework for agile software development, with tips and recommendations contributed by over 1,300 members from 30 countries in IBM. The book itself was developed in an agile way—a successful distributed agile project by itself.

IBM China Development Labs (CDL) has been embarking on the agile journey since 2005. It has accumulated wealthy knowledge and experience on agile development. Particularly, most CDL teams need to conduct product development by collaborating with worldwide teams; distributed Scrum is well adopted in CDL. For example, driven by the agile community, more than 60 teams at CDL have used Rational Team Concert, a collaborative software development environment, to assist agile development. The teams also have done tremendous innovations such as leveraging the 12-hour time difference between development and test teams to maximize agile benefits. Some of the practice have been included with this book; you can read about the details in various chapters.

The methodology of software development has been evolving continuously. Software companies will be more successful only when they can grasp the new methodology. Distributed teams will continue to be a trend in software industry due to the benefits of talent availability and cost reduction, so distributed agile development skill is critical. I highly recommend this book to software developers—you can learn a great deal from the well-structured content, which is practical and can be put into use right away.

Matthew Wang
Vice President
IBM China Development Laboratories

Preface

You know, we do this stuff all the time. We should just write a book about it!

John Sutcliffe

Agile software development is a growing trend as companies look for ways to improve quality, reduce time to deliver software to the market, and more accurately deliver software that meets the needs of their clients. At the same time, globalization, distributed software development work, and telecommuting are rapidly changing how software development teams work.

In 2007, *Dr. Dobbs Journal* reported that agile software development had successfully crossed Moore's technology-adoption chasm in that 69% of agile survey respondents indicated their organizations were doing one or more agile projects (Ambler 2007). Of the remaining respondents, 24% believed their organizations would do so within the next year. Of the 44% indicating a 90%+ success rate for agile projects, co-located respondents were 60% more successful than non-co-located.

Telecommuting is also a growing trend that increases the likelihood that even teams working in the same geographical areas will be functioning as a distributed team at least part time. In a 2008 CompTIA study, a majority of respondents (78%) reported that some employees within their organizations telecommute at least part time (CompTIA 2008). With telecommuting providing significant increases in productivity, cost savings for companies, a reduction in a company's carbon footprint, and a compensation trend for those hiring, telecommuting is a trend that is likely to continue to grow.

A number of great articles on implementing agile in the distributed enterprise environment have recently been presented at conferences, such as the Agile 2008 conference. However, only a few books have been published on distributed agile. Only one book has been published specifically on Enterprise Scrum. This book is complementary to such books in that it provides practical tips, recommendations, and experiences that enrich the knowledge of readers of seeking information on Enterprise Scrum.

This book shares the experience of a community of 1,300 Scrum team members from across IBM business units and geographies. The diversity provides a unique perspective into a broad array of challenges specific to working in a fully distributed software development environment.

Who Should Read This Book?

The target audience for this book is members of software development organizations worldwide, across industries who work with distributed team members and in particular those who are adopting Scrum for agile development. Software developers, testers, technical writers, team leaders, managers, and others who telecommute, work with outsourced teams, or work as part of a fully-distributed team will benefit from the practical guidance provided in this book. Because the book applies to geographically distributed teams, the audience for this book is global.

This book applies not only to the large-scale software top-100 companies but also to smaller companies that perform contract work for larger, distributed organizations and to small companies that find value in allowing their software development team members to telecommute.

Managers who manage distributed teams would be interested in this book as a way to scale agile methods to benefit their organizations.

Why a Practical Guide to Distributed Scrum?

Distributed development is quickly becoming the norm rather than the exception. There are many challenges faced by new teams or teams early in their journey toward distributed development. While creating the content for the book, our aim was to share the challenges that we faced and propose solutions that teams can adapt and adopt. Our goal is not to prescribe solutions, but to present options and to have teams decide what will work best for them in their world.

In all our chapters, we first provide a baseline from the regular Scrum perspective and then we discuss the challenges distributed teams face; we then provide guidance or approaches to make that piece of Scrum smoother.

How We Wrote This Book

IBM Quality Software Engineering (QSE), an organization responsible for helping teams to improve their software development practices, facilitates several communities including the QSE Scrum Community. This book, started at the end of October 2008, would not have been possible without the contribution of its members. The effort was to be a community-developed book, with Elizabeth and Matt serving as authors. Steffan joined the brainstorming group in January 2009 and signed on as the third co-author shortly after that.

Throughout the content development process, the initial core group of contributors and members of the Scrum Community participated in numerous brainstorming sessions, presentations, and content reviews. Thomas Starz, Gregg Gibson, John Sutcliffe, Elizabeth, Matt, and Steffan served as facilitators for many of the sessions and converted many hours of recordings and notes into sentences and paragraphs. We also had the pleasure of hosting a Scrum Community presentation by Roman Pichler, author of Agile Product Management with Scrum, who kindly offered to review an early version of Chapter 3, "Starting a Scrum Project."

One of the most interesting aspects of writing this book was that everyone who participated or contributed in any way in the project was distributed. Elizabeth, Steffan, and Matt wrote a lot of the rough content for the chapters, and the participants from the QSE Scrum Community were just amazing in quickly reviewing these drafts for us and contributing their own ideas and content to help make the book better.

Starting around April 2009, we used two-week Sprints to convert the content from the brainstorming sessions into chapters on specific topics. As authors, we overcame the distance separating us (Elizabeth is in Texas, Matt is in New York, and Steffan is in Quebec) with weekly conference calls and by being very open to changes the other authors felt necessary.

It was our intention to capture experiences and helpful recommendations not just from within IBM, but also from knowledgeable Scrum Team members, coaches, and consultants *outside* of IBM. We felt very strongly that we needed to take an agile approach to developing this book. We wanted to share chapters outside of IBM as they were being developed and gather feedback and quotes that would enrich the content and be helpful to any team using Scrum in a distributed environment. To do this, we had to work to adapt the IBM Press publication and IBM Legal processes. Steve Stansel and Nicole Gallo saw the value of an Agile approach and went out of their way to work with us to make the necessary changes. Peter Santhanam and Dave Hayward provided web server access, so that we could deliver chapters through www.distributedscrum. com. The process opened a door for other authors to take an Agile approach to writing books.

Because of the level of participation from so many contributors, we decided early in the development of A Practical Guide to Distributed Scrum that we would donate all royalties to charitable organizations. Members of the IBM QSE Scrum Community voted on the following charities to benefit from these efforts:

- Children's Hunger
- Alzheimer's Association
- Alzheimer Society

We are thrilled to have had an opportunity to collaborate with so many experienced, thoughtful, and motivated Scrum practitioners through this effort. We hope that this book will make a difference not only for those benefitting from these charities, but for the Scrum and agile community at large.

References

Ambler, Scott. *Survey Says...Agile Has Crossed the Chasm. Dr. Dobb's Journal.* http://www.ddj.com/architect/200001986.

CompTIA. *Summary of "Trends in Telecommuting: Organizations Are Realizing Benefits and Addressing Challenges."* http://www.comptia.org/sections/research/reports/200809-TelecomSummary.aspx, 2008.

Acknowledgments

We are grateful to many people who played a significant role in the development of this book. Each author has provided personal acknowledgments, and together we recognize the community that made this book possible.

Personal Acknowledgments from Elizabeth

Stacia Broderick, a Certified Scrum Trainer, begins her ScrumMaster class with: "Think back to your favorite project. What did you enjoy most about it?" If I were to answer that question today, writing *A Practical Guide to Distributed Scrum* would be at the top of the list. It has been a real pleasure and a blessing to be able to work on this cool project with such a talented group of people.

I want to thank my handsome husband for being my partner in this great adventure of life, for sharing the beauty of each precious day with me, for being supportive, and for "removing blockers." I'd like to thank our older sons, Michael and Zachary, for listening to never-ending Scrum stories and providing continuous stakeholder feedback. I'd like to thank our youngest son, Lawson, for pulling me away to play with blocks and puzzles in support of sustainable pace. I'd also like to thank my mother for always being available for distributed meetings with me, regardless of her normal "working hours."

A few projects from the past had an influence on my passion for writing this book. I would like to thank Roger Tucker for giving me a chance to work on the Central Valley Internet Project, a project that demonstrated the value of short Sprints, continuous stakeholder feedback, and a prioritized backlog. I would like to thank Doug Stephen for the opportunity to work with his agile teams and experience sustainable hyperproductivity. I would like to thank Jim Jones for giving me the opportunity to create and lead IBM's Scrum Community. And, I would like to give Bill

Krebs, Ted Rivera, Paul Gibson, and Matt the recognition they deserve for blazing an Agile path within IBM.

There are a few people that I would like to give an extra "thanks" beyond our group acknowledgments. I would like to thank John Sutcliffe for suggesting the idea in the first place. John's passion and enthusiasm for facilitating teams permeates this book. I want to thank Ming Zhi Xie for leading the IBM Scrum Community in China, for organizing face-to-face meetings and for effectively providing insight to the Chinese culture. I thank Thomas Starz, for brainstorming and presenting the content at Scrum events in Germany, and Gregg Gibson, for spending countless hours facilitating brainstorming sessions and transcribing.

I would personally like to thank Scott Ambler for thoroughly reviewing, sharing his years of experience as an agile proponent, and debating earlier versions of this book. This book is better for his insight.

Finally, I would like to thank my friends and partners, Matt and Steffan. Matt, your enthusiasm and energy for every project you work on is contagious, and this was no exception. It is always a pleasure to work with you. Steff, I can't thank you enough. Your willingness to do what it takes to deliver and fanatical championing of StyleWriter made this project possible. Your unparalleled drive, passion for excellence, sense of humor, and hockey stories made this project a favorite!

Personal Acknowledgments from Steffan

This book has taken me through quite a journey in the past year, and writing this feels like my own little personal Academy Awards moment.

To start, I would like to thank my family, starting with my wife Annie, for understanding that "just one more night of editing" usually meant that I would probably be editing or writing stuff every night of the week. I am eternally grateful for her patience and support while working on this book. I would also like to thank my children, my son Jonathan and daughter Caroline, for always finding a way to make daddy smile, for giving me a change of pace, and for helping me see what is important in my life.

Professionally, I would like to thank and recognize the following people. Steve Teleki, my former manager, for encouraging me to do more writing and for providing constructive feedback and ideas on how to write and present effectively. Robert Begg, for your continued support and for keeping me involved in coaching teams in IBM. Yves Ferland, a former manager of mine in IBM and one of my mentors—we are less in touch, but I always appreciate my talks with you whenever we meet.

I would like to thank Matt and Elizabeth for inviting me to be part of the writing team. Matt, you are such a positive person all the time and easy to work with. It has been a pleasure working with you! Elizabeth, to say you literally turned my life upside down (in a good, fun, and exciting way) in the last year would be quite the understatement. Thank you for being the great leader you are and for keeping us all on track and focused throughout this project!

Finally, I would personally like to thank the core group of participants from our brainstorming sessions; this book is a reflection of all your contributions, and I am grateful to all of you. I have some quick thoughts for some of you, with whom I interacted with a bit more. Leslie Ekas, brainstorming with you is always interesting and fun; we could go on for hours on end. Thomas Starz, you were tireless in taking part in the brainstorming sessions, reviewing materials, and providing feedback on all the chapters. Paul Sims, I appreciated your in-depth reviews, constructive comments, and any discussions we had together.

Personal Acknowledgments from Matt

There are many people that I have crossed paths with in my personal, academic, and business life that have affected me in a variety of ways. To thank them all for their advice and council (and at times pleasant and heated debates) would be impossible, but rest assured, I am indebted to each and every one of you.

There are some people I do need to thank and acknowledge. First and foremost is my management team here at IBM: Monica Piccinini, John Rosato, and Steve Wright. They've always supported my crazy requests to participate in agile efforts across the company, external speaking engagements, or funding my (never-ending list of) conferences. Without them, I would have never succeeded. There are a number of agile zealots like myself inside IBM, and together, we've formed a large following, and interest in the topic that always amazes me. People like Paul Gorans, Michael "Max" Maximilien, Bill Krebs, and Ted Rivera deserve a great deal of thanks (and I'm sure I owe each of them a drink or two) for all their help over the years.

As things get "closer to home," I think about how grateful I am to have both Elizabeth and Steff in my business and personal life. I have never met two more committed, caring, fun, and knowledgeable people. I (and I think IBM) owes them a huge debt of thanks!

Finally, I'd like to thank my family: my wife Karen, my daughter Taylor, and my son Matthew. They put up with a lot from me. Every vacation, baseball game, soccer tournament, and quiet night at home, they find me with a pad of paper writing something. Trust me guys, in between the writing, I saw every hit, kick, and score!

Joint Acknowledgments

We wish to thank our executive reviewers—Matthew Wang, Vice President of China Development Lab; Ponani Gopalakrishnan, Vice President of India Software Development Lab; and Helen McKinstry, Director of IBM Quality Software Engineering (QSE)—for their support of this project.

We are grateful to the team at Pearson Education: Chris Guzikowski, Chris Zahn, and Raina Chrobak, for guiding us through the process and for being so responsive. We are also grateful to Steve Stansel of IBM Press and Nicole Gallo of IBM Legal for their guidance. We would also like to thank Peter Santhanam and Dave Hayward, who provided web server space to host our chapters that we delivered through www.distributedscrum.com.

We also wish to thank our reviewers for sharing their feedback: Ken Schwaber, Roman Pichler, Stephen Forte, Linda Rising, Lisa Shoop, Amr Elssamadisy, and Scott Ambler.

The IBM Scrum Community has engaged in many brainstorming sessions, round tables, and presentations to share their experiences. The following individuals have led sessions, researched, developed content, discussed methods with those outside IBM, shared their experiences, and more:

Jan Acosta	Monica Luke
Corville Allen	Jean-Louis Marechaux
Pushpa Baskaran	Berne Miller
Donald Bell	Andy Pittaway
Diane Benze	Ivan Portilla
Bob Campbell	Hector Rosas
Michael Demeter	Bob Sager
Saurabh Dua	Julio Sanchez
Leslie Ekas	Peter Santhanam
Mike Eversole	Guillaume Senneville
Gregg Gibson	Ryan Shillington
Justin Gordon	Paul Sims
Brenda Hagler	Manmohan Singh
Jeff Hedglin	Maya Srihari
Greg Hendley	Thomas Starz
Jyoti Jalvi	John Sutcliffe
James L. Jones	Teresa Shen Swingler
Alan June	Mike Thompson
Elizabeth Kamau	Jeff Treece
Bill Krebs	Mark Wainwright
John Langlois	Hanhong Xue
Mark Levison	Ming Zhi Xie

About the Authors

Elizabeth Woodward is a Senior Software Consultant with IBM Quality Software Engineering under the Corporate Headquarters Office of Innovation and Technology. She has served as the project manager or development leader on more than 100 globally-distributed projects for IBM and other development companies. Elizabeth coaches distributed software development teams to improve efficiency and effectiveness of their development practices. She has co-chaired the IBM Academy of Technology Conference on Agile Methods, teaches courses on Disciplined Agile Development, and co-leads the IBM Agile Community.

Steffan Surdek is a User Experience Lead and Agile Champion in IBM. He has worked in the software development industry for over fifteen years as a software developer, architect, project manager, and team leader. Steffan has managed and coordinated large-scale projects with teams distributed in as many as five countries—India, Egypt, Israel, China, and Canada. He coaches distributed agile teams, is a co-leader of the IBM Agile Community, and teaches Disciplined Agile Development workshops. He is an active member of the Montreal Agile Community and has written on agile methods and globally distributed development for developerWorks and *Dr. Dobbs Journal*. In his spare time, he does some writing on his website at http://www.surdek.ca.

Matthew Ganis is an IBM Senior Technical Staff Member and ibm.com site architect. Matt was the co-leader of the IBM Agile Community and was an early adopter of agile within IBM. He currently teaches Disciplined Agile Development and has published numerous articles and papers on the use of agile methods within ibm.com—both within its traditional web development and the development/support of their Second Life Island. Matt has been the co-chair and chair of the Academy of Technology's Agile Conferences for the past two years and is a Certified Scrum-Master and Practitioner. Outside of IBM, Matt serves on the editorial board of the International Journal of AGILE AND EXTREME SOFTWARE DEVELOPMENT and is a steering committee member of New York City's Agile Project Leadership Network (APLN) chapter.

Contributors

This book would not have been possible without the valuable contribution of members of the IBM Scrum Community as well as others in IBM. To thank them for their efforts, we created this section of the book to give them some additional recognition.

The following individuals have led sessions, researched, developed content, discussed methods with those outside IBM, shared their experiences, and more:

Jan Acosta is a member of the QSE staff and has been with IBM for ten years. She's a Disciplined Agile Workshop facilitator and enjoys consulting with teams as they work to deploy agile within their organizations. Jan facilitates the QSE Technical Series calls and leads the test-driven development community.

Corville Allen is software engineer for the WebSphere Process Server product within IBM Software Group (SWG) Application and Integration Middleware (AIM).

Pushpa Baskaran is an advisory software engineer and technical team leader working in the Distributed Software Value chain group, in the IBM BT/CIO organization. She has over 14 years of software development experience. She also has J2EE/Java development, C, C++, SQL, shell programming, and ANT scripting experience. Pushpa is experienced in the EAD4J framework and uses the framework to develop J2EE web applications. She has hands-on experience in SOA, web services and Web 2.0 development and uses the technologies to develop applications that support IBM programs. Pushpa and her team are using agile development methodology's for delivering quality software and web applications that support IBM SWG programs. She also has experience developing unit tests for DB2 and Java, using JUnit and TC4DBO, which are included with the team's automated build process.

Donald Bell is a Rational Solution Architect in IBM Rational's Global Services Account Team. He assists project teams in adopting effective software development processes and tools that balance both the client's and IBM's risks and value. He is also contributing to IBM Rational's

Measured Capability Improvement Framework (MCIF) assets so organizations can show through measures how their development processes are improving.

Diane Benze began her career as a proofreader before transitioning to graphic arts in newspapers and commercial print shops. After a five-year detour as an editor at a technical translation agency, she returned to the publishing industry. During a stint as head beta tester for a new publishing application, the software company providing the product decided that it would behoove them to have her on their side rather than on the customer side. She made the leap to software quality testing for companies providing news and advertising software. From there, it was a short hop to testing for telephony and telecommunications software companies. About eight years ago, she accepted a job as a software tester at IBM Tivoli, where she tested the NetView product. She is now testing IBM Tivoli Netcool Management software.

Bob Campbell is a development manager for IBM Cognos "Adaptive Applications Framework"—an applications development framework created by the Performance Analytics group within SWG Information Management. His development teams are distributed around the UK, Canada, and India, and they have been practicing distributed agile development for the past three to four years. Bob has been part of Scrum development teams in various roles, including team member, ScrumMaster, and product owner.

Michael Demeter is a senior software engineer and team lead for UTM Appliances with IBM Global Technology Services (GTS). He also serves as a QSE Development Top Gun.

Saurabh Dua is a project manager in SWG, responsible for the delivery of IBM Smart Business Developers' Toolkit enabling small to medium-sized customers to easily assemble and deploy applications onto Smart Business and Lotus Foundation appliances. He is a proponent for agile development and has been involved in a task force to transition all current processes to the Scrum iterative development agile model in his organization.

Leslie Ekas joined IBM through the FileNet acquisition. She left her development manager position in FileNet 2008 to become a coach in the Agile/Lean Center of Competence. As part of the SWG Strategy and Technology, IBM formed this group to help accelerate the adoption of Agile/Lean best practices throughout SWG. Leslie started practicing Scrum and applying Lean techniques to improve the effectiveness of her teams at the beginning of 2006. She promotes the culture of continuous improvement to invigorate innovation and keep IBM competitive.

Mike Eversole is a manager with SWG AIM Software responsible for Install Strategy and Development.

Gregg Gibson is a development manager responsible for embedded software development in IBM Systems and Technology Group (STG). He has been a developer and team leader on iterative development projects, and is an advocate for agile adoption within STG. He is a senior member of the Institute for Electronic and Electrical Engineers (IEEE).

Justin Gordon joined IBM through the Trigo acquisition in April 2004. Justin has contributed widely and deeply to this product, now known as InfoSphere Master Data Management (MDM) Server for PIM. In 2004, Justin led a rewrite of that product's storage layer to be vastly scalable through a binary storage format that allows reading and writing large semi-structured hierarchical documents, like XML, without any of the parsing costs of XML. During this intense development phase, Justin pioneered the use of test-driven development, JUnit, and other agile development techniques. Justin founded the open source project, the "Dependent Object Framework," which vastly simplifies and accelerates JUnit testing with persistent dependencies. Justin has been passionately writing software for 22 years, focusing on Java for the past 10 years at several startups. Justin graduated in 1991 with an AB magna cum laude in applied mathematics from Harvard and received an MBA from UC Berkeley in 2001.

Brenda Hagler is the team lead for the IBM Human Ability and Accessibility Center Test Lab. Brenda has worked in various product development roles. Her background includes various products, such as AIX, IBM Tivoli Risk Manager, and IBM Tivoli Access Manager for Business Integration. She is a Test Top Gun for the IBM Research division. Her focus has been accessibility verification test (AVT) since she joined the HA&AC in 2004. She supports IBM development and test teams worldwide.

Jeff Hedglin is the manager of Cryptographic Development in STG.

Greg Hendley is a software engineer for FIT-ITE infrastructure development with SWG, Strategy.

Jyoti Jalvi is a lead engineer in the IBM Informix Engineering Operations team. Jyoti is responsible for implementing several key enhancements to the Informix build process. In this role, she has been a change agent in moving traditional Informix builds to a Build Management System (BuildForge), successfully designed and implemented the build infrastructure, and led the effort of build migration. In line with the organizational strategy to use agile development, Jyoti collaborated with the development organization and implemented the Continuous Integration process that provides completely automated build, testing, and regression analysis. Jyoti has 10 years of software development experience. She provides guidance on build/testing best practices and consulting on migration to BuildForge to her team as well as other organizations under Integration Management.

James L. Jones is the manager of QSE Enablement Services, under IBM Corporate Headquarters Office of Innovation and Technology. Jim is responsible for developing the consulting services and resources that will enable teams to improve their software development skills.

Alan June is an executive project manager in STG, responsible for leading the deployment of the industry-accepted practices of Lean/Agile into the z/OS software development processes. He works with ~1200 people on 60 teams working at 5 major sites and a number of local sites to use Lean/Agile development methods to deliver z/OS software. Alan has over 27 years with IBM. He acquired experience in Project and Program Management, Business Management (including First Line and Functional Management), Product Planning, Software Packaging, and Customer Service.

Elizabeth Kamau is a member of the Software Quality Assurance team for Integrated Technology Delivery, Technology Integration, and Management.

Bill "AgileBill" Krebs is founder of Agile Dimensions LLC, trainer and consultant at Davisbase LLC, and is on the board of directors at Rockcliffe University Consortium. He teaches using face-to-face instruction methods and immersive web technology. Bill is a certified Scrum-Master and Practitioner, certified MBTI facilitator, and will receive his Certificate in Virtual Worlds this year in 2010. Bill worked as a developer, performance engineer, and consultant at five IBM Labs from 1983 to 2008. He has used and taught Agile software development methods such as Scrum and Lean since 2001 to over 1,000 engineers and managers worldwide. He has presented at Agile conferences and IBM Research, and served as the co-chair for the IBM Academy of Technology conference on Agile. Bill is a member of Agile RTP, Agile 3d, IEEE, ACM, Scrum Alliance, Agile Alliance, and PMI.

John Langlois is an IBM-certified executive project manager chartered to deliver integrated solutions on the Power Systems platform. From 1996 through 2001, John led the most successful notebook project in history: ThinkPad T series. John's website, www.projectEZ.com, is dedicated to helping project managers guide troubled projects through rough waters.

Mark Levison is a founding partner and consultant with The Agile Consortium, an Agile and Lean consulting company that focuses on helping its customers to deliver working software every two weeks. Mark has been an agile practitioner since 2001, introducing agile methods one practice at a time inside a small team. In the past three years, as an employee of Cognos and IBM, he's been responsible for introducing Scrum to the organization and coaching a number of teams. He also publishes a blog—Notes from a Tool User.

Monica Luke is the test automation architect for System Verification Test for the Rational Jazz products including Rational Team Concert. Monica has 15 years experience doing test automation, the last six of those with IBM Rational.

Jean-Louis Marechaux is a software engineer for Rational at IBM Canada Lab. His main areas of expertise are software architecture, design, model-driven development, and Java Enterprise Edition (Java EE) technologies. He has been applying agile principles with collocated and distributed teams for the past three to four years, both for consulting services and for internal IBM projects.

Berne Miller, PMP, has more than 25 years experience in project management. Certified as a Project Management Professional (PMP) in 1989, Berne has managed activities as large as a ten-year, billion-dollar-plus ship design and construction effort for the U.S. Coast Guard, and as small as a multi-week software modification effort for his current employer. In between, Berne has managed projects in communications, education management, electrical generation and distribution, financial management, natural resources extraction, facilities construction, and regional economic development. Other assignments have included heading the technical services division of a government systems acquisition organization, a stint as a corporate-level strategic planner, postings in executive ranks, and CEO of Southeast Conference (in Alaska). For the last eight years, Berne has served as program manager for the System Availability and Performance Management (SAPM) Project Development Team (PDT), where part of his role is to coach, advise, and mentor project managers for projects in the SAPM portfolio. Berne's particular interest in the agile rollout within SAPM is definition and collection of executive-level project status metrics.

In his spare time, Berne teaches modules in the Austin PMI Chapter PMP exam preparation course. He is also designated a Certified Professional Logistician (CPL).

Andy Pittaway has worked in Information Technology for 27 years, of which the past 11 years have been in various client-facing leadership roles with IBM Global Business Services. He is an executive project manager working currently on assignment in Italy. He is passionate about applying accelerated techniques and driving real business value from the effective and efficient use of these. He has set up and led development centers using Accelerated Solution Delivery (ASD). He has also led Speed to Market initiatives, which focus on the application of accelerators alongside the removal of blockages and implementation of techniques to ensure high levels of business orientation in technical teams. One of the areas that Andy has also been focused upon is the behavioral and cultural aspects that teams need to address in order to make accelerated techniques work.

Ivan Portilla is a certified consulting IT specialist with Business Consulting Services (BCS) at IBM. With almost 25 years of experience, Mr. Portilla is an industry thought leader, speaker, and coach in the areas of Agile Software Development, WebSphere Portal, and Web 2.0 technologies.

Hector Rosas is a systems software test architect with STG.

Bob Sager is with SWG, AIM Software. He is a development manager for WebSphere sMash and Project Zero.

Julio Sanchez is a SUN certified Java programmer. He has over eight years experience in device driver development for Point of Sale (POS) systems and device I/O. Julio is responsible for leading the JavaPOS product. That project used test-driven development to increase software quality by reducing the defect rate within the JavaPOS device driver software. Julio had gained experience by creating unit tests for Java using JUnit, ant, and Code Coverage tools. He is one of the promoters of the Agile and the eXtreme Programming software model within IBM Guadalajara, Mexico.

Peter Santhanam is the senior manager of the Software Engineering department in IBM Research. His current portfolio covers tools and methodology for the end-to-end software life cycle activities. His personal interests include holistic requirements capture, collaborative software development, automated test generation, software metrics, and process improvement. He has published over fifty technical papers in journals and conferences. Dr. Santhanam is a member of the ACM and a senior member of the IEEE.

Guillaume Senneville joined IBM in 2008 through the Cognos acquisition. Working as part of the SWG Information Management Business Intelligence and Performance Management team, he is a development manager leading a team that's actively using Scrum and other agile practices. Guillaume is currently co-leading the Cognos Agile Community, which is set up to complement other IBM agile communities for more local issues. He is an advocate of Scrum best practices and is interested in related topics like Lean Software Development. He has been a Certified ScrumMaster since 2007.

Ryan Shillington is the development manager of the WebSphere Business Services Fabric at IBM. He has worked on and led a few different agile teams, both distributed and completely local. When not pretending to run big blue, he moonlights as the co-owner of both Used Is Better and Austin Star Map.

Paul Sims joined IBM in 1984. Past projects include Series/1-based hardware for the Prodigy videotext service (a joint venture of IBM, Sears, and CBS Records), ISDN basic-rate adapters for 9370 and AS/400 systems, ISDN Q.921 microcode, Communications Utilities for OS/400, CD Showcase CDs to help sell AIX and OS/400 application development tools, IBM Distributed Debugger development manager, ADTC operations manager, WebSphere Commerce system test, and continual test improvement lead. Paul is now a software engineer in the Software Group Scenario Analysis Lab and a Disciplined Agile Development Workshop facilitator.

Manmohan Singh works as a development manager of WebSphere Business Services Fabric and manages the team in Mumbai. He has close to 11 years of experience in the IT industry across different geographies. He is an agile enthusiast and has been contributing to Agile Conferences of Academy of Technology. He is a six sigma green belt certified professional and keen on learning and contributing toward software development process improvements.

Maya Srihari, a member of the QSE staff, leads QSE deployment initiatives in the India software lab. She is responsible for enabling teams in the lab to adopt QSE recommended practices for improvement and establishing local communities and events where engineers can share their best practices and learning. Maya has been conducting the two-day Disciplined Agile Development workshops in the India lab and is part of the lab's Agile focus group, which has been set up to drive agile adoption. She has experience in leading quality initiatives in India and providing process consultancy to other IBM units in AP and Europe.

Thomas Starz is a software developer and agile coach with IBM SWG and works as part of Tivoli Service Automation Manager team. Thomas was among the early adopters of agile methods in his organization. He gathered his first agile experiences through practicing with student teams before he introduced agile practices in product development. He is a Certified Scrum-Master and Practitioner and an active member of the IBM Scrum Community. He regularly teaches an internal IBM Disciplined Agile Development class and works as a mentor and coach for several teams and individuals in various locations.

John Sutcliffe is a software development manager and Certified ScrumMaster working with distributed teams at IBM, in the Information Management group working for the Cognos Software Group. John has been deeply involved with the Cognos team in its conversion to Agile practices and their integration into IBM. John recently served a term as a member of the QSE Scrum Community Leadership Team. John was recently made a QSE Fellow for his contributions to the QSE team. John has spoken on facilitation skills and their importance at several IBM internal conferences and virtual events.

Teresa Shen Swingler is an advisory software engineer focusing on user interface design for storage management. She has worked in a distributed agile environment with IBM Director as part of STG.

Michael Thompson is a staff software engineer for WebSphere Application Server's Security team. He has a background in open source, Linux, and C/C++ development, and currently develops in Java with JUnit. He is a QSE TopGun, agile coach, and TDD advocate for the WebSphere organization, and has taught IBM Agile and TDD/unit test classes. With a passion for improving development processes and practices, Michael has embraced agile and champions unit test and static analysis within as part of development and continuous test activities. Michael is a graduate of Clarkson University with a BS in Computer Science.

Jeff Treece is a software development manager for IBM Software Group Information Management.

Mark Wainwright is a software engineer and coach on the Agile/Lean Center of Competence team where he uses his experience of leading agile development teams to help and encourage other SWG teams adopt agile practices. Over a period of 20 years, he has worked in services, sales, and the software group as a programmer, project manager, pre-sales technical support, architect, and integration test architect. He has been promoting agile development since 2006.

Hanhong Xue is an IBM senior software engineer leading a software development team in communication protocols for high-performance computing in IBM Systems and Technology Group. He has been practicing agile with a globally distributed team and within a waterfall-oriented environment since 2006.

Ming Zhi Xie is a CDL Testing Center (Testing as a Service) technical leader, an agile coach, and an agile practitioner. Ming Zhi frequently leads agile sessions and workshops at the IBM China Lab. He has published a series of papers on agile and agile testing via conference and IBM internal and external websites. He is also an agile consultant serving IBM China internal and external customers in dealing with agile deployment and agile testing consulting services.

CHAPTER 1

The Evolution of Scrum

If we don't change, we don't grow. If we don't grow, we aren't really living.

Gail Sheehy

Scrum is an iterative framework for managing software projects according to agile principles. It enables teams to deliver the right features on time, on budget, and with great quality. Scrum helps a software development organization adapt to changing business requirements and stakeholders' needs while protecting the team from unproductive disruptions to their workflow.

A **Team** of five to nine members works to produce a tangible deliverable the customer can review at the end of short periods of time with a fixed duration—**Sprints**. At the end of each Sprint (also referred to as an "**iteration**"), the team reflects on its performance and considers ways to improve. Scrum helps a company to compete by focusing the team on the highest-value client requirements.

When Ken Schwaber first introduced Scrum at the 1995 International Conference on Object-Oriented Programming, Systems, Languages, and Applications (OOPSLA), it was common to have collocated development teams (Schwaber 1995). Much of the available documentation on Scrum reflects those roots. For example, Scrum describes **Daily Scrum** meetings as occurring at the "same time and place" each day. Requirements and tasks are on small notecards tacked on physical task boards located in a common area. During the planning cycle, everyone sits around a table, openly discussing the requirements and displaying their planning "poker cards" simultaneously. This often-used technique in Scrum is called **Planning Poker**™.

For an increasing number of software projects, collocation is no longer the norm—in fact, recent surveys have shown that only 45% of agile teams are collocated, and the rest are distributed in some manner (Ambler 2009). Although most people would agree that collocation and face-to-face communication are ideal, today's business environment often demands that managers organize globally distributed development teams. So, teams need to figure out how to work effectively as part of a distributed team. Given Scrum's roots in collocated teams, this means Scrum practices need some extension and reinterpretation to fit the way we work today.

Thousands of companies, from the very small to large-scale enterprises, use Scrum because of the competitive advantages it provides. And many of those companies are finding techniques that enable them to use Scrum successfully within a distributed environment.

This chapter reviews the fundamentals of Scrum. It describes the different arrangements of distributed teams and provides practical guidelines for organizing Scrum Teams. Finally, this chapter describes the IBM® development environment and the Scrum adoption within IBM as an example of how distributed teams use Scrum within a large-scale enterprise.

Core Principles of Scrum

Before making any changes to Scrum, it is important to understand Scrum's underlying principles. We recommend that you review Ken Schwaber's *Agile Software Development with Scrum* before continuing with this book. Throughout this book, we discuss techniques that distributed teams can use to increase their chances for success with Scrum.

Those who have experience with Scrum may want to skip this section. However, we have found that with time, teams can drift in their understanding of what is pure Scrum. We recommend reading this section to ensure that you understand the baseline used throughout the rest of this book.

An Agile Project Management Framework

Scrum is a disciplined framework for agile project management made up of a few simple roles, structured meetings, and artifacts. Ken Schwaber, the co-creator of Scrum, compares Scrum to a game of chess. There are a few pieces and a few simple rules, but the strategy and possible permutations of execution can be complex.

Scrum Roles

Scrum defines three roles as part of a Scrum Team: the ScrumMaster, the Product Owner, and the Team. The **ScrumMaster** is a servant to the team. This person is responsible for ensuring the Scrum Team adheres to Scrum values, practices, and rules (Schwaber 2009). The ScrumMaster ensures that meetings run smoothly and makes sure that everyone on the team has what they need to be successful. If the Scrum Team faces a **Blocker**, an issue that prevents progress, the Scrum-Master is responsible for ensuring its quick resolution.

The Scrum **Product Owner** is the person who owns the **Product Backlog** (a list of stakeholder needs for the product), ranks the work items by priority, and defines the acceptance conditions. The Product Owner is responsible for everything that goes into the product release.

The Product Owner meets with stakeholders, preferably covering all four of the following groups, to gather their needs (Kessler and Sweitzer 2007):

- **Principals**—Customer representatives who decide whether to buy.
- **Insiders**—Those within the software development company directly impacted by the project.
- **Partners**—Solution providers, integrators, and others.
- **End users**—Stakeholders who will use the product that is in development.

The **Team** is a self-organizing, self-managing, cross-functional group of people, such as developers, testers, information developers, architects, and any other participants the team needs to deliver the work described in the Product Backlog. The Team selects the Product Backlog and turns it into increments.

A **Scrum Team** consists of the Product Owner, ScrumMaster, and the Team. It is responsible for taking the work in the Product Backlog and figuring out how to deliver small demonstrable increments of the work in each Sprint while they are managing their own work in the process. Team members are collectively responsible for the success of each iteration and of the project as a whole (Schwaber 2004).

Scrum Artifacts

Scrum Teams work from a single, prioritized **Product Backlog**, as shown in Figure 1.1. The Product Backlog is the master list of work for the entire project. It contains the prioritized requirements and size estimates for both business value and development effort. Anyone on the team can add items to the Product Backlog.

Although Scrum does not define the format for stakeholder needs, many teams use **User Stories** because they can help teams to focus on the value they will deliver to stakeholders. User Stories typically follow the format "As a <role>, I need to <goal> so that <business value>." They include deliverable acceptance conditions and brief notes from the team based on conversations with the Product Owner and stakeholders. The User Stories help teams focus on the value they will deliver and show to stakeholders at the end of each Sprint. This guide substitutes the terms "User Stories" and "stakeholder needs" interchangeably. For more information, refer to Mike Cohn's *User Stories Applied* (2004).

The detail level for each of the stakeholder needs in the Product Backlog varies. The high-priority stakeholder requirements the team must address early in the release need more details. The less-critical items the team will address further along in the release may have fewer details and will serve mainly as placeholders for discussion. The Product Owner is responsible for using his or her technical knowledge as well as knowledge of the team and of the business value to assess stakeholder needs and order the backlog in a priority sequence. The conditions to define these priorities can include the return on investment (ROI) for the development effort, knowledge of the development team's abilities and capacity, and the technical value of items for future development. In enterprise environments with complex projects, the Product Owner is more likely to rely on an Architecture Owner to understand technical implications and to facilitate major technical decisions with the Scrum Team. Although the Product Owner considers technical input from the Architecture Owner, the Product Owner is ultimately responsible for prioritization.

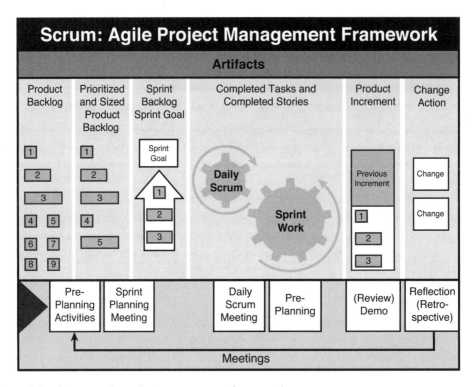

Figure 1.1   Scrum: agile project management framework

The cross-functional Scrum Team is responsible for sizing the effort needed to deliver each requirement in the Product Backlog. By having cross-functional representation in sizing, the team will include all relevant project tasks, including architecture review, development, testing, end user documentation, user experience tasks, and others in the estimate. Because the team as a whole is responsible for delivering the User Stories, the act of estimating as a team helps to build team ownership. Team ownership is a key idea of Scrum and a key to a team's success with Scrum.

The Sprint

The team works to complete tasks in the Sprint Backlog throughout the Sprint. Sprints are a powerful technique to time box the project and channel resources to work on the highest-priority requirements. The literature varies on how long a Sprint should last. Ken Schwaber recommends one month. If the complexity demands more control because of greater risk, he recommends shorter Sprints. Shorter Sprints pay for the risk management with the additional planning. Sprints should be a consistent length, so the team establishes a regular pattern of delivery. Most teams within IBM use a consistent Sprint length of either two weeks or four weeks. In industry, the most common sprint length is two weeks (33% of teams), followed by four weeks (23% of teams), and then three weeks (17% of teams) (Ambler 2008).

Team members register completion of their tasks in a common tracking tool (that is, spreadsheet, notes on a board, or other tools such as IBM Rational Team Concert™). Each team member is responsible for updating the tool to show that his or her work is complete. This removes the time-consuming project management task of collecting status.

On the first day of every Sprint, the Scrum Team meets with the Product Owner to plan the Sprint. The length of the meeting will vary, depending on the length of the Sprint. For a thirty-day Sprint, the team will likely meet for the entire day. For a two-week Sprint, Scrum Teams typically meet for half a day. During the first half of the meeting, the team discusses the high-priority items from the Product Backlog. Effective communication is essential for the team to understand the Product Owner's and stakeholders' expectations for the items. Often the discussion will include high-level sketches to help the Team understand the Product Owner's vision. In the second half of the meeting, the Scrum Team goes over the Product Backlog and identifies the User Stories from the list that it will commit to completing during the Sprint. For each user story, the team will detail all tasks, including architecture review, development, testing, end user documentation, user experience tasks, and others.

Each day of the Sprint, the team gets together for a "Daily Scrum," also referred to as a "Daily Standup." Each team member answers three questions: What did you do yesterday? What are you going to do today? Do you have any blockers?

At the end of the Sprint, the team demonstrates working code for the User Stories they completed during the Sprint to the Product Owner and stakeholders. The team does not show User Stories from the Sprint they did not complete; instead, they move them back to the Product Backlog. The Product Owner will set a priority for those stories once again, and the team may decide to complete the work in the following Sprint.

After the demonstration, development team members get together to reflect on the Sprint and to identify ways they can improve. They conduct a reflection meeting in which they discuss their thoughts on what went well and how they can improve. The development team then identifies one or two items on which they can improve in the next Sprint.

The Shift to Distributed Development Teams

Since the emergence of agile methods in the mid-1990's, the business of software development has changed dramatically. Today's software development organizations are more likely to outsource at least part of their development. They are also more likely to expand their business into other countries—including high-growth countries like Russia and China. In other words, their business is more likely to be distributed. And with increasing access to high-speed Internet service and improvements in distance collaboration tools, even employees within the same city are more likely to telecommute and work with their colleagues in a distributed fashion at least part of the time.

Globally Distributed Teams to Reduce Costs

How do teams become distributed? A software development organization may outsource a particular function to another company in another country, or the software development organization may be hiring their own workers in an emerging country. With a well thought-out plan to best leverage the talent in multiple countries, it can be less expensive to develop a product. Working with distributed teams where the talent is available to do the work can sometimes reduce labor and business operations costs.

Reaching Market More Quickly with the "Follow the Sun" Model

The team with members in the U.S. and China essentially has the possibility of working on a project 24 hours a day and making significantly more progress than a team working on a standard (8-hour) workday. By working with distributed teams, it is possible for companies to work a full 24-hour day and get their product to market more quickly.

As a first example, assume that a team has 10 stories in a Sprint that would take 20 working days to get done for a team working 8 hours a day. That would be two days per story. If the team can split those stories between the two smaller cross-functional teams—one in California and one in Beijing—the product could get to market in half the time (assuming equal velocity). Each team would complete five stories in ten working days. By working in parallel on the User Stories, the product gets to market more quickly. For a second example, assume the team has most of their developers in California and most of their testers in Beijing. Developers develop a small piece of code during their eight hours and testers test the code during their eight hours, both of which are in the same 24-hour period. If you have more integration testing and performance testing that needs to be done toward the end of the Sprint, this is done during the Beijing day. You may not get to market twice as quickly the way you are able to with the first scenario, but your product will get to market more quickly. And, if your competition is limited to an 8-hour workday during every 24 hours, your product will likely get to market more quickly than your competitor's product.

Distributed Teams Expand Access to New Markets

Most of foreign affiliate sales are local sales, and local sales in emerging markets increased between 1994 and 2002 (Borga 2005). To parent companies, this underscores the importance of investing in foreign affiliates.

The world's top 100 non-financial transnational corporations, ranked by foreign assets in 2003, showed the UK, Netherlands, Japan, France, Spain, Germany, Switzerland, the United States, Malaysia, Australia, Norway, the Republic of Korea, and Ireland are all home to leading corporations that invest heavily outside their home country. An average of 41 percent of the employees in the top 20 transnational corporations work outside of the home country (United Nations).

IBM continues to drive growth in emerging markets, which accounted for 18 percent of IBM's overall geographic revenue in the second quarter of 2008, and represented a growth rate of 21 percent year-to-year (Azzi 2008). The Brazil, Russia, India, and China subset grew 31 percent in the second quarter of 2008, led by strong growth in India. IBM continues to grow, nurture, and develop software development team members in these markets. In January 2009, the IBM Scrum Community included software development team members from more than 30 different countries as a result.

Acquisitions

Another trend that increases team distribution is market consolidation, which results in an increase in acquisitions. These acquisitions are likely to result in distributed teams as the combined companies begin working together to integrate their products. Within IBM, Cognos® is a good example of this. Cognos bought several companies with development teams in multiple locations before IBM bought them. After joining IBM, the different Cognos branches began working with IBM teams in even more distributed locations.

Expanding for Innovation and Thought Leadership

Another business trend that is increasing team distribution is the search for knowledge, intellectual property, and innovation. Studies have found that multinational companies produce more ideas than their purely domestic counterparts (Criscuolo 2005). Having more researchers and access to a larger "worldwide pool of information" fosters the generation of more ideas.

In a knowledge-based economy, innovation and thought-leadership are critical to the success of a business. Hiring software development team members in other countries as part of the search for innovation naturally increases distribution of teams.

Telecommuting

Telecommuting is also a growing trend that increases the likelihood that even teams working in the same geographical areas will work as a distributed team. In a 2008 CompTIA study, 78 percent of the respondents reported that some employees within their organizations telecommute at least part-time (CompTIA 2008). Telecommuting can provide a significant increase in productivity, cost savings for companies, and a decrease in their carbon footprint.

Employers are also using telecommuting as an incentive that attracts new employees who see an opportunity for improved work-life integration. As a result, telecommuting is a trend that is likely to continue to grow (Levison 2008).

Improvements in Distributed Collaboration Tools

Improved tools for distributed communications and server-based, multiuser tools for product development are removing barriers, and more teams view distributed collaboration as an alternative. Today's communications tools enable teams to identify when their teammates are available online and to communicate quickly with one or more through a chat session. They enable teams to share what they are seeing on their screen with others. Tools enable team members to sketch their ideas on a virtual whiteboard. And today's development tools enable anyone anywhere to view work requests, view status of work, identify defects, and more.

Because of the business value of distribution and the increasing improvements in the tools that make effective distributed collaboration possible, it is likely that teams will become even *more* distributed over time.

Types of Distributed Teams That Have Emerged

As software development teams have become more distributed, they have adopted different patterns or models of distribution. Each model of distribution has a different set of challenges associated with it. Scrum Team members will recognize there are four general levels of challenges with each of the different Scrum activities. The subsequent chapters in this book provide suggestions and recommendations for dealing with Scrum practices at each of the levels of distribution. By increasing distribution, these levels are as follows:

1. Collocated
2. Collocated Part-Time
3. Distributed with Overlapping Work Hours
4. Distributed with No Overlapping Work Hours

Figure 1.2 provides a visual representation of this relationship.

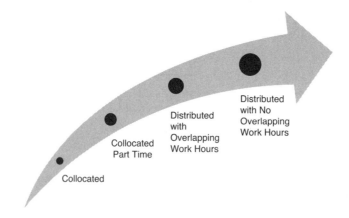

Figure 1.2   Levels of distribution

Collocated

Collocated teams have members that are all in the same physical location. Team members may have their own individual or shared offices, or they may work in a radically collocated environment where all team members have desk space in one large conference room. In order for a team to be considered collocated, they have to meet face-to-face frequently. There are cases where a team may sit in cubicles on the same floor and still never overhear discussions between their teammates or rarely meet for face-to-face communication. To be collocated, a team must meet frequently.

The first level describes all the challenges that collocated teams normally face with Scrum. Delivering a tangible working product within each Sprint heightens any existing dysfunctions and communications challenges in a team. We will discuss these challenges in the other three successive levels of distribution.

Collocated teams are becoming less common in our global workplace. Elizabeth Woodward, an agile coach within IBM, has noted the following:

> *In teaching our two-day Disciplined Agile course throughout IBM, I have met only one collocated team—a team of developers working on a federal government contract. They were on the same floor within a building in Washington, D.C. In general, though, students in every other class that I have taught have all been part of a distributed team.*

The existing literature provides proven techniques for managing collocated Scrum Teams. This guide will provide new techniques for dealing with remote teams working in the other three levels of distribution.

Collocated Part-Time

Collocated Part-Time teams have members that are usually all in the same physical location, with some members who occasionally work off-site. Team members may occasionally work from another business location or perhaps out of their home offices.

Collocated Part-Time teams experience some of the challenges experienced by distributed teams. However, in general, team members are in the same time zone and have the opportunity to meet face-to-face if necessary. For these teams, Scrum meetings such as the Daily Scrum and **Sprint Planning** meetings gradually become more challenging, depending on how available the off-site team members are. Useful collaboration tools are critical to involve off-site team members.

Team members can start to experience difficulties with some of the core Scrum principles even with this scenario. Take the daily Scrum meeting. If most of the team members are physically present in the room and just a few are remote, it can be difficult to remember the people on the phone. Remote team members can begin to feel out of touch with the rest of group. On the other hand, if the team uses teleconferences for the Scrum meetings and most of the members are remote, the meeting can drag on. Without facial gestures or expressions to help signal that someone is taking too long to complete their turn, the person may continue to drift further off topic— turning a 15-minute Scrum into an hour-long yawn-fest.

A second example of the challenge for Collocated Part-Time teams is a Sprint Planning meeting with most of the team in one room and one person calling in. In such meetings, it is likely the team members gathered in the room will be insensitive to the remote caller. The team may neglect to draw the remote worker. As the adage goes, "out of sight, out of mind." Steffan Surdek, a User Experience Lead within IBM, made the following observations:

> *I have been working remotely (with a one-hour time difference) with my team for about 18 months. My biggest challenge is making sure that people invite me to the planning*

and design sessions that happen with the rest of the team. To help with this, I keep in close contact with the team leads that are aware of the different meetings that are going on. When they plan meetings, they put me as an optional invitee so I can decide which meetings I need to take part in.

Because of the time difference, I also face times when people schedule meetings during my lunch hour or after my regular working hours. The biggest challenges, though, are always ensuring that I'm invited to meetings, a dial-in number is available, and the rest of team joins the conference call at the appointed time.

Distributed with Overlapping Work Hours

The next tier of pain related to working as a distributed team is the case where the team is **Distributed with Overlapping Work Hours**. With this model, team members have at least a few hours during each normal workday in which they interact with each other.

One example of this model is a Scrum Team of eight members of all disciplines, where five members are in Europe (the UK) and three members are in India (Pune), with an overlap of 3.5 hours (see Figure 1.3). On such teams, the development team must try to schedule the Daily Scrum meeting during the overlapping work hours. Not everyone is at the same point in the work-day during the call.

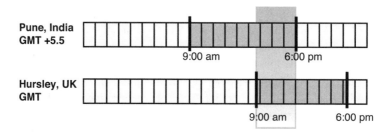

Figure 1.3   Distributed with overlapping work hours

The Sprint Planning meeting is more difficult to schedule than the Daily Scrum. The Sprint Planning meeting typically happens on the morning of the first day of the Sprint. A Scrum Team with members in the UK and in India will face an obvious scheduling challenge. If the team schedules the Sprint Planning meeting for 9:00 in the morning in India, members in the UK need to be available at 3:30 in the morning to attend. If the Team schedules the meeting for 9:00 a.m. in the UK, then half the day is over in India.

At the end of the last day of each Sprint, the team schedules a demonstration meeting. For our Scrum Team with members in the UK and India, at what time should the team schedule the meeting? In the afternoon of the UK or India? The team has to make a decision that works best for the team. Suggestions and guidelines are provided in Chapter 8, "End of Sprint Reviews."

Another common challenge with distributed teams is to be sure the Scrum meetings are efficient. Even if the team is able to find a good meeting time, it is more difficult to know if remote people are actively engaged or not due to the lack of body language. Compared to a face-to-face meeting, it is also much more difficult to know how members are reacting to different messages.

Cultural differences and language barriers also become more acute in this tier. Beyond scheduling issues, these teams face more challenges in that team members may not have the same communications styles. Working as a distributed team is already challenging, and team members who are not native speakers of the language used for meetings will likely have a much harder time being understood and understanding others during a teleconference. The extreme scenario would be a team split—for example, between the UK, Germany, and Spain. The time difference here is negligible (one hour) but the cultural challenges can be quite large.

John Langlois, an IBM Executive Project Manager, shares a story about cultural impact on communication where nodding and acknowledgment do not indicate agreement:

> *A U.S. Product Owner complained that our development organization in Japan had not worked on a key feature they had agreed to develop during a Sprint. "Did Yokemura-san say: I agree to work on the feature?" I asked. In fact, his actual words were: "Ah so des ka," which loosely translated means "Is that so?." Yokemura-san had simply confirmed that he heard you. The next time, ask him directly, if he agrees.*

To be a successful distributed team, teams that are significantly distributed may need to address cultural and language barriers, as well as barriers related to time zone differences.

Distributed with No Overlapping Work Hours

Teams that are **Distributed with No Overlapping Work Hours** have no opportunity to interact during each other's normal working hours and live in the most challenging tier of pain.

One example of such a team is a cross-functional team that has members in California (U.S. Pacific time zone), in Texas (U.S. Central time zone), and in Beijing, China (see Figure 1.4). When it is the beginning of the workday in Texas (8:00 a.m.), it is only 6:00 a.m. in California, and it is 9:00 p.m. in Beijing.

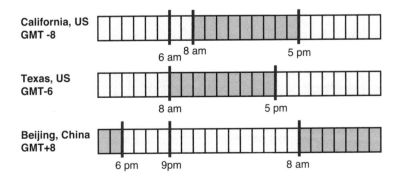

Figure 1.4   Distributed with No Overlapping Work Hours

Every Scrum meeting is a challenge for these teams. With no overlapping time at all, when do you schedule these meetings? Working together throughout the Sprint is also much more difficult, given that most of the daily communication must be handled asynchronously, using tools like email.

Ways of Handling Distributed Teams

In addition to the different levels of distributed teams, Scrum Teams will also be organized in ways that will allow Scrum to be used for development of large-scale projects. It is almost impossible to provide recommendations for distributed Scrum Teams in the enterprise without taking into consideration how multiple teams work together to deliver a project. Jeff Sutherland and Guido Schoonheim describe three different models that you can consider when using Scrum with distributed teams (Sutherland and Schoonheim 2008), as follows:

- Isolated Scrums
- Distributed Scrum of Scrums
- Totally Integrated Scrums

Isolated Scrums

In the **Isolated Scrum model**, each location has a cross-functional Scrum Team. Teams work apart from one another. Each team is independent. There is no need for collaboration between teams.

This is the ideal scenario because teams are essentially at the first two levels of distribution—Collocated or Collocated Part-Time. The teams can more easily use Scrum as originally prescribed.

The closer that a team can get to setting up Isolated Scrums and staying within the first two levels of distribution, the less effort will go into overcoming challenges related to distributed communication. Effective face-to-face communication breeds success, regardless of whether the team is using Scrum or some other development method.

Consider a software development organization that has a combination of development, test, user experience, information development, architecture, and other key skills at each of four sites in Germany, India, China, and the United States. In the best-case scenario, the organization would create a cross-functional Scrum Team in each location: Germany, India, China, and the United States. In the worst-case scenario, each Scrum Team may include members spread across time zones that have no overlap during a normal workday. Typically, not all the necessary skills will be available at each site. So, the organization will need to compromise by forming distributed teams. In this case, it is important for the organization and for the teams to find ways to reduce the pain as much as possible.

Distributed Scrum of Scrums

The second model, the **Distributed Scrum of Scrums**, places a separate, cross-functional Scrum Team at each location, but the teams use a regular **Scrum of Scrums meeting** to coordinate efforts between them.

If separate Scrum Teams at different sites are working together to integrate their deliverables into an overall project or product, the team coordinates the work through a Scrum of Scrums meeting. Obviously, some representatives will need to attend remotely.

Ken Schwaber (2004) recommends conducting the Scrum of Scrums daily as a 15-minute meeting where representatives from each Scrum Team answer the following four questions:

- What did your team do yesterday?
- What will your team do today?
- What blockers have you met?
- What blockers might you be throwing into another team's way?

The last question is an addition to the three Scrum questions used in a collocation model. Mike Cohn (2004) suggests holding longer meetings, fewer times a week, to give members more time to communicate. Regardless of which method the team uses for the Scrum of Scrums, the key point is that isolated teams need to communicate effectively following a model similar to the Daily Scrum. This means using brief, to-the-point communication that looks for ways to remove obstacles and move the team forward through project execution.

The Product Owner faces the added challenge of coordinating the work from not only one, but multiple teams. In fact, there may be multiple individuals in different locations who make up a Product Owner team. As a result, it is important they communicate effectively and speak with a single voice.

Totally Integrated Scrums

The third model of distributed Scrum is the **Totally Integrated Scrum**. In this model, each Scrum Team has members in multiple locations. It may be that all testers are at one location while all developers are at another location or that each of the cross-functional team members telecommutes. Where multiple Scrum Teams are working together to deliver a project, all of these teams were required to have a single integrated, integration-tested increment at the end of every Sprint.

The Totally Integrated Scrum Team falls into the third level of distribution if members are in time zones with overlapping work hours and into the fourth level if they have no overlap in work hours.

Totally Integrated Scrum Teams are common at IBM. Cross-functional Scrum Teams have members in three or more locations, in multiple time zones, and with members whose native language is not the primary language used for team meetings.

John Sutcliffe, a ScrumMaster with IBM Cognos, shares an example of totally integrated Scrum Teams within the company:

IBM Cognos' Performance Management (PM) team has a long history of using totally integrated teams spread across many geographies and time zones: North America, Europe, and India. Many of the groups making up the IBM Cognos PM team had joined Cognos via an acquisition that forced these teams to work with the other teams within

*Cognos. As the companies became a part of the larger organization, they found them-
selves working with Development, Quality Control, Documentation, Release Engineering, and other teams. These teams had members spread across York (England), Ottawa
(Canada), Minneapolis (U.S.), Princeton (U.S.), Littleton (U.S.), Pune (India), and
other locations. The ScrumMaster was in Minneapolis MN with one or two developers,
another developer was in Portugal, another in Luxemburg, the Quality Control team
was in Ottawa, or spread between Ottawa and Littleton, and the Product Owner was in
central England.*

In working with Totally Integrated Scrum Teams, we also use the Distributed Scrum of
Scrums to coordinate the work of the teams. This follows Sutherland and Schoonheim's description of the Distributed Scrum of Scrums, except that each team sending a representative is a
member of a totally integrated Scrum Team, rather than a separate collocated Scrum Team.

In the article on outsourced development teams, Jeff Sutherland describes how he has been
able to coach distributed teams to a hyperproductive state where productivity is 5 to 10 times
industry average. The chapters in this book elaborate on techniques used by distributed teams to
increase their productivity. This book also shares valuable insight about what not to do.

IBM's Experience in Distributed Scrum

Many of the examples in this book come from members of IBM Scrum Teams. These teams oper-
ate within all four levels of distribution and as Isolated Scrum Teams, Scrum of Scrums, and
Totally Integrated Scrum Teams.

IBM is an incredibly large and diverse organization. To give some sense of the scale, the
company produced more than US$98 billion revenue in 2007 with a net income of US$10.4 bil-
lion. This exceeds the Gross National Product of 120 small countries. In 2009, there were over
416,000 employees in more than 200 countries. The largest two business units have over 35,000
software engineers between them.

The company has software engineers of diverse cultures working in nearly every time zone.
They work on teams that use different tools, programming languages, and development applications that make sense for their particular projects. The variety of software under development
varies: Some teams are developing applications, others are developing middleware or operating
systems, and still others are developing firmware for hardware products. There are many software
development projects launched internally, whereas other projects enter through acquisitions. In
fact, the company brought in projects from more than 75 companies through acquisitions
between 2000 and 2008.

IBM Software Group averages about 120 individuals on each product. Some of the smaller
teams may have 50 members. Larger teams can have up to 600 people working on a product.
Figure 1.5 shows the distribution level in the IBM WebSphere® Portal V6.0 project (McKinney and
Rivera, 2008). The 224 members of the development team for this project are in two locations:

Boeblingen, Germany and Raleigh, North Carolina in the United States. Four smaller locations share the remaining 114 members of the team. Ten other teams contribute and provide extra assets.

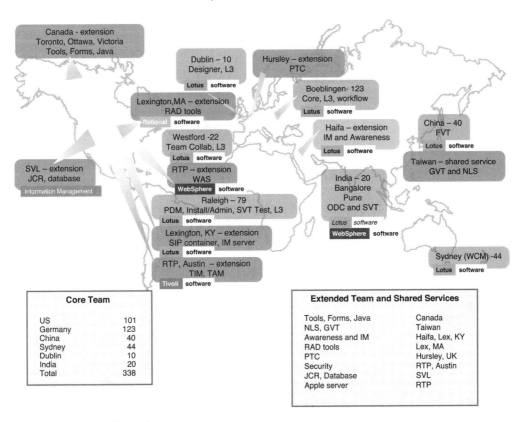

Figure 1.5   Portal V6.0 development

History of Agile in IBM

Given the landscape of diversity within IBM, teams became aware of Agile methods at different rates and with different levels of interest. In fact, the internal Agile movement began as a grass-roots efforts and eventually gained real momentum through executive support.

During the 1980's, like most others, the company promoted the use of waterfall development where progress flows steadily downward through prescribed phases from concept, through design, test, and maintenance. In the 1990's, however, the focus shifted toward more iterative development methods. Internally, teams used a customized version of the Rational Unified Process (RUP), developed methods for sharing through community source and component reuse, and began stressing the end-to-end customer experience of the product lifecycle.

Software engineers in different parts of the business and on different teams began to adopt and promote Agile development internally. This began in the 1990's as Scrum gained recognition through Ken Schwaber's 1995 presentation at OOPSLA and Kent Beck introduced XP practices through "The Chrysler Payroll Project" presentation in 1998. Grassroots Agile adoption began gaining momentum in 2003—two years after the 2001 signing of the Agile manifesto—as a group of four individuals set up an internal Agile community, using a wiki, social software, and discussion boards. Initially, there were 160 internal community members.

Bill Krebs, one of the four founding members of this Agile community, shares his experience from the grassroots perspective:

> *In 2001, someone infected me with JUnit at an information IBM session, and they mentioned it was part of XP and there was a conference. I learned about pair programming and iterations, and tried them in 2003–2004 at NC State University. I wrote a paper that showed good results and presented at an XP conference. We knew we were on the right track, but it was hard to get traction at first. Somehow the words "Extreme" and "Agile" turned people off. We did get traction when people started talking about Lean. It is hard to argue with cutting out waste. And, of course, executive support helps. Acquisitions also helped. We continuously bring in new perspectives and look for ways to leverage what works for them.*

Matt Ganis, another of the founding Agile@IBM members, recalls when they first started with Extreme Programming:

> *Like many development teams, we had some frustration with spending time sizing and analyzing requirements, that in the end, our customer did not want or tried to alter at the last minute. We would always disagree on the deliverable and the time frames after committing to a plan. This was simply because we didn't have time to react, having spent large amounts of time doing some early planning. Since we were a relatively small shop, our solution, with our customer, was to try an Agile approach to see if we could improve this "explosive" situation. The results were outstanding. From the first project onward, our customer insisted we use Agile for all projects. From the start, it was a "win" for the team. Since then, we've moved from a more XP-centric method, to a Scrum model, simply because more than just our developer have adopted these methods.*

Teams were looking for relief from these and other issues within their own organizations. As a result, this grassroots effort centered on the Agile@IBM wiki, which served as a clearinghouse of internal experience reports, discussions, and lists of Agile enthusiasts willing to coach other teams within the company.

In April of 2006, IBM Software Group (SWG) shared their key initiatives at a Technical Leadership Exchange Conference, an IBM-only event that fosters collaboration, networking, and the exchange of ideas by top technical talent and business executives. They identified Lean and Agile as their primary focus. In December 2006, software transformation leadership teams began teaching a two-day Disciplined Agile Development class internally across many of the divisions. At the same time, Vice Presidents began expressing their support through communications to their teams. Teams are rapidly adopting Agile principles and Scrum. In January 2007, only 5 out of 550 projects in SWG were Agile; by 2008, this number increased to 220 projects.

Summary

As you can see, adopting Scrum at IBM has been both a grassroots and top-down effort resulting in the current worldwide transformation. Like many other enterprise organizations today, IBM is transitioning teams to Agile development methods. Many teams have been actively using Scrum for years, some are preparing to begin their first Sprint, and others are considering whether Agile development methods can work with distributed teams. This book captures experiences, answers questions, and provides teams with guidance on how to adopt and use Scrum effectively within a distributed organization and as a distributed Scrum Team.

Ideally, an organization will scale by using Isolated Scrum teams, each with cross-functional skills. However, many business reasons are prompting teams to become more and more distributed. To succeed and compete, most teams need to be able to develop software and work effectively within a distributed organization. The goal in structuring teams should be to minimize pain according to the levels of distribution. Larger teams should consider self-organizing into smaller teams that minimize distribution. Where distributed teams cannot be avoided, Chapter 2, "A Magnifying Glass on Our Dysfunctions," will provide some overall, general guidance for working as part of a distributed team. Each of the subsequent chapters in this book will delve into tips and techniques for engaging in each Scrum activity as a distributed team.

The heart of Scrum is enabling teams to work together as efficiently and effectively as possible. Teaming and good team dynamics are compulsory for the successful use of Scrum. Many people will question whether you can even have a Scrum Team if members are not consistently working together on the same schedule. This guide will show that it is possible to develop a high-performance distributed Scrum Team...if the team makes an effort to draw everyone into the game.

The team will decide whether or not they can be an effective and Agile team given the geographical and cultural distances. If they decide the distributed team *can* function well and that all they need to do is work out *how,* they will be right. They will have an attitude to minimize the issues. If they decide that the distributed team will *not* work, they will also be right because their actions will make the team less effective or even dysfunctional. Sometimes people state openly, with such a strong view, that the distributed team cannot work, it is difficult for them to "keep face" if it does actually start to work well. This can also drive unhelpful behavior. At the end of the day, attitudes, behaviors, and culture are critical factors in determining the success of Agile teams—regardless of the level of distribution.

References

About IBM. http://www.ibm.com/ibm/us/en/. Retrieved February 26, 2009.

Ambler, S.W. (2008). *2008 Agile Adoption Survey*. http://www.ambysoft.com/surveys/agileFebruary2008.html.

Ambler, S.W. (2009). *November 2009 State of the IT Union Survey*. http://www.ambysoft.com/surveys/stateOf ITUnion200911.html.

Anderson, A., Beattie, Ralph, Beck, Kent, et al. "Chrysler Goes to 'Extremes'." *Distributed Computing* (October 1998), pp. 24–28.

Azzi, M. *IBM Growth in Emerging Markets Fuels Lotus Momentum*. http://www.marketwire.com/press-release/ Ibm-NYSE-IBM-884845.html. July 31, 2008.

Borga, M. "Trends in Employment at U.S. Multinational Companies: Evidence from Firm-Level Data." Brookings Trade Forum—2005, pp. 135–163, September 2005.

Cohn, Mike. *User Stories Applied for Agile Software Development*. Boston, MA: Addison-Wesley, 2004.

CompTIA. Summary of "Trends in Telecommuting: Organizations Are Realizing Benefits and Addressing Challenges." http://www.comptia.org/sections/research/reports/200809-TelecomSummary.aspx, 2008.

Criscuolo, C.H. *Global Engagement and the Innovation Activities of Firms*. Cambridge: National Bureau of Economic Research, 2005.

DevSource. *IBM to Mentor Developers in Emerging Markets*. Retrieved February 26, 2009, from DevSource: http://www.devsource.com/c/a/Architecture/IBM-to-Mentor-Developers-in-Emerging-Markets/, 2005.

Employment and Training Administration—U.S. Department of Labor. *Employment and Training Administration Status Report*. Retrieved November 2, 2008, from Scribd: http://www.scribd.com/doc/1717081/Department-of-Labor-BRG-SR-July07-Web, 2007.

Hall, Edward T. *The Silent Language*. Garden City, NY: Doubleday, 1959.

Kessler, Carl, and John Sweitzer. *Outside-in Software Development: A Practical Approach to Building Successful Stake-holder-Based Products*. Upper Saddle River, NJ: IBM Press, 2007.

Levinson, M. *Survey: Telecommuting Improves Productivity, Lowers Costs*. http://www.networkworld.com/news/2008/ 100708-survey-telecommuting-improves-productivity-lowers.html?hpg1=bn, October 7, 2008.

List of Mergers and Acquisitions by IBM. Retrieved February 26, 2009, from http://en.wikipedia.org/wiki/List_of_ IBM_acquisitions_and_spinoffs.

McKinney, S., and Rivera, T. The Economics of Agile: The Competitive Advantage of Developing Commercial Software with Agile Methods. *Agile2008 Conference Proceedings*. Toronto, 2008.

Schwaber, K. SCRUM Development Process. OOPSLA'95 Workshop on Business Object Design and Implementation. http://www.tiac.net/users/jsuth/oopsla/oo95summary.html, December 10, 1995.

Schwaber, K. *Agile Project Management with Scrum*. Redmond, WA: Microsoft Press, 2004.

Schwaber, K. *ScrumGuide*. Scrum Alliance, 2009. http://www.scrumalliance.org/resources/598.

Sutherland, J., and G. Schoonheim. Fully Distributed Scrum: The Secret Sauce for Hyperproductive Outsourced Development Teams. *Agile2008 Conference Proceedings*. Toronto, 2008.

United Nations. *United Nations Conference on Trade and Development: World Investment Report*. Retrieved February 26, 2009, from 2005 Transnational Corporations and the Internationalization of R&D. http://www.unctad.org/en/ docs/wir2005ch1_en.pdf.

CHAPTER 2

Challenges Faced by Distributed Teams

The hardest thing to explain is the glaringly evident which every had decided not to see.

Ayn Rand

What challenges does your distributed team have? Are they failing to meet some expectations? Are they having trouble working as a team? Is team morale a problem? Scrum can't fix every problem, but it can bring them out into the open where the team can evaluate and correct them. Scrum puts challenges under a magnifying glass. As the image under the glass grows larger, they scream for attention, and your team's performance will improve after they address the challenges and correct dysfunctions.

In the ideal case, a distributed team has a mix of skills at each location so they can work and make progress independently. However, it is more common for different work areas to be at different sites—such as team leads at one site, testers at another site, developers at another site, and writers at another site. Distributed teams heighten the need for clear, timely communication between sites. Recognizing and confronting communication inefficiencies can be critical to the success of the project.

This chapter identifies some of the challenges distributed teams experience whether they use waterfall or agile methods. This chapter also provides general tips for improving team communications regardless of where the team is within the Sprint. During team formation, the team will develop a process for social etiquette, communications, and other aspects of distributed collaboration. The team will evaluate their performance at the end of each Sprint during the retrospective to find opportunities to improve, although the team is expected to make continuous updates throughout the Sprint as needed.

Communicating with Distributed Team Members

Distributed teams experience the same problems as collocated teams, plus they have some extra ones. Many of the problems are communication issues at their core because of the added difficulties posed by distance. Even when team members are on the same continent or in the same region, not working face to face can complicate communication. The complexity increases with distance as time zones, language barriers, and cultural differences get in the way.

Even when all members of the team speak the same language and have the same cultural background, there can still be significant communication problems. An important part of communication is nonverbal, and a huge challenge in communication between distributed team members is missing the nonverbal cues. Edward T. Hall (1959), a renowned social anthropologist, argued that in a normal conversation, more than 65 percent of social meaning occurs through the nonverbal channel. In a remote meeting by telephone, since the typical nonverbal cues to meaning are not available, only 35 percent of the normal communication channel is available to us! As a result, remote team communication can be challenging. A videoconference is a good compromise, but you never have all tools at your disposal in a remote communication. IBM ScrumMaster Thomas Starz offers the following observation:

> *In the daily standup meeting, I watch the speaker the least. I spend more time watching the reactions of the team members to the speaker, which is often impossible with a distributed team.*

Knowing the remote participants can compensate to some extent. We highly recommend that team members have an opportunity to meet face-to-face if at all possible. If not all members can meet physically, consider having at least a few members meet at the beginning of a project or initiative. This helps the team members to get to know each other's personalities, mannerisms, communications styles, and cultures.

Time Zones and Working Hours

Misunderstandings about meeting dates and times occur more often with a distributed team working in different time zones than with a collocated team. The strategies in this chapter can help teams deal with issues related to dates and times.

When working with global teams, team members need to be mindful of different time zones. When identifying dates in communications, it is important to always state the time zone or, at the beginning of the project, agree on the time zone the team will use and stay consistent. Many global team members have experienced dialing into a meeting early only to find that no one calls in at the supposedly scheduled time. At best, the person has dialed in hours *before* the meeting. At worst, the person has *missed* the meeting.

It is important, too, to remember the format of dates varies throughout the world. The order of day, month, and year differs, as well as separators. For example, November 12, 1909 is 11/12/09 in the United States, 09/11/12 in Japan, and 12/11/09 in Spain. Getting a note saying the expected date for something is "5/6" can cause confusion and possibly negatively impact the project. To clarify for everyone on the team, spell out the month and use the four-digit year.

Working in different time zones is discussed throughout this book. One way to try to reduce the impact of different time zones is to actively and creatively look for ways of taking advantage of it. Even if the full "follow the sun" approach described in Chapter 1 cannot be used, there are often activities that can be progressed by one part of the team while the other part of the team is not working. These kinds of activities can also help team work, as high levels of collaboration will be required. The key is that the team needs the mindset and attitude to try to turn a constraint into an advantage whenever possible!

Cultural Differences

Cultural differences can also impact the effectiveness of a team's communication and collaboration. These differences become more obvious when a team works closely together as part of a Scrum team throughout a Sprint.

As an example, in some cultures, it is inappropriate for someone to say they do not understand the speaker. The primary symptom of this is finding that some team members say "yes" without ever challenging or questioning statements. This can be problematic for a distributed team where communication in general is much more challenging. Identifying points that need clarification is especially critical to align the team's efforts with the expectations of the Product Owner.

Steffan Surdek relates the following example:

> *I spent hours with the team designing a solution to a problem, and at the end of the meeting, everyone understood and agreed the solution was the right one. When the developer delivered the code, I realized the problem was still there. I spoke with the team, and they said the original solution did not work so they went in a different direction instead. After listening to their explanation, it became obvious they did not understand the solution at all.*

Steffan resolved this by pair-programming to ensure the other members of the team understood step-by-step what they needed to do. His example shows team members need to speak up when they do not understand something and to communicate details often to ensure everyone is on the same page. The documentation level should be "just enough" to ensure a common understanding.

Thomas Starz related the following experience:

> *Some years ago, I was responsible for developing a complex, important, but relatively independent software component. A person in Moscow was to complete this work. Whenever we scheduled a meeting at least two days in advance, he always attended. But whenever we tried to schedule a daily meeting, or a meeting on short notice, he would not attend, even though the meeting was during his normal working hours.*

Thomas attributes delayed and missed meetings with the developer's discomfort in letting others know he was experiencing difficulties. *Country-based* culture may explain this reaction, but the developer may also have had previous experience with a *company or team* culture that stressed individual blame over whole team ownership.

Working with team members of different cultural backgrounds also means team members need to be more aware of cultural differences in their communications. Be particularly careful when using humor. What is humorous at best in one culture may be puzzling in another. At worst, misdirected humor can result in anger and harm relationships. Consider the Jyllands-Posten Mohammed cartoons controversy in which a Danish newspaper published depictions of the prophet. While Danish Muslims held public protests, more than fifty other countries published the cartoons. Riots led to deaths of more than 100 people. The Muslim community and the cartoonist in Denmark viewed the cartoon differently. The lesson: Religion, politics, body parts, and animals are all sensitive subjects for different cultures worldwide.

Another area where culture impacts communication is how symbols can differ between countries. For example, the swastika symbol can mean different things depending on society and context. The word "swastika" comes from the Sanskrit words *su* meaning "good," and *asti,* meaning "to be" (Rosenberg). Today, Buddhists and Hindus often use the swastika as a religious symbol, but for many other countries, the symbol quickly conjures negative images of the Nazi party and the associated tragedy—even though the Nazi party reversed the direction of the symbol. The use of color is another area where cultural differences can surface. The color black has a connotation of completeness in English as in a "black lie." The connotations of red in Japanese include "complete" or "clear."

Obviously, the team would be wise to invest some time exploring each others' cultures to get a better understanding of their cultural differences. We encourage distributed teams to explore each other's cultures, as this will help with communication and team bonding and is very rewarding at a personal level. People generally like to be asked about their culture, and people also generally like to learn new things! Andy Pittaway of **IBM** Global Services in the UK provides the following example of his team's approach when they were brought together for a face-to-face meeting at the start of a project:

In a team where people from Italy and India were working together for the first time, a team lunch was being organized in Italy whereby many volunteers prepared food. When planning the lunch, the team discussed the usual array of very nice Italian food. Then someone had the idea to ask the Indian team members to bring a taste of their food. The Indian team members took this to heart and home-cooked a variety of very interesting and delicious food. The Indian food was the most popular on the day. It caused a lot of discussion, requests for recipes, and general conversation, and it is still being talked about almost a year after the event. This really helped the teams get to know each other a little better. These kinds of events may seem unimportant but are often pay great returns on relatively little investment.

Cultural differences impact both communication and collaboration. Scott Ambler notes the following:

> *Some cultures do not promote risk taking, yet others do. Some promote deference to management, whereas some promote challenging everyone. Some promote trust, some do not. An environment without trust makes non-solo development difficult, for example. So, cultural differences affect how you interact with each other, how you communicate, and how you organize.*

Language Differences

A team distributed across regions or countries may also face language differences that will impact their ability to communicate effectively. Language challenges appear in several forms. Some or all distributed team members may not have the same first language, some members may not speak the language used by the team, or team members may not be able to easily understand one another because of accents. A Scrum environment where team members communicate often will highlight communication challenges and make them more obvious.

Keeping Language Simple

For team members whose first language is not the primary language the team uses to communicate, complex language can make communication less effective. Keep sentences simple and concise, use common words, and do not get creative by using the most obscure words in the dictionary. Develop a common low-level vocabulary where you understand one another and build from there.

Readability tools will enable you to find out the complexity of your writing. Readability formulas for U.S. English came about in the 1920s in the United States in response to demands by junior high school science teachers who wanted books that were at a level their students could understand.

Of course, it is not possible to measure all features that promote readability mathematically. Standard words a team will use to describe a product may be unusual and unrecognized by the readability tool, and trying to achieve a certain number on a readability test is not likely to produce good communication. The tests can, however, help you to consider more carefully the complexity of the words and sentence construction you are using. The Flesch-Kincaid Readability Test in Microsoft® Word provides one tool to calculate readability for English documents. Use the Help feature in Microsoft Word to learn more about this feature. If the primary language of your team is not English or if you use a word processing program other than Microsoft Word, you may want to explore other options for determining the readability of your text.

The more complicated the sentences that you use in documents and email, the harder it will be for others who are nonnative speakers to understand. Most readability experts view the average word length, number of syllables, and number of words in each sentence as influencing the complexity of the written material. To foster global communication, keep each sentence simple and direct.

Team members may use informal language when writing email and sending instant messages. If you are working with a distributed team with nonnative speakers, keep in mind that using proper spelling, grammar, and punctuation can make communications less confusing.

Slang, idioms, and clichés can also negatively impact the communication in distributed teams. "BTW" may be universally recognized as meaning "By the way" in an English chat session, but that shorthand will not be understood in another language. In U.S. English, someone who is "blue" is sad. In German, "blue" is *blau*, and someone who is *blau* is drunk. In Ontario, Canada, which has a large German population, someone who is *blooeyed* is drunk. Using "blue" as an idiom can clearly cause miscommunication when working with global teams. Avoiding idioms, slang, and clichés is a best practice for communication in general, but it is even more important when communicating with a globally distributed team.

Also, using pronouns in English can force the listener to find out the related noun. Clarify the sentence for global communication by replacing pronouns with nouns where suitable. Consider replacing he, she, it, that, and this with nouns to help clarify communications.

Giving Everyone a Chance to Speak

On a teleconference, team members have a difficult time knowing when they can interject their ideas without interrupting someone who is speaking. Occasionally, several people will start to speak at the same time. At other times, there may be a long period of silence when each person thinks the other person is about to say something. The language barrier can make it more difficult for nonnative speakers to step into the conversation and supplement other team members' ideas. Jean-Louis Marechaux shares his technique for engaging everyone on the team:

> *I usually facilitate the sharing of ideas by calling on each person to give them a chance to speak and to make sure each person's contribution is captured. This is even more valuable when some team members speak a first language other than the one used in the meeting. The pause gives them time to translate their thoughts into words and to contribute to the conversation.*

Using Group Chat During Meetings

When team members speak different languages, a chat tool can be way for team members to let others know they are having communication issues without feeling as though they are disrupting the call. They can use the tool to say they did not understand something, to ask for a translation, or to ask that a speaker slow down.

Even when everyone uses the same language, chat can be helpful for team members to share web links and pointers to materials they need the team to look at or consider during the Sprint planning meeting. IBM Rational Team Concert (RTC), a distributed development environment, builds chat functionality right into your development environment. This enables you to discover who is currently online, whether they are available, and then optionally log any ensuing chat against a requirement or defect on which you are currently working.

Providing a Translator

When the distributed Scrum team members speak more than one language, the team should agree on one primary language and use that language during global team meetings. Side conversations in various languages can have a negative impact not only on the global team meetings, but also on teaming in general.

If language is a significant issue, consider having someone with fluency available to help with translating. John Langlois remembers one conversation that required translation between an American and a Japanese development team:

> *The American was emphasizing how important the project was to our business strategy by declaring that we were "betting the farm" on the project. The facial expressions on the Japanese team members suggested they were puzzled by the expression, but no one raised their hand to ask for clarification. Eventually a person leaned next to me during a break and asked why we were talking about farm animals. I was also asked to explain the meaning of a "straw man."*

Confirming What Team Members Understand

Do we have the same understanding of a matter? We can ensure a common understanding by asking leading questions or by having members summarize in their own words to confirm their understanding is correct. Typically when one person summarizes, others can quickly determine if their own understanding was correct or ask additional questions to clarify.

Formal inspections, such as Fagan Inspections and some of its predecessors, have been proven to help with reviews of key inputs and deliverables. A key to the review process is restating the content in the code or deliverable by using different wording. Although they can be a little "painful," as they require a formal meeting with roles and a certain structure, the outcome of the meeting is a high level of confidence that all attendees have a common and agreed understanding as to what has been reviewed. Elizabeth Woodward shares a story from a non-IBM project:

> *I was working with a team that was developing software for hosting, conducting, and supporting virtual conferences. Some members of the team had spent time diagramming the feature and briefly documenting the use case for a conference attendee to play back a recorded lecture during a specific presentation time slot for the conference. Though we were all using the same words, when we met to review the work, we discovered there were two valid ways to interpret the recorded lecture diagram and text. Had we not taken a structured approach to inspecting the content, we might not have discovered the problem until the demo at the end of the Sprint—essentially wasting a good portion of the Sprint.*

You can measure the quality of a communication by the amount of response that you get. If you do not like the response, then change something about the way you are communicating! Having a culture where the communicator not only feels responsible for sending the message but also for ensuring the message was received as intended can help in situations where different languages and culture exist.

Tools

The right tools can help facilitate good communication. Requirements repositories, software configuration management, software repository, version control, build software, defect tracking, and project management tools used by a distributed team should provide good performance across the geographies where the team resides.

Daily builds, although important to collocated teams, are even more critical to distributed teams. These builds help to ensure that distributed teams can work continuously. In the worst case, a broken build will block the other team's entire workday.

Locations with a less-advanced communication infrastructure than others can pose problems for the distributed team. For instance, Liz Kamau shares the following story:

> *I worked with a team in India that had to work through a specific person when they took part in conference calls; they could not dial in on their own. We had to cancel conference calls when that person was not available. In other cases, team members that I worked with did not have Internet or phone access at their homes, which made contacting them during their off-hours impossible.*

To increase productivity of distributions teams, issues with communications tools must be identified and addressed. Do not assume the tools and environment available to team members in one location are the same for team members in another location. Ask questions.

Instant messaging tools can be used to help ongoing communications between distributed team members. However, their use needs to be managed in such a way that they do not become too distracting. This can be managed easily in most chat tools by changing your status to "Please do not disturb" or "In a meeting."

File Sharing

Not knowing where to locate files and the correct versions of files to be working with are dysfunctions that plague many distributed teams.

A collocated team working in one large room or separated only by cubicle walls can mask inefficiencies. A team member can step over to ask the person sitting next to them for the latest version of a document, notes from a discussion, or the right version of code. This makes the disorganization less obvious. There is a cost to disrupting work and searching for answers that a collocated team can hide. When there is a four-hour shift in the workday from the person who knows the answer, there is a much longer wait before getting the information. The pain is sharper, and the costs are higher and more obvious.

Teams need to define their methods of work and document them clearly. All team members should follow them to ensure the entire team works in the same way. If you have no documented procedures, you cannot expect all members of the distributed team to be in step. Help the team by ensuring that information flows freely among the team members and that all team members (and distributed teams) feel like equals.

Technical problems that occur with security—firewalls and access lists—can also create barriers that become more challenging with the geographically distributed teams.

Software Engineering Practices

Good software engineering practices are important for both collocated and distributed teams. But, for distributed teams, poor engineering practices are much more obvious and are a greater problem.

Three extreme programming practices that we have found to be particularly valuable to teams are test-driven development, continuous integration, and test automation.

With test-driven development, developers cycle through writing a test, writing the code to pass the test, and then refactoring their code. This helps the entire product team to work quickly and effectively because development is delivering high-quality tested code. As a result, work can proceed with fewer defects. This means teams spend less time debugging and recreating issues. Additionally, test-driven development is a low-level design approach that allows the team to evolve the design over time. Finding defects earlier in the software development process is less-costly and time consuming than finding and addressing defects later. Given the decrease in efficiency of communication for distributed teams, good practices that reduce problems later in the Sprint are even more important.

Continuous integration is another valuable software engineering practice that ensures members of a team can integrate their work frequently (Duvall, Matyas, and Glover 2007). This approach uses automated tests to detect integration problems quickly, so they can be addressed closer to the time the problems were injected. It is valuable for collocated teams to use continuous integration, but even more important in an environment where there are more opportunities for communications issues.

And, finally, test automation is a valuable practice that is even more important for distributed teams. Test automation can help teams to more quickly execute their tests. As a result, it can help the team to more efficiently test code and more quickly implement and execute tests for new code.

Whether or not a team is using good software engineering practices becomes much more obvious when a distributed team is working together to deliver value in two-week or four-week Sprints.

Schedule Differences

Scheduling team actions and tasks becomes more challenging with increasing levels of distribution. Within IBM, each site has a local holiday schedule. Although these are consistent for sites within a given country, holidays across countries can vary. The Chinese celebrate their New Year for a week, beginning between January 21 and February 20. The U.S. teams typically take vacations during the last two weeks of December. Some in India celebrate the five-day festival of Diwali beginning on the new moon that occurs between October 13 and November 14.

Elizabeth Woodward provides an example of the added complexity of international holiday schedules:

> *I was responsible for setting up a call with many potential business partners in India for a demo with a team in the U.S. and Canada. We had received a good response from people who said they would attend. On the day of the call, only two people from India showed. As it turned out, we had scheduled the meeting in the middle of a weeklong holiday in India!*

A best practice is to solicit the national holidays from each team member at the beginning of the project and to ensure the team's commitments take into account those holiday schedules. Having the schedule is particularly helpful for complex projects where the team needs to coordinate commitments for upcoming Sprints with other Scrum Teams.

Team Dynamics

Peer pressure can be both positive and negative. There are times when some members of the team exert positive peer pressure to encourage a certain behavior. But distance can make this difficult. As a result, it can become easy to avoid confronting problems and just let them fester.

Also, it can be difficult to identify what is happening when distributed team members stop communicating. An IBM ScrumMaster provides the following story that highlights the need for constant communications:

> *An acquaintance was forming a test team in Bangalore. All went well for some time. They educated the team, discussed the design, and planned responsibilities of the remote team. The remote team lead was helpful. When the time of transfer of the responsibility approached, I planned a final call with the team lead to confirm the transfer would happen as scheduled, but I could not reach the team lead. After four days of investigation and confusion, my acquaintance found out the team lead left the company without further notice. We had to cancel the responsibility transfer because the rest of the remote team was unable to continue the efforts without their leader.*

Distance can make some team members feel isolated, especially if they have a specialized skill that is used only at certain times during the development effort for each work item. If the team only engages the writers on their team after a feature has been demonstrated to stakeholders, writers can feel they are not part of the team. Team members that are on a waterfall team may not engage with one another for long periods of time. Not having regular contact with other members of the team can weaken the social skills of remote team members. They may feel less comfortable with dealing with one another.

A Scrum Team helps relieve some of the issues with isolation by keeping members involved, engaged, and feeling ownership and responsibility. Corville Allen talks about the comments he usually gets from writers who are new to Scrum:

Writers and other distributed members of the team begin to feel relevance immediately because of the team attitude in Scrum. Like other team sports, you win or lose based on a team effort and leave no one behind. So, the team members have a vested interest in engaging everyone and making sure they do their part of the work. The writers feel included and treated as equals and enjoy working with the team.

A successful Scrum Team brings team members back into the fold. Making the Daily Scrum a priority is one example of how to keep the whole team engaged. Each person talks and gives their status. This is similar to the practice used in U.S. preschools that get children comfortable speaking in public, communicating, and overcoming their fears. Scrum helps remote workers to build and preserve their communications skills.

Successful distributed Scrum Teams make the effort to include all team members, to get to know each other personally as well as professionally, and to work together despite the distance.

Telephone Dynamics

A distributed Scrum team works together daily and will likely be on telephone conference calls much more often than members of a distributed waterfall team. Scrum will magnify the problems inherent to telephone conversations. The following are some of the problems teams may face and some of the ways to mitigate the problems.

Providing Access to the Call

The first challenge teams experience when working with global teams and using international calls is making sure everyone can access the conference.

You may want to provide toll-free teleconference numbers, so team members dialing into the teleconference from home outside normal working hours can take part without incurring toll charges. Not all teleconference providers offer toll-free numbers to all countries, and sometimes the toll-free numbers they provide may not work when dialed using cell phones in some countries.

A second point related to setting up the teleconferences is to make sure everyone knows how to dial into the teleconference and how to dial international numbers to reach their colleagues. Not everyone may be familiar with dialing to another country. Elizabeth Woodward, an Agile Transformation coach at IBM, shares the following story:

The United States provides a "9-1-1" emergency service. If you dial 9-1-1, you reach emergency services that will then send an ambulance, a fire truck, or the police to help you. This is not a number to use lightly. We had a teammate from New Delhi, India. The international code for India is 9-1 and the first two numbers for New Delhi are "1-1".

So he gave his number as "91-11-xxxxxxxx". A teammate tried dialing the number from the United States without dialing the international call prefix "0-1-1" first. The first time he tried to call his colleague in New Delhi, he dialed "9-1-1..." and reached his local emergency services.

Working with Telephones in a Meeting Room

Another teleconference problem teams should be aware of when part of the team is calling in from a conference room is the difficulty of hearing everyone in the room. When people sit around a table with the telephone in the center of the room, it can be difficult for the people on the call to hear each person in the room. People who speak more softly, speak quickly, or don't speak clearly are difficult to understand by phone.

People who are listening may be reluctant to voice a concern if they are unable to hear because they may have to disrupt the flow of the conversation repeatedly to report they can't hear or understand the conversation. As a result, many teleconference meetings are ineffective. The Scrum team, and in particular the ScrumMaster, should take responsibility for making sure everyone can hear and participate in the conference call.

One way to solve this is to move the phone closer to the speaker. We have found two approaches that help: Either gather the on-site team close around the phone or consider shifting the phone closer to each person as they speak. Moving the phone from person to person every two minutes can irritate those on the call if they hear the loud screeching sound of the phone sliding across the desk, so be gentle if you decide to take this approach.

Another approach is to use a phone with microphone extensions or to pass a wireless speaker around the room so people on the phone can hear everyone.

Unfortunately, some telephones can make it difficult to hear people speaking in a large room. Some speakerphones (half-duplex phones) may only allow one speaker to be understandable at a time. If someone speaks without pausing, it can be impossible to interrupt their monologue verbally. Fortunately, the telephone buttons still work while the person is speaking. When using a half-duplex phone, press a non-function button to let the speaker know he needs to pause to give others a chance to speak.

Scott Ambler, Chief Methodologist/Agile at IBM Rational, shares his experiences with teleconferencing:

I'm hearing impaired, and in particular I can have significant problems when some people on the conference call are using VOIP phones or mobile phones. Sometimes I need to ask people to rejoin the conference call using a land line, if available, for me to hear them. This can be particularly frustrating for them when it means incurring additional telecom costs as a result. The point is that you cannot assume that just because a technology works well for you that it will work well for everyone on your team.

Identifying the Speaker

A newly forming team may have difficulty recognizing who is speaking on the phone. This can become more challenging with unfamiliar accents or team members with similar voices. If the team members are not familiar with each other's voices, everyone should identify themselves before speaking until the team becomes more familiar with each voice. The ScrumMaster can help by reminding team members to identify themselves or by announcing who is speaking. This becomes important in a collaborative meeting where being able to speak directly to the person who made a comment is necessary. Also, being able to follow the thread of a conversation between multiple people and interject your ideas is a key to a successful planning meeting. To do this, you have to be able to recognize who is speaking.

Some teleconference services provide a way to identify who is speaking either through a website or through chat. A screen identifies the each participant, and a speaker bubble appears beside the avatar of the active speaker. Work with your teleconference service to find out if a similar feature is available. This can be helpful with keeping up with a teleconference conversation.

A best practice is to include a clear photo of each team member in the chat profile when possible. The Scrum Team can also create a wall, wiki, or website of team members with pictures, location, and personal and contact information. Seeing the face of a speaker can help distributed team members associate the voice with a person.

As the team forms, identifying the speaker will become much less of a problem.

Handling Visual Cues

A teleconference problem the team is likely to face more often is the lack of visual cues. Team members should state what they assume people are doing but cannot see for themselves to help the team communicate more effectively. Ask, "Marion, are you shaking your head and wincing right now?" or, "Bill, are you smiling at that last comment?," rather than have unconfirmed visual cues like this in your mind.

An even more direct application of this tip is to have people explain what they see themselves or others are doing that may be invisible to distant team members. You might say, "I'm holding up that report we did last month because I'm afraid we've already forgotten it," or, "You guys should see Lee right now; she's holding her hands around her throat like she's choking."

Use gestures when you speak. Even though remote team members cannot see the gesture, they can hear the change in voice inflection and feel the emotion that naturally accompanies a gesture.

If the team needs to share diagrams, consider using a whiteboard tool or preparing graphics with a graphics program the team can display with a screen-sharing tool. Team members can quickly become alienated from a meeting if they are unable to see diagrams that other team members are discussing.

Encouraging Participation

Quieter individuals may have an even harder time trying to speak up on the telephone, since there's no way to use body language to signal an interest in saying something. By keeping a list of participants' names in front of them and noticing who is not speaking, team members can encourage participation and ask for information from those members. This gives them an opportunity to join in and speak up. You can also use an agreed-upon signal in a chat session to "raise your hand" to speak.

Act as "gatekeeper," or appoint someone to do this job. The gatekeeper watches the gate of participation and opens it to those who have not said much, while closing it to those who have had a disproportionate amount of talk time. The gatekeeper might say something like, "Thanks for your comments, Jane. Mary, what are your concerns?"

Appoint a scribe to keep notes for the meeting and shares them afterward, asking everyone to review and confirm understanding. A scribe pays special attention to key decisions made, important information shared, and action items the team needs to follow up on, and checks for unclear wording.

Amr Elssamadisy with Samadisy, Inc. suggests the following:

> What I've seen work is to have a ritual at the beginning of the meeting of going round-robin and getting everyone to acknowledge their participation 100% or their lack of focus because of ongoing situations. I find that when someone commits in the beginning, there is a change in their focus.

It is easier for team members to detach themselves when their colleagues are unable to see them. Most people who often use teleconferences have experienced a call where it was obvious at least one team member was reading email or doing other work instead of taking part in the call. Engage people at the start by asking them how relevant the topic is to them. Make it clear to everyone in the meeting they have certain responsibilities, such as supporting group decisions, honestly expressing their views, sticking to the agenda, and respecting others.

To keep everyone engaged, team members should call on people by name, especially if they have not heard from them for a while. Throughout the call, check in constantly:

- "Did everyone follow Ed's explanation?"
- "Can anyone clarify further?"
- "Any more comments before we move to the next topic?"

Keep the meeting short and focused. People are likely to pay attention in a focused 15-minute meeting and more likely to lose focus in a 60-minute meeting. Jim Jones, a manager with IBM Quality Software Engineering, offers the following suggestion:

> Don't assume every meeting has to last one hour. The conversation will expand to fill the hour, and some people will lose focus. Last year, I set my default meeting length in my calendar tool to 45 minutes. I found that we were able to complete the same work in 45 minutes that we usually would have accomplished during a one-hour meeting. This year, I'm setting the default to 30 minutes.

Limiting Side Conversations

Side conversations are another common problem for distributed teams. This can be particularly troublesome because the background noise distracts the people who have dialed into the teleconference. If it is already difficult to hear everyone in the room giving their status clearly, it is even more difficult when there is background noise and other voices interrupting the main speaker. John Sutcliffe, manager of a Scrum Team for IBM Software Group Information Management, shared the following story:

During a Sprint planning meeting, part of the team was actively discussing a certain module that two members of the team would not be working on. Those two team members were in the room and used the time for a side discussion related to another user story the team would be discussing shortly. While this behavior was annoying to the members talking about the story, it made it nearly impossible for team members dialed into the meeting to keep up with what the team was talking about.

The ScrumMaster must promote good team collaboration and ensure that everyone on the team feels included. Are there splits on the team? Are some people in one location grouping and excluding others? Are there side discussions that exclude some of the people on the call? Are there new team members who do not know what's going on because the side conversations do not include them either? These are all not healthy team behaviors.

To promote teaming and to give everyone a chance to speak without disruptions, members of the development team or ScrumMaster should end any side conversations quickly. The Scrum-Master should also make sure the meeting remains focused and the team postpones unrelated items so they can address them later.

With teleconferences, the facilitator (typically the ScrumMaster) will need to ask questions that address the few, not the many. If they ask, "Did everybody get the agenda?" or "Can everybody see that line in the database?," the chorus of "yes" can drown out the lone "no." However, the answer to "Is there anybody who didn't get the agenda?" will get attention.

Muting the Lines

With teleconferences, one person in a busy location with background noise can derail a call. It difficult for those on the call to concentrate when there is significant background noise.

One IBM ScrumMaster described a call disrupted by a team member dialing in while at the subway station. The person thought he was on mute and was not paying attention to the call. All members had to hang up the phone and dial back in. To prevent this from being an obstacle for your team, ask everyone to put themselves on mute if they are not talking and take themselves off mute to speak. Some teleconference programs have a mute feature built in by pressing a certain combination of keys. For example, pressing #6 will use software to mute some phones.

Teleconference services usually provide a button code each participant can use to silence the line they are using, but the mute button on their phones typically work just as well. Some teleconference services provide the ability for the teleconference leader to mute individual lines. This can be a handy feature when an individual is disrupting the call because they are not on mute and their environment is noisy. The team member who was dialing in from the subway would have been far less disruptive if the teleconference service used by the team had offered a way to mute a line.

Checking for Agreement and Disagreement

To confirm a decision, check with each individual to find out whether they agree and will support fulfilling the decision and its outcome. Without visual stimulation to keep participants engaged and alert, it is easy to check out or to give up ownership for decisions the group is making.

Make sure all team members voice their individual concerns before closing on a decision.

Identifying an Advocate to Represent Remote Team Members

Someone from the team can volunteer to be in charge of calling out any non-remote friendly behaviors such as side conversations or people talking too far from the microphone. Typically someone who has been a remote employee will be better at identifying unfriendly behaviors than those who have always been part of a collocated team.

The advocate can also keep track of remote attendees' questions (sent through instant messages, for example). That person can also encourage participation from remote attendees by keeping track of who has not spoken yet.

When Nothing Else Works, Everyone Dials In

If you find you are having trouble working with some people in a conference room and others dialed in, consider asking that everyone dial into the meeting. In certain situations, having all members dial into the teleconference can be a better alternative than having most people in one conference room and a couple of people dialed in from different locations. Each person dialed in is in an equal position to everyone else. There is no longer an advantage of those in the room being able to use nonverbal communication those on the call are unable to see or interpret. Everyone is speaking directly into the phone, which can make it easier for everyone on the team to hear the conversation. This makes verbal side conversations less of a problem.

Although it may seem that having everyone use low-bandwidth communication will reduce the effectiveness of communication, doing so may improve communication overall. If the team is having trouble with a mix of some people dialing in individually and others dialing in from a conference room, the net result of having all dial in separately can actually be a significant improvement.

Reminders

Collocated teams may pick up on reminders about meetings from teammates through chats in the break room or random hallway discussions. With remote teams, it becomes more important for the team to use reminders. If your company has a calendar tool that sends reminders, enabling that feature can be helpful. Otherwise, it may be useful for the ScrumMaster to send a reminder the day before the meeting. This is not a question of whether the team is responsible, but rather helping to compensate for clues that are just not available when working as a remote team.

Impact of Communication Problems

Some obvious problems occur when communication channels fail. Team members may not be doing the right task, doing the task correctly, or doing the task at the expected time.

However, there are more subtle problems that can occur. For instance, tasks outside the team's mission can pull away team members to work on lower-priority matters. It is common to expect a team to handle both release content, support, and maintenance tasks, but the team may not be in a position to focus adequately on either. Although this is a problem for either a collocated or distributed team, members in a distributed environment may not know one of their teammates is not working on the expected tasks until it becomes difficult to recover from.

Scrum helps mitigate this problem through the daily Scrum meeting. However, the more distributed a team is, the more challenging it becomes to have a Daily Scrum meeting and the more tempting it may be to skip the Daily Scrum meetings. A team is more likely to achieve success with Scrum if it understands the purpose of the Daily Scrum as defined by its creators and identifies a distributed model that aligns with it.

KEY POINT   The more closely a distributed team can adopt Scrum as designed by its creators, the more likely a team will experience success. The design of Scrum promotes good communication. At the same time, with some minor adaptations for distributed teams, Scrum can help teams deliver the right product, at the right time, with the right quality.

You may be familiar with the Forming-Storming-Norming-Performing model of group development (Tuckman 1965). Given the communication challenges that occur and the reduced contact between team members, is it reasonable to expect distributed teams to get to the performing level? Yes!

Thomas Starz has had experience working with many distributed teams:

Distributed teams easily block at the storming stage. A team can start over at the forming stage when team changes occur, sometimes even little changes. The performing stage can be fragile. Because of the limited personal contact, remote teams take longer to get through this stage.

Elizabeth Woodward has worked with more than one hundred teams, mainly distributed, to develop software and other deliverables:

I have found that having the ability to select from the best talent globally provides a competitive edge. The more distributed a team is, the more challenging it becomes, but

I have had first-rate distributed teams that outperformed many collocated teams. Work-
ing with a distributed team means actively working on communication, making sure
teams have the right tools, addressing issues head-on, and always seeking ways to
improve. I like Schwaber's philosophy of Scrum as the "art of the possible."

Communication can impact team members' understanding of what they should be doing. If
the team does not work from an organized Product Backlog, the team does not break down tasks for
the Sprint Backlog, and team members do not claim tasks, the team will have trouble being successful. A smaller, collocated team may be able to deal with some disorganization, but a distributed
team will typically have much more difficulty.

How Does Scrum Help?

How does Scrum help fix any of the tricky problems discussed in this book? It does not. It just
puts a spotlight on them so the team can identify and address them. It prevents the team from
overlooking them while they quietly drain performance from the team. Leslie Ekas, an agile
coach, shares a story:

I was working with a team that had some festering problems. The team was not getting
to the root causes of their problems and fixing the right things. The team had those
problems from day one, but it wasn't until they began using Scrum that they started
seeing what the root problems were and addressing them.

Short time-boxed iterations either show results or they do not. It quickly becomes obvious
whether you are making adequate progress. Problems surface in daily meetings. Regular retrospectives invite discussion on identifying and fixing productivity problems. When other tasks
outside the team's mission are pulling team members off their work, it becomes obvious almost
immediately. The team can adjust quickly to their problems.

Leslie Ekas shares the following experience of how Scrum serves as a magnifying glass on
a team's dysfunctions:

We had an environment where the development team was in a central location and the
QA teams were in two other locations. The development team drove the move to agile
and so drove the Scrum meetings and defined the user stories. As was typical when they
were doing waterfall, QA fell behind at the beginning of the project. Their commitment
to work on user stories was vague and their participation in the daily Scrum was inter-
mittent. The development team continued to "drive" how the team worked, and because
this behavior was similar to how it had been in the past, no one took action.

The team continued in this way until it came up in a reflection. Development com-
plained that QA did not buy into the new approach, so they did not engage as needed.
After a brief discussion, it became clear that QA's real challenge was they were behind

and had no way to catch up. The development team realized that to achieve in agile, they had to take the "whole team" approach and get QA caught up.

It was easy to ignore the problems for a while because QA was not local and thus the trouble they were getting into was not so easy to discover.

Summary

Scrum changes the way a team works together. A team of specialists working in a waterfall fashion waits for their work assignments. In an agile team, the team pulls the highest-priority work and works together throughout the Sprint to complete it.

Each of the issues mentioned can be a parasite to the team's performance. It might be tempting to let some of these go and see if they work themselves out. However, most projects eventually reach a "crunch time"—a period where collaboration needs to be quick and efficient to finish the work needed to reach a project deadline. Waiting until the project nears the deadline to identify and fix communication problems is too late and puts the project in jeopardy.

References

Astels, Dave. *Test-Driven Development: A Practical Guide*. Upper Saddle River, NJ: Pearson Education, 2003.

Duvall, Paul, Matyas, Steve, and Glover, Andrew. *Continuous Integration: Improving Software Quality and Reducing Risk*. Boston: Pearson, 2007.

Fagan, M.E. "Design and code inspections to reduce errors in program development," 1976, *IBM Systems Journal*, Vol. 15, No. 3, pp. 182–211.

Hall, Edward T. *The Silent Language*. Garden City, NY: Doubleday, 1959.

Rosenberg, Jennifer. "History of the Swastika," at history1900s.about.com/cs/swastika/a/swastikahistory.htm.

CHAPTER 3

Starting a Scrum Project

In preparing for battle, I have always found that plans are useless but planning is indispensable.

Dwight D. Eisenhower

Scrum includes three levels of planning: Release Planning, Sprint Planning, and Daily Scrums. The Release Plan shows what stakeholders can expect from the completed project, how the teams will work together, and what progress they can expect at the end of each of the Sprints that make up the release (Schwaber 2004).

The Release Plan focuses on how the team will turn the vision for the project into a winning product by identifying goals, Product Backlog priorities, risks, features, and functionality. Every Sprint Review and Sprint Planning meeting provides an opportunity to adjust the Release Plan and Sprint Plans. Daily Scrums provide an opportunity to adjust short-term plans each day.

Scrum does not discuss what the vision includes and how to create it or how the Scrum Team should create a Release Plan. There are many project startup considerations and tasks that are not part of Scrum that complement Release Planning and have an impact on the success of the project.

Each company and organization has its own ways for selecting projects and identifying who will work on them, as well as different approaches for completing them. Those working on the project may all be employees of the organization. A company may also outsource all or part of the work. Or, they may buy another software company and modify their software. Each approach involves different release planning and project initiation activities.

This chapter provides *general* guidance, tips, and considerations for starting a Scrum project in a distributed enterprise environment. It begins with identifying stakeholders, capturing needs, minimal modeling of solutions, and identifying the priority of features—information that defines a *vision* for the product. Subsequently, we discuss considerations for converting the vision to a Release Plan with a Release Roadmap that maps the work the team needs to do into Sprints. Finally, we discuss project startup tasks, such as selecting tools, selecting Agile software development practices, scaling the Product Owner role, and other project startup tasks.

How to Identify the Problems Your Product Will Solve

The first step in developing a new project or product is to understand the value proposition it will offer and why executives should sponsor it. To reach this understanding, you need to know the following:

- Who are your stakeholders?
- What problems will the project address?
- What are your solutions to the problems?
- What is the return on investment?

Who Are Your Stakeholders?

Stakeholders provide information to the Product Owner about features and work the Scrum Team needs to do. They also regularly review deliverables and discuss them with the Product Owner to confirm the work of the Scrum Team will meet their expectations and deliver business value. Finally, they need to work with the Scrum Team during the entire release.

Table 3.1 reviews the four types of stakeholders Scrum Teams need to work with, as discussed earlier in Chapter 1, "The Evolution of Scrum" (Kessler and Schweitzer 2007). Each of the types brings their own different insights to the project.

Table 3.1   Summary of Stakeholder Types

Type	Description
Principals	Stakeholders who champion the need for your software and have the authority to buy and put it in place.
End users	Stakeholders who personally interact with your software.
Partners	Stakeholders who make your product work in real life, such as operations teams, business partners, and system integrators.
Insiders	Stakeholders within your own organization, such as developers, support engineers, sales, architecture, and marketing teams.

When the project is an application for a single customer, that customer will likely identify who will act as their stakeholder to represent their interests and work with the Team during the project (see Figure 3.1).

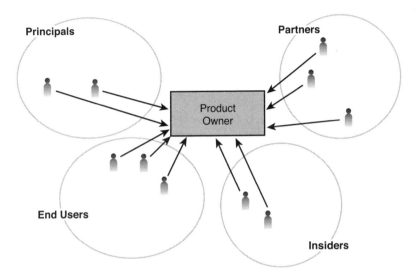

Figure 3.1   Product Owner working with key stakeholders

Because there is typically a much larger group of customers and potential stakeholders, it is more challenging to identify key representatives in an enterprise environment. In cases like this, the Scrum Team needs representation from different stakeholder categories and market segments. As Figure 3.2 shows, while gathering information about requirements, the Product Owner will identify key stakeholders to represent various groups while the Scrum Team is developing the release.

Having the right stakeholders review and discuss deliverables will impact the quality of the comments received and the actions the Scrum Team will take to improve the deliverables. Distributed teams are more likely to be working with geographically and culturally diverse distributed stakeholders who also need to provide insights based on their location and culture.

Elizabeth Woodward offers the following example:

Years ago, I worked on a product that we expected to deliver worldwide. We reviewed and discussed the product with many different stakeholders. Unfortunately, we did not include representatives from various geographies, and in certain geographies, screen resolution was typically no better than 800x600. The team built the screens assuming a minimum resolution of 1024x768 with no way to scroll or size the screens. The team would have found this problem earlier if they had included representatives from target markets worldwide as reviewers.

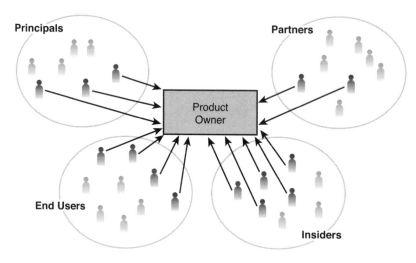

Figure 3.2   Product Owner engages stakeholders

Identifying key stakeholders allows the Product Owner to set up a growing relationship and continuously gather information from individuals who are familiar with the project. This information is useful when preparing the backlog before the Sprint Planning meetings and to get timely responses to questions from the development. Engaging stakeholders during release planning also helps identify potential participants for Sprint reviews and identify who can work with the Scrum Teams when they need details outside the expertise of the Product Owner.

When multiple teams are working with the same set of stakeholders, they may need to work with the same people at different times. This can make it challenging to coordinate their availabilities. For example, a stakeholder who takes part in a review for a Scrum Team at the end of their Sprint may not be available to return a week later to review the work of another Scrum Team. If the first team waits until the Sprint review of the second team, they will be partway in their own Sprint and they may not be able to address the comments until their next Sprint.

What Problems Will the Project Address?

After identifying the stakeholders, the Product Owner needs to gather their requirements. In a small-scale development project where a Scrum Team is developing an application for a specific client, the Product Owner is more likely to meet face-to-face with collocated Principals and End Users type stakeholders to discuss their needs. There may be no Partners at all and only a few Insiders to engage on the project.

However, in a large-scale project or an enterprise environment, the Product Owner needs to gather information from many different stakeholder types and companies to identify needs and priorities. Some of the alternate sources a Product Owner can use to collect information include competitive intelligence, third-party research, brand research, partner research, user groups, customer councils, websites, and event surveys. Although they may meet face-to-face with some stakeholders, they may also send out surveys or meet with user groups and engage them to gather information and understand their needs.

In an enterprise environment, the Product Owner should work closely with market intelligence teams, product management, sales, and other insider organizations that interact with customer stakeholders to understand their needs.

Often a stakeholder will review and discuss a proposed solution, rather than the problem they are experiencing. Although there is value in understanding their view of what a solution might look like, understanding the root problem helps the Scrum Team to deliver a solution that solves their problem.

Karen Rosengren, a Senior Technical Staff Member with IBM, shares the following story:

> *A stakeholder requested a set of service routines to delete indices from a database and restore them. This was clearly a solution, rather than a problem. After exploring to understand why the customer wanted this specifically, the team determined the problem was an ever-shrinking window of opportunity to take the database offline for maintenance. Nonindexed databases take less time to backup. By deleting the indices, creating a backup, and rebuilding the indices, the backups were faster. The root problem was the shrinking window of opportunity to have the data unavailable. The team was able to look for solutions to back up data because they understood the business needs of their stakeholders.*

The Product Owner may want to use User Stories to get to the root problem and to make sure they capture the stakeholder type in the comments. The format of "As a <role>, I need to <goal> so that <business value>" forces the conversation to center on what the stakeholder is trying to achieve and the cost of the problem to their business. Identifying the cost helps the Product Owner to understand the value the product will deliver and later, to identify the priority of the features for the release.

While gathering information from stakeholders, the Product Owner needs to capture both functional and nonfunctional requirements. The team can add the latter to User Stories as acceptance conditions or to an overall document that identifies conditions all user stories need to meet.

Once the Product Owner understands the needs of the stakeholders, he or she explores whether there are existing products that fulfill their needs. Part of starting up the project involves understanding what is already available because there may be existing software that will help reduce the development effort. Knowing what is on the market can also help you identify if there may be existing patents for the solution you are working on and avoid patent infringement issues.

Grouping the stories into problem areas can help the Product Owner to organize the information and identify a shortlist of high-value requirements for the system. An affinity diagram (see sidebar) is a common tool that helps with organizing information that comes from many different sources. By grouping the information, you can then begin to analyze and decide the solutions needed to address the problems.

It can be helpful to think of the groupings as **problem areas** or **feature areas** instead of **themes**. This helps make sure the Scrum Team does not lose the problem as well as the value. As an example, consider the difference between a theme of **poor performance** and a problem area of **need to reduce time needed for backups**. Poor performance is broad and could cover many different high-level features. It can be difficult for the Scrum Team to identify User Stories to address from the theme perspective but easier for them to think of solutions from the problem area perspective.

KEY POINT   Grouping ideas into themes, problem areas, or feature areas helps the team understand *why* they are building what they are building.

AFFINITY DIAGRAMS

An affinity diagram (also referred to as the KJ method) is a common tool that helps with organizing information that comes from many different sources. By grouping the information, you can then begin to analyze and decide the solutions needed to address the problems. The general steps of the method are as follows:

- Write each idea on a separate card.
- Group the ideas that seem similar.
- Identify the natural themes, problem areas, or feature areas for each group.
- Confirm the ideas are in the proper groups.

For collocated teams, the Scrum Team will use physical cards or sticky notes to capture the problems. In a distributed environment, teams may use a whiteboard tool to create sticky notes that all members of the distributed team can move.

Let's use an example to talk through using the method. Figure 3.3 shows some ideas a Product Owner gathered in a discussion of needs for a Virtual Conference. Before the start of the meeting with the Scrum Team, the Product Owner transcribed the ideas on sticky notes and put them on a virtual whiteboard.

The Product Owner reads through the cards and invites the members of the Scrum Team to group the sticky notes together in silence. They can move any card, anywhere they want, but ideally they should look for cards that may have the same solution or solution set.

Figure 3.4 shows the two groups the team came up with after moving the sticky notes. At this point, the team starts working with the Product Owner to identify any natural themes that come out of the groupings.

After looking at the groupings and discussing them, the team identified two problem areas, as shown in Figure 3.5.

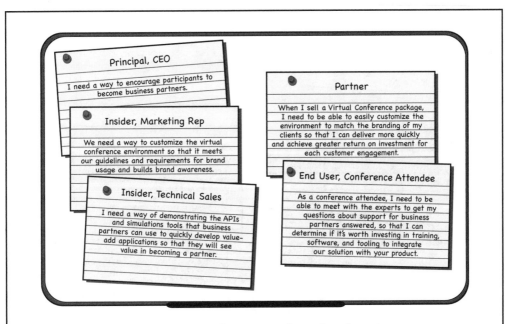

Figure 3.3 Idea cards from a Virtual Conference discussion of needs

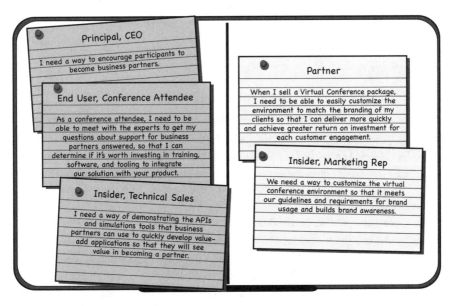

Figure 3.4 The team groups the related idea cards.

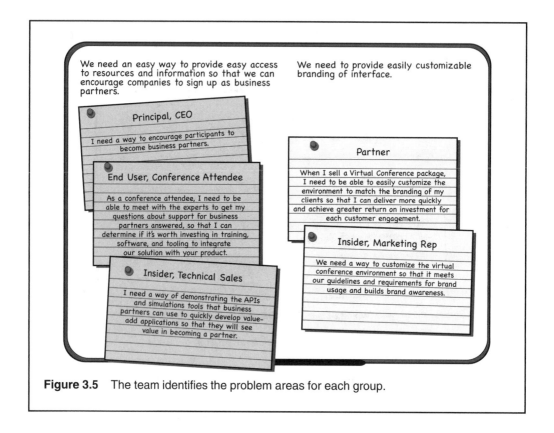

Figure 3.5   The team identifies the problem areas for each group.

What Are Your Solutions to the Problems?

To identify the priorities for the work the team will do, the Product Owner needs to be able to compare the investment needed against the benefits of carrying out the solution.

Once the Product Owner has collected and grouped needs, a Scrum Team starts discussing and sketching the early solution. Scott Ambler describes an agile approach to early architecture envisioning in his *Introduction to Agile Modeling* (Ambler, http://www.agilemodeling.com/essays/introductionToAM.htm).

When there is no Scrum Team identified to work on the project, the Product Owner still needs to engage a cross-functional group of representatives. The goal is not to design solutions in detail, but to gain a common understanding among the Scrum Team and stakeholders of one or many proposed solutions. Leveraging lean principles of deferring commitment, developing more than one solution in parallel can be more cost-effective where there is significant risk and uncertainty (Poppendieck 2007).

The early modeling is *not* about developing documentation, but about *simplifying communication*. Remember, user stories include *conversation* as well as the card "As a <role> I need to <goal> so that <business value>." Architecture envisioning and agile modeling simplify communication.

For the Product Owner to identify the priorities for the work in the Product Backlog, they need to understand the effort needed to carry out the solution. Additionally, the Scrum Team needs an opportunity to provide comments on risk, feasibility, technology assumptions, special skills needed (that may not be on the Scrum Team), and other conditions that will impact the priorities.

Using the Virtual Conference as an example, the Scrum Team will model alternative solutions to the "**Need to provide easy access to resources and information, so we can encourage companies to sign up as business partners**" problem area. The development team and Product Owner may all agree that a virtual tradeshow booth where attendees can directly communicate with vendor experts and access takeaway documentation would solve the problem.

However, some team members may imagine a solution that provides provisioning of virtual machines where sample API code is available for hands-on demonstrations, and another team member may imagine a solution that simply provides HTML links to video demonstrations. The cost of each solution could vary dramatically. By working with the team to model the solution briefly, the Product Owner has a better understanding of costs, risks, dependencies, and other conditions that will impact the priorities.

Modeling may also identify more questions the Product Owner will need to discuss with stakeholders.

At this point in Release Planning, the Scrum Team will likely need to give time for the Product Owner to work with stakeholders to better understand the solutions that will address their problems. Distributed stakeholders may be in different parts of the world, and the Product Owner needs enough time to contact them and understand their position.

What Is the Return on Investment?

Once high-level proposed solutions (possibly documented as large user stories or *epics*) are in place, the Scrum Team will estimate the size of the solutions so the Product Owner understands the relative effort needed to build the solution. Teams can use the Planning Poker technique (see sidebar) to do these early estimates.

Besides sizing the user stories as part of release planning at the beginning of the project, the team will spend some time each Sprint revisiting their estimates as part of grooming the Product Backlog.

To identify the priorities of the release, the Product Owner evaluates the problems of the stakeholders, their proposed solutions, and the discussions about them with the Scrum Team. There are several methods for systematically and consistently comparing the relative value of features:

- **Roger Burlton's Pain-Gain matrix** looks at how much benefit stakeholders can get from an improvement, and how much pain their current way of working causes them. It gives different weight to different stakeholders' opinions (Sehlhorst 2007).

- **Steve Tockey's work** explains how to use financial value to prioritize the investment in software. The formulas and approach are the same techniques that business startups use to find out and show viability of their business plans (Tockey 2008).

- **The Analytic Hierarchy Process** is a decision technique that enables you to compare solutions based on the weighted conditions that you identify. These may include number of customers, size of potential market, new or existing markets, risk of new technology, impact on other products, or any other suitable conditions.

It is important for the Product Owner to review the priorities with stakeholders, so there is buy-in and agreement the Scrum Team is working on the most important, valuable deliverables first.

PLANNING POKER

A common technique used for agile estimation is a version of Planning Poker described by Mike Cohn in *Agile Estimating and Planning*. In a collocated work environment, each team member discusses a user story. Then, at the same time, all collocated members display a physical playing card that points out how big they think the story is.

The numbers on the playing cards represent abstract story points or ideal days (Cohn 2006). Story points are an abstract, relative unit of measure. The team asks itself, "Is Story B half the effort of story A? Is Story C bigger than both A and B combined? Where does Story D fit? Story D is similar effort to Story B." So, a user story that is two story points is about one-fourth the size of a requirement that is eight points and twice as big as a requirement that is one point. Ideal days are the second method for measuring size. Ideal days are from the time that something would take without any interruptions. Email, meetings, and other corporate overhead aside, a story estimated at one ideal day may take around two "real" days to complete. Within IBM, most teams prefer story points to ideal days (Surdek 2009).

To apply Planning Poker in a distributed environment, the ScrumMaster can read a user story, the team discusses it, and the team types a number into a group chat window. For new teams, calling out "Ready, set, go!" will help in getting everyone to type their values into the chat window at the same time. The purpose is to prevent one team member's estimate from influencing other team members' estimates. Teams that are more comfortable with one another and more comfortable with sharing their opinions don't need the "Ready, set, go!" The ScrumMaster will say "What do you think?" or "What's your estimate?" and the team will respond with their numbers.

When using a group chat window, you will want to define clearly where the set of new estimates begins. Otherwise, a long list of numbers entered by the team members will make it difficult to distinguish between the sizing for one user story and the next.

As an alternative, you can use PlanningPoker.com (Cohn, http://www.planningpoker.com/). If security is an issue for your organization, you may not be able to enter user stories; however, the ScrumMaster can verbally identify the stories and the team can respond by selecting cards. PlanningPoker.com has a built-in timer the team can set after discussing the user story to limit time spent on it.

Define the Vision

In communicating with stakeholders, gaining an understanding of needs and evaluating solutions, the Product Owner is *creating a vision* of what the product or project will be. Developing the vision provides the information to create a business case and to decide if and how the project should continue (Pichler 2010).

Briefly documenting this vision and communicating the vision to the Scrum Team and stakeholders helps to create a "shared vision" that provides a common focus (IBM Rational® Software 2009).

Jim Jones, a manager with IBM Quality Software Engineering, relates this story:

> *In the 1960s at NASA (National Aeronautics and Space Administration), no matter who you asked what they were doing—control center staff, janitors, programmers— everyone would respond they were putting a man on the moon. A vision like this motivates and excites people and moves them in a common direction to meet it.*

Getting the team to have a common business view of the project is key to enabling faster delivery of business benefit. It encourages an orientation on business benefits rather than on the technical solution.

The **vision** provides a high-level view of the business opportunity. It describes the business and functional requirements, market demographics, stakeholder needs, the competition, and a description of how the product will fit into the market and address needs. In a traditional enterprise environment, the team that develops the early product vision is usually a business team that includes market analysts, upper level management, key technical visionaries within the company, product management, and Product Owners. Upper-level management and decision-makers within the company who are responsible for deciding funding of projects may also influence the product vision. In an enterprise environment, there may be several different models in play that will affect how involved the development team and ScrumMaster are in developing the vision.

Taking an agile approach of asking the perspective of the development Team and Scrum-Master provides a more robust vision. When creating the vision for a new product, there may not be a Scrum Team assigned to it in the early stages; however, there may be an organization within the enterprise developing products in the same "family." Development team members working in the same family of products can help create the vision, even though they may not be the ones who engage in development.

Andy Pittaway describes the approach his team uses for the vision:

We look to have these expressed in business terms so to base the team on the business values rather than the technical tasks. On Agile projects that I am involved in, we put a big focus on understanding and communicating the following three points:

- *The Mission (or Vision)—Ideally, a one-line inspirational sentence easy to understand by all, such as **Sell a new product on the Internet by December 1st**.*

- *The Business Outcomes—Ideally, quantities or descriptive factors that allow us to recognize that we have achieved the Mission, such as **Product must have certain characteristics**.*

- *The Business Drivers—We would like to know from the business what the relative priority of the following are: cost, speed of delivery, feature set, and need to balance risk and opportunity. Based on this information from the business and stakeholders, we will craft a delivery solution that gives the business what they want.*

Create the Product Roadmap

Once the product vision is in place, the Product Owner or product manager uses the vision to sketch the **product roadmap**. This is nothing more than an effort to document where and roughly when you plan to deliver a specific set of features or themes. Within that roadmap, there are milestones—releases—that more precisely define the themes the team will deliver along the way. The near term releases have more detail in their feature descriptions than those that are further out on the timeline because the team has the most information.

Planning too far in advance leads to waste because the team is deciding when they have the least information. Facts, priorities, and the business climate can change before the team is able to start work on those features that are in later releases; just-in-time planning is the cornerstone of agile and Scrum.

Themes are high level but are useful for grouping and selecting requirements when it comes to Sprint Planning. They also provide some "wiggle room" to allow teams to react to lessons learned along the way. For enterprise software, this gives the business decision makers an opportunity to assess the overall product strategy and how the product fits in their portfolio strategy, and shows the expected high-level return on investment over a sequence of releases.

The product roadmap describes contents of several releases at a high-level. On the other hand, the release plan focuses on the next detail level for a single release.

Organize the Scrum Teams

As mentioned in Chapter 1, you will want your teams to experience the lowest distribution level possible. If you have the opportunity to organize the teams, look for ways to create cross-functional, collocated teams working on independent features. If that is not possible, look for opportunities to create cross-functional teams within similar time zones.

Scrum Teams are five to nine people in size. Teams greater than nine people should consider self-organizing into a smaller team to reduce the lines of communication needed to keep everyone in sync. They should also consider geographic closeness and proper distribution of skills as well as team size.

How the team self-organizes will impact how they assign user stories to Sprints. A team of ten people may complete a larger story in a two-week Sprint, but two smaller Scrum Teams may need to break down the same user story into two parts to complete their work within the Sprint. This could impact the layout of user stories across each Sprint.

Coordinating teams is more problematic because of dependencies when organizing teams by components. Organizations should encourage having feature teams over component teams.

KEY POINT   Individual Scrum Teams should aim to have the lowest distribution level possible.

A Scrum Team that self-organizes into two cross-functional smaller teams in different parts of the world, such as China and North America, may have an easier time and maybe even an advantage. Their distribution level allows the teams to work a combined 16 hours each day, where each team is working on independent user stories.

Create and Prioritize the Backlog

Once the Product Owner prioritizes the solutions, and the Scrum Teams are identified, the development team is ready to begin identifying the user stories to address the solutions.

The team may need to develop more than one feature to address a single solution. The Scrum Team will disaggregate the higher-priority features into user stories that can fit within a Sprint and will leave the lower-priority features as larger stories until they get closer to working on them.

The Scrum Team and key stakeholders engage in a user story writing workshop to define the requirements for the release.

The Product Backlog includes everything needed to launch a product, as follows:

- Work items to address the features of the product
- Development requirements, such as setting up systems to begin development
- "Spikes" or time-boxed work items to help the team to gain technical understanding needed to size a user story
- Exploratory work items to help with technical decision-making for developing the product
- Fixes for known bugs

As mentioned in Chapter 1, Scrum does not mandate any particular approach to developing requirements. However, many teams prefer **user stories** because they help them to understand the needs of the stakeholders and focus on the value they will deliver (Cohn 2004). Those working with medical devices or requiring more precise requirements traceability may choose to work with use cases or a combination of user stories and use cases.

In a collocated story writing workshop, participants write user stories on the front of paper cards and then identify acceptance conditions on the back of the card (Beck 2004).

In a distributed environment, physically working with paper cards is not possible. Electronic planning tools for Scrum provide a repository for distributed team members, Product Owners, and ScrumMasters to add their user stories. In cases where not all stakeholders have direct access to the tool, a scribe may be responsible for documenting user stories as the team is discussing them on the teleconference and putting them into the Scrum project management tool.

It can also be valuable for a scribe to take note of user stories throughout the discussion while displaying them to others using a distributed screen-sharing tool. Having the stories displayed allows participants to build from each others' discussion points.

Estimating the Stories as a Team

In an enterprise environment—especially one just transitioning to agile development—it can be tempting to have a few people meet and decide for the larger team either because of scale or distribution of the team across time zones. Excluding members because of their geographic location or status or only including certain members because they are the technical experts could result in significant team dysfunction. Scrum values the team.

A core principle of Scrum is that team members responsible for delivering the work should estimate it. Everyone involved in getting the work done needs to be part of estimating the stories—developers, testers, information developers, architects, user experience professionals, and others. Each story should include all facets of completing the work during the Sprint, not just development. Any one person is unlikely to know all the work needed to complete a user story.

Enterprise organizations transitioning to Scrum may feel the need to only include the "experts" in estimating sessions but they should include both experienced and new team members. The team may not know who is going to be working on the story. A new person may see the problem as larger than a more experienced person and may ask questions that make the experienced person reconsider or may have a different view of how to solve the problem. For these reasons, estimation should involve new members as well as experienced members.

When a few people provide a rough estimate earlier in the project if there are no specific teams assigned to the project, the Scrum Team that will do the work needed to revisit the estimates before committing to do it.

Prioritizing the Backlog

The Product Owner creates and prioritizes the backlog using a 1-n prioritization scheme based on information from the Scrum Team and stakeholders. A small-scale collocated Scrum Team works from a single Product Backlog the Product Owner keeps in a priority sequence. At the start of each Sprint, the team selects the stories from the Product Backlog it will deliver during the Sprint.

Larger-scale distributed teams integrating their work in a single product face added challenges. These teams need to decide early in the Release Planning on how to manage their Product Backlog; there are many approaches they should consider to find out which might work best for them.

One approach is to have the members from all distributed locations working as a single Scrum team with a single Product Backlog. One of the challenges in selecting this way of working is having the entire Scrum Team present at the Sprint Planning meeting. Given how distributed some teams can be across multiple geographies, it can be challenging to find a convenient time for the Sprint Planning meeting.

Single Backlog for Multiple Scrum Teams

Another approach shown in Figure 3.6 is to have all Scrum Teams at all locations work from a single Product Backlog. This model works well if the different skill sets the team needs to deliver user stories are available across each distributed location. When some skills are missing in a location, it may be possible for team members from another Scrum team to compensate and help rebalance the skills.

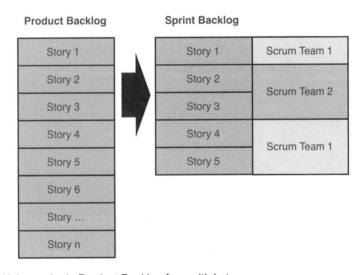

Figure 3.6   Using a single Product Backlog for multiple teams

Single Backlog with Sections for Multiple Teams

Another possible approach is a single Product Backlog that contains the work all teams need to do on the product. The Product Owner separates the Product Backlog into sections that show the user stories (features or components) the Product Owner is targeting for each of the teams. The

Product Owner orders the work within each of the sections of the backlog according to priority. Each Scrum team pulls work for the features assigned to the team in priority order.

Figure 3.7 shows a Product Backlog divided by features each Scrum Team is responsible to deliver. This provides visibility into the overall progress of the project and gives the Product Owner the perspective of the amount and the kind of work targeted for each team. Each team can more easily identify the work for their team, as well.

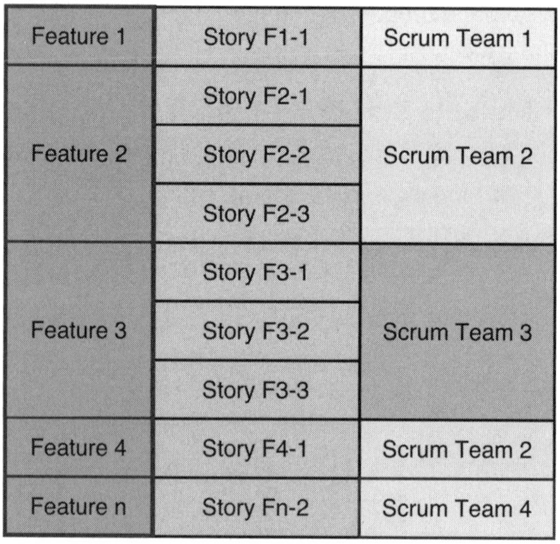

Feature 1	Story F1-1	Scrum Team 1
Feature 2	Story F2-1	Scrum Team 2
	Story F2-2	
	Story F2-3	
Feature 3	Story F3-1	Scrum Team 3
	Story F3-2	
	Story F3-3	
Feature 4	Story F4-1	Scrum Team 2
Feature n	Story Fn-2	Scrum Team 4

Figure 3.7   Using a single Product Backlog with multiple sections for multiple teams

Separate Backlogs for Multiple Scrum Teams

Figure 3.8 shows unique Product Backlogs assigned to multiple teams. This approach works for teams with products having multiple large standalone components that are the responsibility of specific Scrum teams. For example, a product may have a core component and multiple content pack components that customers can install on top of it.

In cases such as these, there is one overall Product Backlog that provides visibility into the overall product (see Figure 3.8). To help guide their work, the team can extract team-specific backlogs when using component teams. The Scrum teams work independently from one another and have their own individual Sprint backlogs, but the Sprint dates are the same. Each team works independently during the Sprint. They discuss their interdependencies in the Sprint pre-planning sessions or in a Daily Scrum of Scrums. The teams also need to make sure they consider important dependencies in the lookahead planning to avoid trouble.

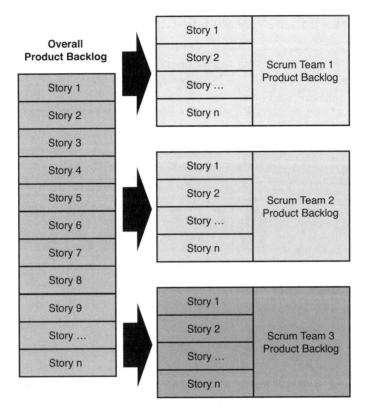

Figure 3.8   Using multiple Product Backlogs with multiple Scrum teams

Any multiple Scrum Team model become problematic when there are differences in skills between the teams or when the delivery of a story best fits a specific team. For example, it may be the highest-priority stories "belong" to one of the teams that has skills best suited to the stories. When all the highest-priority stories belong to one team, it causes the second team to have to search for lower-priority work that may not be as well understood or as refined in the Product Backlog. It may also cause some resentment or raise feelings of inadequacy in the "second team."

Additionally, the team that owns the highest-priority stories may not be able to complete all the stories the Product Owner had projected for a Sprint. The Product Owner needs to supply enough work for the two differently skilled teams in the Product Backlog priorities, which can be a bit more tedious. Dividing work between teams with different skills adds yet another layer of complexity to our multi-team model. The Product Owner must also work with the team to refine the user stories and order them for the next Sprint or two based on the team velocity.

Single Backlog Populated by Multiple Other Teams

Figure 3.9 shows another case for multiple Product Backlogs. In this scenario, items from the Product Backlog of multiple product teams populate the Product Backlog of another team. A real-life example is a suite of related products supported by a single virtual team responsible for creating all the installers for the suite.

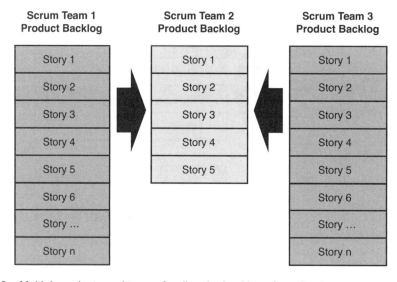

Figure 3.9   Multiple projects and teams feeding the backlog of another team

The Product Backlogs of each of the individual product teams in the suite has its own set of installer-related user stories they would like to include in their product. If the Product Owners set priorities for these installer user stories by comparing them to the new product work, installer stories may drop lower in the Product Backlog and lose visibility.

Because the virtual installer team delivers these users stories, they need to pull in the list of stories from the Product Backlog of each of the product teams and build their own backlog (see Figure 3.9). After the team creates the new Product Backlog, their Product Owner needs to set the priorities for the installer user stories across all the products in the suite.

Create the Release Plan

After setting the priorities of the Product Backlog, the Product Owner can start creating a Release Plan and lay out the user stories across the Sprints. Before creating the plan, the Product Owner needs to have the following information:

- What is the Sprint length?
- What is the estimated team velocity?

- What are the dependencies?

- What are the risks?

After gathering this information, the Product Owner starts grouping the user stories from the Product Backlog into Sprints. The planning for the first few Sprints typically has more details. The Product Owner groups together the stories for the later Sprints because changes in the scope of the release are likely to occur before the start of those Sprints.

For enterprises with dependencies between multiple teams, the planning horizon needs to be longer. Instead of grooming the Product Backlog just before the next Sprint Planning meeting, the team breaks down and refines requirements for the next two or three Sprints to identify dependencies between them and level the workload across the teams. This provides each team with a better understanding of how their progress impacts other teams. Coordination is critical, and the teams will need to map out user stories for a larger number of Sprints to keep the teams aware of dependencies and to keep their momentum. Mike Cohn describes the technique of **lookahead planning** in Agile Estimating and Planning. The number of Sprints to map out and use with lookahead planning will depend on Sprint length, dependencies, and needs of the teams involved.

When mapping user stories to Sprints, you should be sure to balance the expected work effort with the local holiday schedules of distributed team members.

Figure 3.10 shows a sequence of stories mapped into Sprints.

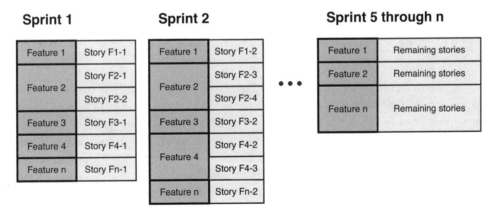

Figure 3.10   Mapping stories into Sprints

Although an ideal Scrum project focuses on creating a releasable version of the product each Sprint, in large-scale development, this is not always possible. There is a greater need for Sprints focused on modeling early in the project and to focus on "endgame" tasks, such as packaging the product, training teams, and formatting end-user documentation at the end of the project. When mapping user stories to Sprints, the Release Plan will likely reflect this reality (Ambler 2005).

What Is the Sprint Length?

The Product Owner needs to know the Sprint durations the Scrum Team will use throughout the release. We recommend the Sprint duration remain consistent during the release to create a rhythm, and that Scrum Teams that work together use the same Sprint durations and beginning and end dates. This simplifies their planning and how they will manage the dependencies between them.

> **KEY POINT** Teams that work on a set of related products should synchronize their Sprint lengths and start dates.

Figure 3.11 shows two teams working together using different Sprint lengths; when these teams talk and refer to Sprint 1 or the end of Sprint 4, it is not always clear which Scrum Team they are referring to. It is more difficult for team members to keep track of dependencies when they are using different Sprint identifiers and start and end dates.

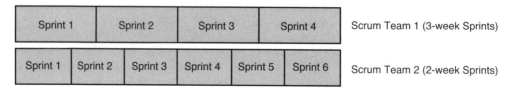

| Sprint 1 | Sprint 2 | Sprint 3 | Sprint 4 | Scrum Team 1 (3-week Sprints) |

| Sprint 1 | Sprint 2 | Sprint 3 | Sprint 4 | Sprint 5 | Sprint 6 | Scrum Team 2 (2-week Sprints) |

Figure 3.11   Confusion for teams with different Sprint lengths

Occasionally, teams decide to run on different Sprint lengths as a way to further increase their productivity. One example is when a team finds they are more effective delivering in shorter Sprints, perhaps two-week Sprints, when others are delivering in longer Sprints of four weeks. Teams that have interdependencies will need to communicate often to manage expectations for the delivery of dependencies. We recommend the teams synchronize their Sprints on divisor of the longest Sprint length used by one of the coordinating teams.

Scott Ambler, Chief Methodologist/Agile for IBM Rational, offers the following example:

Eclipse has a six-week iteration, so subteams go for one-, two-, three-, or six-week iteration lengths. That way, the integration rhythms of the subteams line up with the integration rhythm of the overall team. Ideally they are all the same length, but for small subteams, that doesn't make much sense sometimes.

As shown in Figure 3.12, Scrum Team 1 is using a four-week iteration and Scrum Team 2 is using a two-week Sprint. To simplify reporting through the product chain and to manage interdependencies, Scrum Team 2 uses letters to identify the shorter Sprints and keep the same Sprint number as the other Scrum Teams.

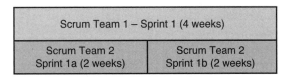

Figure 3.12   Synchronizing two related teams

There are also cases where it may take longer for teams to be able to synchronize because of mismatched Sprint lengths or Sprint dates that are out of synch. When this happens, the teams need to work out their dependencies. One approach is to base the delivery date on the date of the last day of the Sprint of the team delivering the item. The dependent team can consume the deliverable in their next Sprint.

KEY POINT   Where there are likely to be dependencies between teams, it is important to synchronize as often as possible if the teams are not on the same Sprint duration.

What Is the Estimated Team Velocity?

Velocity is the average amount of work a team can do within a Sprint. For teams estimating their user stories using story points, their velocity is the number of story points for each completed user story in a Sprint.

When a project involves multiple teams, estimating the velocity becomes more challenging because of the skill differences between the teams. The development team doing the work should always estimate the stories they will work on because teams have different scales. A story worth one story point for one team may be worth three for another.

Teams must work together for a few Sprints before they are able to start estimating their velocity; this is why it is important not to use the first Sprint of a new team as an indicator of expected velocity. For new teams, the Product Owner should measure two or three Sprints worth of work, perhaps through early prototyping, to start forecasting the project velocity.

Velocity is important because it allows the teams to help estimate how much work they can deliver. Figure 3.13 shows how to estimate the work a fictional team can complete by a fixed date. The Scrum team in the example has 1,000 story points of work in their Product Backlog and 15 iterations planned for the release. By using their lowest historical velocity of 30 story points, they estimate they will be able to complete a minimum of 450 story points in the release. Their highest historical velocity of 40 story points enables them to estimate they will be able to complete a maximum of 600 story points in the release.

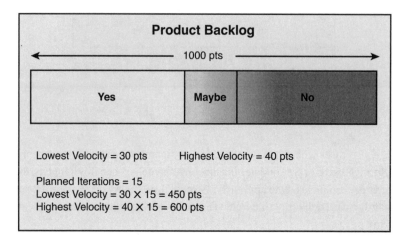

Figure 3.13   Using velocity to estimate how much work the team can complete by a fixed date

These estimates suggest the Product Owner should make sure the highest-priority work for the release is in the top 450 story points in the Product Backlog. They should also place any work that is important but not critical for the release in the 450 to 600 story point range. These estimates also suggest the Scrum Team will not be able to complete any work after 600 story points in the Product Backlog.

KEY POINT   With a predetermined end date, the content needs to be flexible.

Some teams may be working with fixed content instead of a fixed date. In this case, the teams need to identify the end date by which they will complete their work. Figure 3.14 shows a team with 1,000 story points planned for their release. By using their lowest historical velocity, they estimate that it should take them about 33 iterations to complete the work. Their highest velocity allows them to estimate that it should take them about 25 iterations to complete the work.

These estimates suggest to the Product Owner the team will need between 25 and 33 iterations to complete all the work in the Product Backlog. As the team starts executing the work and tracks their velocity after each iteration, the gap in the estimate will start to close and the team will be able to predict their end date.

KEY POINT   It is not realistic to expect teams to deliver specific content identified at the start of the project (sometimes 12–18 months in advance) by a specific date.

```
Lowest Velocity = 30 pts        Highest Velocity = 40 pts

Planned Points = 1000 pts
Lowest Velocity = 1000 / 30 = 33 iterations
Highest Velocity = 1000 / 40 = 25 iterations
```

Figure 3.14 Using velocity to estimate how much time the team needs to complete the work

What Are the Dependencies?

External dependencies will impact the layout of user stories across Sprints. Some stories may not be able to start until an external team completes or resolves dependencies. During an enterprise transition to agile methods, not all parts of the business will instantly be able to support an agile project.

As an example, it is common for translation to take place at the end of a project. When laying out Sprints, the team may need to add specific user stories for translation, rather than translation being part of fully completing each user story.

When working on the release plan, it is important to recognize these dependencies between the Scrum Teams working on the release and other organizations or companies. For example, a story may need translation before the team can consider it "done." Companies that deliver in multiple languages often employ their own translation department or outsource the translation to another company. Because of these dependencies, it may be necessary to add a release Sprint or add user stories toward the end of the release. This will enable the team to focus on translating stories from earlier Sprints.

Elizabeth Woodward provides the following example:

> I worked with one client that provided their content to a third-party translation company toward the end of the release of each project. At first, we created separate work items for translation that took place toward the end of the project. However, we were able to work with the translation company to develop a new way of working to allow us to work more closely and to translate user stories within the Sprint or in the following Sprint. While the idea was new, the company found that having smaller items in their work queue allowed them to more efficiently meet the needs of several clients. At the same time, this helped the development team to complete their user stories at the end of each Sprint.

Ming Zhi Xie, an agile coach for China Development Lab, provides another example where his team provides certain test services for other teams within IBM:

> CDL provides test services for many teams. We have someone with deep test expert assigned to each of our client Scrum Teams. They take part in all planning, including the Daily Scrums. They work with the ScrumMaster and Product Owner to set up the

Product Backlog for test teams at CDL. The test team at CDL pull highest-priority requirements from the test backlog, according to the expertise of the test teams.

Figure 3.15 shows the backlog model of the CDL.

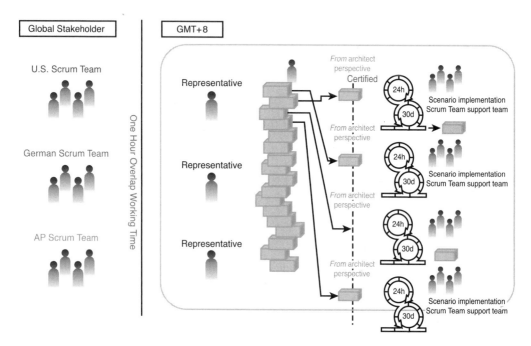

Figure 3.15 Backlog model of the China Development Lab

Agile teams will not try to account for every possible dependency at the start of the project, but will look ahead two or three Sprints to ensure that teams are ready to deal with dependencies.

For distributed release planning, limiting dependencies between teams is even more important. The acronym INVEST reminds us that good user stories are **I**ndependent, **N**egotiable, **V**aluable, **E**stimable, **S**mall, and **T**estable.

The Product Owner looks for ways to organize and write user stories so a cross-functional, collocated team (if possible) can develop each story without significant dependencies on other teams. The more dependencies, the higher the likelihood for problems to arise when a team's pace suggests they can't commit to the work originally identified for each Sprint laid out in the release plan. Additionally, dependencies can impact whether a team is able to work at a higher pace than expected during planning. If the team is depending on others who are unable to deliver as quickly as them, they may wind up functioning at a velocity that is lower than their potential.

What Are the Risks?

During the Release Plan, the Product Owner will want to identify the risks associated with the project and, when possible, the mitigation plan for each of them. This is another good place where affinity diagrams can help the team group the risks into different themes or problem areas.

When the risks affect high-priority user stories, the team may want to create some extra user stories to do some research or early prototyping to help mitigate the risk. When they are dependencies or issues the team cannot handle without help from upper management, it is important to identify these as early as possible in the release.

Coordinate Multiple Product Owners

With a smaller project, one Product Owner is responsible for communicating with stakeholders and ordering the work in the Product Backlog. In large enterprises, it is common for a product or project to involve hundreds of people on multiple Scrum teams. Often, there is too much work for one person to serve as the liaison between the team and stakeholders. As a result, as shown in Figure 3.16, larger products often use a hierarchy of Product Owners (Schwaber 2004).

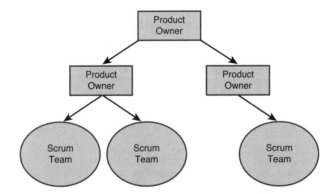

Figure 3.16   Hierarchy of Product Owners

One Product Owner provides the overall direction and priorities for the product. The highest-level Product Owner provides a liaison to each team. The lower-level Product Owners coordinate the priorities of their team's Product Backlog with other teams contributing to development of the product. One individual may serve as the Product Owner for more than one team, but should not serve more teams than would be effective.

Product Owners take part in the Daily Scrums and in the Scrum of Scrums to understand implications of actions on stories in the current Sprint and those in the backlog. Product Owners also meet regularly to discuss Product Backlogs, dependencies, and links between and boundaries between user stories.

In a complex hierarchy of collaborating Product Owners, the Product Owners at the various levels have a tendency to become specialized. The lower-level Product Owners work more closely with the teams, for instance, whereas the top-level or chief Product Owner takes on most of the stakeholder management work.

Scott Ambler describes the role of the Product Owner team:

The product ownership team is a grouping of the Product Owners of each subteam and is responsible for coordinating the requirements effort across the subteams. They will need to negotiate requirements with the larger body of stakeholders whom they represent and properly divvy them out among the subteams. They will also need to negotiate the unavoidable disputes between subteams about whom should do what and what a requirement means.

Use Agile Project Management Tools

Transparency is one of the key points of Scrum (Schwaber and Beedle 2001). Making the ordered backlog visible to the team, to management, and to stakeholders helps everyone to work together toward successfully delivering the highest-priority features at the end of each Sprint. It also helps in ensuring the features meet the needs of the stakeholders.

The team will need to be able to view the backlog, but it is also important the team be able to move requirements from the backlog into the Sprint where they will do the work. When using paper cards, the team would physically move the requirements from one section of a whiteboard or from the Product Owner's stack of cards to a different section of whiteboard. In a virtual setting, the team will want to be able to move text from one location to another.

There are a few ways the Product Owner might make the backlog visible to the team during Sprint Planning:

- **Using a separate backlog displayed with a screen-sharing program.**The problem with using a screen-sharing program is the team will be unable to change the Product Backlog to move requirements from the Product Backlog into the Sprint.

- **Using a separate backlog as a shared document.**This method enables everyone to change the document shared by the Product Owner. However, if the Product Owner keeps a separate backlog, the team may need to copy and paste between the backlog and whatever repository they are using to hold the requirements for the Sprint.

- **Using a shared tool with read and write access.**Several tools on the market provide a central storage location for a Product Backlog the team can then work with to move user stories from the Product Backlog into the proper Sprint backlog.

The best solution to help with distributed communication is to use a shared tool with read and write access. However, it is important the team recognize that filling out fields in a tool is not Scrum. The tool may help with communication, but it will not replace good Scrum practices.

In fact, a team can complete every field in a tool and not be using Scrum. Keep the tooling as simple as possible.

When selecting planning tools, we need to consider the tasks that are part of planning. To plan successfully as a distributed team, the team will need to be able to do the following quickly and easily:

- View the prioritized backlog.
- Add estimates to requirements in the Product Backlog.
- See the Product Owner adjust the priorities of the Product Backlog because of team discussions.
- Disaggregate user stories into smaller user stories and add user stories to the Product Backlog.
- Move high-priority items from the Product Backlog to the Sprint backlog.
- Identify tasks to carry out to satisfy a requirement.
- Estimate the tasks.

The distributed Scrum team can benefit from using a multiuser networked tool for Sprint Planning. It is important for members of the team to be able to add tasks and to estimate tasks simultaneously. Not having such a tool will slow down the Sprint Planning procedure for the distributed Scrum Team. As a best practice, make sure that everyone is familiar with the tool at the beginning of the project. Consider hosting a lunch and learning webcast to demonstrate every new tool.

Invest in Smarter Development

Test automation and continuous integration help teams complete user stories within a Sprint. Both practices are even more important when multiple teams are working together or for distributed teams. Teams transitioning to agile may need more time to focus on getting test automation in place or setting up a continuous integration infrastructure that will provide long-term benefits. These actions will impact the speed of the teams. There are two common approaches to handling these kinds of stories, as follows:

- Do not place them on the Product Backlog. Complete them outside the context of the user stories needed to produce the deliverables.
- Include them on the Product Backlog with a certain number of points assigned to each Sprint.

We prefer the second approach because it gives clear visibility and awareness of the actions as important to the development team and to the business. If the team assigns no points to the effort, it will have no visibility. This makes it more likely they will not complete the work within the Sprint. Although there may be short-term benefits, there can be a significant long-term impact to the team's productivity.

We recommend the team identify small stories that it can complete within the different Sprints and that will significantly improve productivity in incremental steps.

Coordinating Agile and Non-Agile Teams

In a large-scale enterprise transitioning to agile, some teams may be agile whereas some might still be using traditional methods. Including the non-agile team in the Scrum-of-Scrums meetings is a good way to coordinate the teams and to expose the non-agile team to agile methods.

Making sure that all teams meet at the beginning of the project helps the team members to feel more engaged and included in the overall project.

The non-agile team may not be able to adjust as quickly as the agile team. Therefore, making sure the non-agile team is aware of the priorities of the agile teams and keeping dependencies visible can help to prevent blockers between the teams. The agile team can build an application programming interface (API) or simulation layer of what they think the non-agile team will deliver and test against that. Providing the non-agile team with access to a distributed Scrum tool can also help with visibility into what the teams are working on, what is pending, and how the teams are progressing.

In a mixed environment of agile and non-agile projects, teams may need to plan how they are going to report status of the release. The resulting status may be a mix of agile and non-agile, depending on how far along different teams and different parts of the enterprise are in their transition to agile.

Reporting on Release Status

During release planning, you need to define how you will report on the status of the release. In working with multiple teams, you will need to roll up the view of the work completed by the different teams into one view that depicts the status of the overall release.

Ongoing Updates to Release Plan and Vision

The Product Owner should continuously be watching for the latest changes in the market and meeting with stakeholders to understand their evolving needs. Feedback during reviews provides one way of identifying shifts, but the Product Owner in an enterprise should continuously gather feedback from additional stakeholders to keep in tune with shifting markets. The Product Owner should regularly revisit both the Vision and the Release Plan. Both are living documents.

Important Note about Meeting Face-to-Face

If there is any chance of the Scrum Team meeting face-to-face during a project, we recommend they meet during the early project startup—in particular, when building the Product Backlog and helping the Product Owner to create the release roadmap. Face-to-face, the Scrum Team will be able to sketch out alternative solutions quickly, see confusion or understanding on each others' faces, add to other's diagrams, or modify each other's diagrams to gain understanding quickly. Most importantly, it enables them to begin to build trust and relationships they can sustain during the distributed development efforts.

Engaging in these project startup tasks as a distributed team will take longer, and it will take longer for the team to become a team. If you have team members in significantly different time zones, consider that someone will likely be on the call outside their normal working hours for extended periods. You may want to reduce the amount time spent each day on project startup tasks, which will extend the *duration* of the project startup tasks.

Summary

In the large-scale enterprise, release planning often means the Product Owner will need to coordinate multiple, distributed teams. To be successful, the Product Owner, ScrumMaster, and development team must address additional complexities when engaging in release planning.

Besides knowing what the release will include and how to map the user stories into the Sprints and dates for the release, it is also important to consider special consideration related to the enterprise environment. These may include working with multiple teams at different stages of transition to agile development. Although the release plan should be at a high-level, the release planning process should help the team, Product Owner, and ScrumMaster begin preparing for Sprint Planning, as discussed in the next chapter.

References

Ambler, Scott. *An Introduction to Agile Modeling*. http://www.agilemodeling.com/essays/introductionToAM.htm.

Ambler, Scott. *The Agile System Development Life Cycle*. http://www.ambysoft.com/essays/agileLifecycle.html#Iteration0.

Beck, K. *Extreme Programming Explained: Embrace Change*, 2nd. ed. Boston: Addison-Wesley, 2004.

Beck, Kent, Mike Beedle, Arie van Bennekum, Alistair Cockburn, Ward Cunningham, Martin Fowler, James Grenning, Jim Highsmith, Andrew Hunt, Ron Jeffries, Jon Kern, Brian Marick, Robert C. Martin, Steve Mellor, Ken Schwaber, Jeff Sutherland, and Dave Thomas. *Agile Manifesto*. 2001. http://agilemanifesto.org/.

Cohn, Mike. *User Stories Applied for Agile Software Development*. Boston: Addison-Wesley, 2004.

Cohn, Mike. *Agile Estimating and Planning*. Boston: Addison-Wesley, 2004.

Cohn, Mike. http://www.planningpoker.com/.

IBM Rational Software. *Shared Vision Practice*. http://www.ibm.com/developerworks/rational/practices/shared_vision/.

Pichler, Roman. *Agile Product Management with Scrum: Creating Products That Customers Love*. Boston: Addison-Wesley Professional, 2010.

Pichler, Roman. *True North*. http://www.scrumalliance.org/articles/115-the-product-vision.

Poppendieck, Mary and Tom. *Implementing Lean Software Development: From Concept to Cash*. Boston: Addison-Wesley, 2007.

Schwaber, Ken. *Agile Project Management with Scrum*. Redmond, WA: Microsoft Press, 2004.

Selhorst, Scott. *Stakeholder Value-Delivery Matrix*. 2007. http://tynerblain.com/blog/2007/10/25/stakeholder-value-matrix/.

Surdek, Steffan. *Agile Planning in Real Life*. DeveloperWorks, 2009. http://www.ibm.com/developerworks/linux/library/l-agile-plan/index.html?ca=drs-.

Tockey, Steve. *Return on Software: Maximizing the Return on Your Software Investment*. Boston: Addison-Wesley, 2008.

Preparing for Sprint Planning

It is a mistake to look too far ahead. Only one link in the chain of destiny can be handled at a time.

Winston Churchill

In traditional Scrum, planning for the Sprint typically consists of two seamless back-to-back meetings referred to as the **Sprint Planning meeting** (Schwaber 2004). The two meetings have distinct purposes and actions. In the first one, the Product Owners review the highest-priority items in the Product Backlog with the Scrum Team, and they decide *how much* work they can do within the Sprint based on their velocity in the previous Sprints. In the second one, the Scrum Team decides *how* it is going to get the work done by breaking down the user stories into tasks and then commits to the Sprint Plan.

The first half of the Sprint Planning meeting can be very painful for teams when there are no priorities in the Product Backlog or when the team does not have a common understanding of the deliverables for a given story. Another challenge these teams face is asking questions the Product Owner can only answer by contacting stakeholders who are not available in the meeting. All of these actions take time, and being in this position is a good sign these teams are not ready to do their Sprint Planning meeting.

There is no official Sprint preplanning meeting in Scrum, but it is one approach that some teams take to get ready for their next Sprint. To be effective, the Scrum Team needs to have the following information ready before the Sprint Planning meeting:

- A prioritized Product Backlog
- User stories the team can complete within a Sprint
- Clear acceptance conditions for each user story

Figure 4.1 depicts the tasks to create a prioritized and sized Backlog as the **Sprint preplanning meeting**.

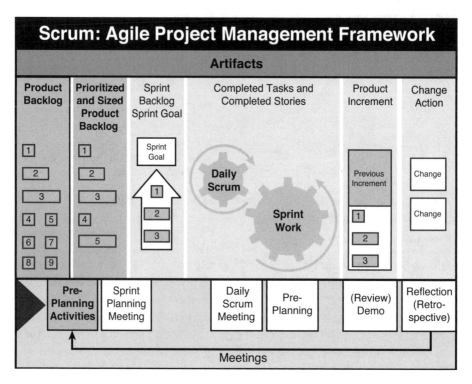

Figure 4.1   Preplanning in Scrum

This chapter focuses on how teams can use a Sprint preplanning meeting to prepare for the Sprint Planning meeting ahead of time. It identifies some of the actions the participants will want to do and some of the approaches that teams take to do their meetings.

Sprint Preplanning Activities

The purpose of Sprint preplanning is to make the Sprint Planning meeting more effective. Ken Schwaber suggests the first half of the Sprint Planning meeting can take less than the targeted time box of 4 hours for a 30-day Sprint if the success preconditions are in place (Schwaber 2007).

KEY POINT   Two preconditions of a successful Sprint Planning meeting are having enough of a detailed prioritized Product Backlog and knowing how much work the Team can complete within a Sprint.

To provide the right preconditions, the participants need to take the following actions during the Sprint preplanning meeting:

- Discuss and clarify acceptance conditions for high-priority user stories.

- Provide a relative estimate of the size of user stories to help the Product Owner identify their priorities in the backlog.

- Break down high-priority user stories into smaller ones that will fit within a Sprint.

- Consider dependencies between user stories owned by different teams—for this Sprint and the next Sprint or however many Sprints the team is using for lookahead planning.

- Consider dependencies on specialized skills and workload for each team in a scaled environment.

Clarification of the User Stories

In preparing for Sprint Planning, the participants discuss the highest-priority stories from the Product Backlog, including the story and acceptance conditions. When they cannot clearly identify the scope of work for a user story or the value it will bring stakeholders, it is a sign that the team needs to clarify the scope.

The participants can then confirm the story has the same meaning to everyone and that everyone understands what the deliverable for the story is. Culture differences may make seemingly obvious stories unclear across the language boundaries of distributed teams.

Jean-Louis Marechaux describes how his team makes sure everyone has a common understanding:

In a project with a distributed team, I ask the team members to explain the high-priority stories in their own words during the Sprint Planning meeting. This allows us to ensure a common understanding despite language barriers or the cultural differences.

The participants will then bring up questions the Scrum Teams may ask about the user story at the Sprint Planning meeting. This Product Owner will then either answer them right away to help them understand or will work with stakeholders after the meeting to find the answers. Some questions may be of a more technical nature and may need some investigation by some team members.

Asking questions in the preplanning meeting gives extra time to the Product Owner to get answers from stakeholders in different time zones before the Sprint Planning meeting. It also gives time to team members researching issues to discuss their technical implications with others who were unable to attend the preplanning meeting. Once the people looking for answers find relevant information, they will add this new information to the story in the tool the team is using to track their stories.

When discussing the user stories, the participants should also try to confirm if the estimates still seem accurate or if they need to revise them based on their latest knowledge. Clarifying acceptance conditions also helps the team to find out whether there are dependencies they need to consider or specialized skills they need to complete a story. This clarification helps the Product Owner set the priorities of the Product Backlog.

When discussing a user story, if the participants find there is only one task to do, it is either too small or may be a component-based story instead of a feature-based one. In this case, they can decide to either keep the user story as is or to combine it with another one.

Breaking Down User Stories

In the early Sprints of a release, some teams may still have many large stories in their Product Backlog. When these teams only look at the user stories at the Sprint Planning meeting, they may spend a long time disaggregating stories in that meeting instead of planning for the Sprint. Teams in this position typically create many user stories from Sprint to Sprint and never understand the quantity of work they need to do for the release.

KEY POINT   The earlier in the release the team breaks down large user stories, the earlier they will understand how much work they need to do. Teams should not create the user stories for the release from Sprint to Sprint.

During preplanning, participants can help by identifying the highest-priority user stories from the Product Backlog that are too big to fit in a Sprint, break them down, and clarify them. The next section on estimating user stories provides guidance on how to handle getting estimates in the preplanning meeting. The Product Owner will need them to help identify their priorities in the Product Backlog.

When participants cannot identify the scope of work for a user story, it can also be a sign that it is too large and they need to break it down in smaller, more manageable chunks. They first need to clarify the user story to make sure they gain a common understanding of its meaning.

When breaking down user stories, Teams need to look for ways to reduce dependencies and, as discussed in Chapter 3, "Starting a Scrum Project," having feature teams instead of component teams is an important key to doing this. Additionally, the granularity of user stories should help isolate dependencies.

Depending on the duration of the Sprints, there is also a risk that sizing the story to fit the Sprint can create stories that are larger than they appear because they forgot some pieces of the work. Teams with Sprints longer than two weeks should take a closer look at their user stories and consider disaggregating the ones that contain a large amount of work or have tasks that take more than two to five days.

Estimating User Stories

During a Sprint, the Scrum Team and stakeholders may add new stories to the release backlog. These new stories may not have any sizing information. As part of Sprint preplanning, the development team may also estimate the size of any new stories to help the Product Owner identify their priority in the Product Backlog. As discussed in Chapter 3, it is critical the development team doing the work is the one to estimate their user stories.

At times, there may not be enough representation from the development team that will work on a user story to be able to estimate it right away. In such cases, the ScrumMaster or Product Owner should work with the team later to make sure they estimate these user stories.

Occasionally, it may be suitable for a group of representatives to provide an early estimate. Figure 4.2 shows a case where three cross-functional teams are working from a common backlog and pulling highest-priority work off the top. If each team has 9 people, that is 27 people who would engage in a distributed meeting. The meeting could be less productive than if each team identified a few representatives. However, the representatives should go back to their teams and decide if the early estimates are reasonable or if they need to adjust them.

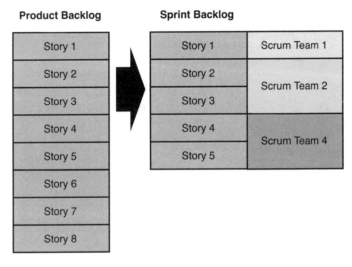

Figure 4.2   Where representatives can be helpful

In the example presented in Figure 4.3, multiple teams are working on features identified in the Product Backlog. Each feature team contains five to nine people, so each feature team as a whole team estimates the stories that Team will complete.

The example in Figure 4.3 is similar to the example in Figure 4.4 where different teams with different skills expect to work on different sets of stories from the Product Backlog. Again, each team should estimate stories as a whole team. Not all teams and team members need to estimate all stories.

The team achieves team ownership, buy-in, and commitment when the people who are doing the work provide the estimates.

Feature 1	Story 1	Scrum Team 1
Feature 2	Story 1	Scrum Team 2
	Story 2	
	Story 3	
Feature 3	Story 1	Scrum Team 3
	Story 2	
	Story 3	
Feature 4	Story 1	Scrum Team 2
Feature n	Story 2	Scrum Team 4

Figure 4.3   Feature teams

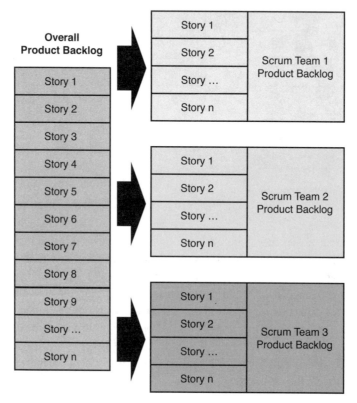

Figure 4.4   Independent teams

Dealing with Dependencies

Development team members need to look for ways to minimize the dependencies between user stories in the Product Backlog. A good user story is independent and does not have any dependencies. This is even more important in a scaled environment, where this can create dependencies between different Scrum Teams pulling the highest-priority stories from the same Product Backlog into the Sprint. Those dependencies need some coordination and may result in one team not being able to make progress because they are waiting on another team.

James C. Porter, an IT Architect for IBM Global Business Services®, suggests there are three types of dependencies (shown in Figure 4.5) that teams typically face, as follows:

- Simple dependencies
- External dependencies
- Intertwined dependencies

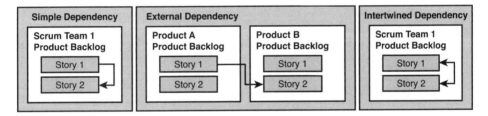

Figure 4.5   Three types of dependencies teams face

Simple dependencies happen when one user story depends on another one that can stand on its own. One way to remove this unidirectional dependency is to combine or split the user stories differently. When this is not possible, the alternative is to set a higher priority for the standalone user stories with the greatest number of dependencies than their dependents. The team will then address the standalone stories in earlier Sprints and dependent stories in later Sprints.

External dependencies happen when a story is dependent on outside teams. In this case, the teams need to negotiate integration and delivery dates and adjust the priorities of the stories. The team working on the dependent story should not commit to completing the dependent story within a Sprint until the other team delivers their user story. In *exceptional* cases, the dependent team may plan for a stub-out of the interface, but this is *risky* because your system is no longer potentially shippable until you replace the stubs with the real code. Examples of external dependencies include an interface, a data feed, or a web service.

Intertwined dependencies are when two or more user stories are co-dependent, and each cannot complete without the others. Ideally, the team should look for ways to break all the connections or look for ways to turn the intertwined dependencies into simple dependencies instead. Dealing with the dependencies across Scrum Teams is a critical responsibility of the Product Owners working with the Scrum Teams.

Some Examples of Managing Dependencies

This sidebar presents some examples of user stories that have dependencies and the steps teams can take to manage them.

Example 1: Handling Unidirectional Dependencies

A team working on a Virtual Conference software project has the following two user stories in their Product Backlog:

- Story 1: As a virtual conference attendee, I can add events to my personal conference schedule.
- Story 2: As a virtual conference attendee, I can remove events from my personal conference schedule.

An attendee needs to be able to add events to the personal event schedule before being able to remove them. This points out that Story 2 has a dependency on Story 1.

In cases like this, there are two possible actions the team can take, as follows:

- If the stories are small enough to fit within a Sprint, they may combine them into a single "As a virtual conference attendee, I can manage events on my personal conference schedule."
- They could make a note that Story 1 needs to have a higher priority than Story 2.

Example 2: Dealing with Intertwined Dependencies

A team working on a Virtual Conference software project has the following two user stories in their Product Backlog:

- Story 1: As a conference moderator, I need to be able to chat with attendees in a given presentation session.
- Story 2: As an attendee, I need to be able to chat with the moderator of a given presentation session.

These stories share some common code because both need the ability to chat and both need the chat session to be limited to the people attending a presentation. Another consideration is the moderator is also an attendee at least for the chat. This causes a circular dependency where each story needs the other one to be complete.

In cases like this, the second story will typically take less time to complete once the Scrum Team finishes the first story. In the Product Backlog, the original estimates for both stories may be five points, but after completing the first story, the value of the second one goes down to two points.

Here are the possible actions the team can take:

- Assuming the velocity of the Scrum Team is at least seven points, they can combine them into a new story: "As a conference participant, I need to be able to chat with others attending a given presentation session."
- When the velocity of the Scrum Team suggests they cannot commit to both stories in a single Sprint, they may split the stories differently to create a simple dependency instead. The following stories set up the development incrementally, in the Product Backlog, Story 1 should have a higher priority than Story 2:
  - Story 1: As a conference attendee, I need to be able to chat with other attendees.
  - Story 2: As a conference attendee, I need to be able to chat with the moderator for a given session.

Planning with multiple teams forces the Scrum Team to look beyond the next Sprint to deal with dependencies. How far ahead the Scrum Teams need to look will depend on how long their Sprints are, how many teams are coordinating, and how often the team identifies dependencies between the teams. During Sprint preplanning, the team should use lookahead planning, described in Chapter 3, to identify dependencies that are coming in the next Sprints.

KEY POINT Lookahead planning can help the team identify dependencies that may affect their ability to deliver user stories in future Sprints.

Figure 4.6 shows that team A and team B identified they will need to use the results from team C to complete their user stories. If team C completes the user story at the end of Week 4, team A will be able to use that code for their Sprint ending Week 6. Team B will be able to use the code during Week 8 because they are on four-week Sprints.

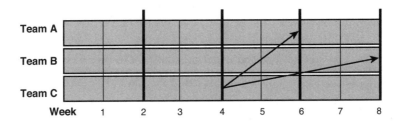

Figure 4.6 Lookahead planning and dependencies

The later teams identify their dependencies, the longer they will have to wait to complete their stories. Notice that being on two-week Sprints allows team A to take advantage of team C's code earlier than team B can take advantage of it. In environments where dependencies are an issue, teams may want to consider shortening their Sprints to allow for greater adaptability.

Teams working together should also identify potential dependencies during the Scrum of Scrums meetings and bring up this information during Sprint preplanning to guide the priorities of user stories.

For multiple teams are using a common backlog, each of them may have a special area of expertise. When setting the priorities of user stories, the Product Owner needs to consider the available skills and the velocity of each team to maximize their use.

Cleanup of the Product Backlog

The Scrum Team continuously updates the Product Backlog. The Product Owner and the Scrum development team need to pay close attention to make sure the high priority stories in the Product Backlog make sense for the current release. The preplanning meeting provides an opportunity to the participants to review the Product Backlog regularly and to make changes based on the knowledge the team gained in the last Sprint.

Armed with their latest knowledge, the Scrum Team may decide that some user stories in the Product Backlog would not bring any added customer value to the current release. There also is a possibility that some user stories would bring value to the product, but are not as critical as others. The Product Owner should lower the priority of these stories in the Product Backlog.

Another possibility is that a team member added a new story to the Product Backlog, but the sizing shows the team is unable to complete the work in the current release. Stories such as these can be valuable enough for the Product Owner to keep in the Product Backlog, but their priority should be lower.

The Product Backlog should not become a parking lot for every possible feature that could potentially be in the product. The quantity of work in the Product Backlog should reflect what the Scrum Teams are likely to be able to address. When requirements change often, there may only be a few months worth of work in the Product Backlog; when they are more stable, the Product Backlog may contain work further into the future. Feel free to let some features fall off from the Product Backlog. If something is a good idea, you will hear about it again from your stakeholders, and it will make its way back on the Product Backlog (Surdek 2009).

KEY POINT   The Product Backlog is not a parking lot for every possible feature that could potentially be in the product.

Approaches for the Sprint Preplanning Meeting

There are different approaches teams can take to prepare for the Sprint Planning meeting. Some teams hold a single meeting each Sprint to help with preparing for the Sprint Planning session, others meet weekly, while others meet as needed. The advantage of a regular weekly meeting is the team can get into a rhythm, and it can also help to bring down interruptions related to requests for help with sizing user stories.

The preplanning meeting should not take on a life of its own. We recommend time boxing it to a reasonable amount of time, such as one hour per meeting, to remain focused. As a general guideline, in their Scrum Primer, Peter Deemer, Gabrielle Benefield, Craig Larman, and Bas Vodde (Deemer, Benefield, Larman, and Vodde 2009) recommend teams spend between five to ten percent of their time for a Sprint preparing for the next one.

Thomas Starz, a ScrumMaster with IBM Systems and Technology Group in Boeblingen, Germany, uses a single preplanning session each Sprint:

> *We have a Sprint preplanning session every two weeks to keep the Sprint Planning session short. Our review and planning happens every other Monday. The Wednesday before that, we have a meeting we call a "design" meeting, but it is not a design meeting. We get together to break apart our user stories. Our architects take part in this session, though they do not always take part in the Sprint Planning session.*

Hanhong Xue, a developer with IBM Systems and Technology Group's Systems Hardware Development, also uses a preplanning meeting the team refers to as a "design" meeting:

> *In our environment, the ScrumMaster works with the Product Owner to come up with decisions about what they want to do. Then they have design meeting with the team and Product Owner to talk about the items they want to do. This is a high-level design to understand the difficulties and dependencies. Then, when they know what it is they are going to do, they sit down together for Sprint Planning.*

However, not all teams have a single meeting to prepare the Product Backlog. Alan June's z/OS® organization with IBM "...prefers to deal with the new stories as they come in, rather than waiting." Whether this approach will work for you may depend on how often the team adds new stories to your Backlog. Clearly, if the Product Owner is often engaging with the team on stories other than those the team is addressing in the current Sprint, this could negatively impact their productivity.

The rest of this section will outline some other ways that distributed teams are successfully carrying out a preplanning meeting. In all the approaches we will discuss, the meeting participants are taking their best guess, based on the priorities in the backlog, at the stories the team will decide to select for the next Sprint. At the Sprint Planning meeting, the team may decide that they are unable to commit to all the stories the preplanning team identified. They may also decide to commit to some user stories the preplanning meeting participants did not discuss in their meetings.

KEY POINT   The purpose of the preplanning meeting is not to be a command and control center. The Scrum Team decides the user stories they will commit to in the Sprint Planning meeting.

The participants then focus on clarifying these stories and making sure the team has all the information they need to be ready to work on those user stories in the next Sprint.

The Full-Team Approach

The Full-Team approach is a regular meeting that involves the entire Scrum Team. This approach is good for smaller Scrum Teams or for collocated and collocated part-time teams.

For large distributed teams, having all Scrum Team members from all locations attending a single meeting may be unrealistic, especially for teams distributed without overlapping hours. This approach *can* work for distributed teams with or without overlapping hours as well, but the team will face the added challenges of cultural differences and language barriers. The more distributed team members you have in the meeting from different locations, the bigger the challenge will be to find a good meeting time. You will want to make sure the meeting time works for as many team members from all locations as possible.

Larger teleconferences are usually less effective than smaller teleconferences because of the time needed to compensate for the lack of visual cues. (Refer to Chapter 2, "Challenges Faced by Distributed Teams," for some helpful techniques.)

There are several benefits to the Full-Team approach as this approach is ideal and adheres to the core spirit of Scrum. Because it involves the entire Scrum Team, it provides a stronger sense of ownership. Everyone has a chance to ask their questions and have their opinions heard.

Because everyone doing the sizing of the stories is a part of the meeting, another benefit is the team can also use this meeting to size new and existing stories. Having the whole team take part in the sizing also identifies tasks and issues that a smaller group may not have considered, which helps the sizing be more accurate.

The drawback of this approach for several Scrum Teams working together on a single Product Backlog is that having many team members in the same meeting may need significantly more time. Another drawback is that having many team members in the same meeting will create many questions and thus may need a stronger facilitator to keep the meeting on track.

Table 4.1 summarizes the pros and cons of the Full-Team approach.

Table 4.1   Pros and Cons of the Full-Team Approach

Pros	Cons
• It provides a sense of team ownership. • All team members can ask questions or voice concerns. • The team can use meeting to do sizing of stories. • It allows the Product Owner to get information from stakeholders before the Sprint Planning meeting.	• It is harder to keep the focus of the meeting with many distributed participants. • It may be difficult to schedule a time that works well for all Scrum Team members.

The Preplanning Team Approach

The Preplanning Team approach is a weekly preplanning meeting that involves the Product Owner and the smallest subset of team representatives able to select and describe stories. Distributed teams with or without overlapping hours often use this approach because it works well for larger distributed teams where not everyone will work on every story. Each team can select representatives to represent particular roles.

The benefit of using this approach is that having a smaller group of people involved in the meeting will keep the meeting participants focused on what they need to do. It also brings down the disruptions on other team members and allows them to focus on their work for the current sprint.

Leslie Ekas shares the following story:

We found that having a smaller group of people involved earlier in a preplanning meeting was quicker than involving the whole team at once. We used a preplanning meeting with the team leads and the Product Owner to avoid pulling people out of the iteration. They would sometimes pick some stories wrongly but most of the time, they picked the right stories and were in a better position to discuss the stories on planning day.

The biggest drawback of using this approach is that not having the entire Scrum Team take part in the discussion may also result in a loss of communication. This is why it is important for the participants from the distributed locations to work with their teams to discuss the stories, estimates, and priorities. They need to be able to go back to their teams and be able to answer their questions at the Sprint Planning meeting.

Table 4.2 summarizes the pros and cons of the Preplanning Team approach.

Table 4.2   Pros and Cons of the Preplanning Team Approach

Pros	Cons
• A smaller group of participants is more effective for teleconferences.	• There is a potential loss of communication or information by not having the full team present.
• At allows the Product Owner to get information from stakeholders before the Sprint Planning meeting.	• Neglecting to go back to the whole team for their contribution can result in a loss of team ownership.
• It reduces the disruptions on the work of team members for the current Sprint.	• This approach can easily shift from Scrum to a command and control center.

The Balanced Team Approach

The Balanced Team approach is a compromise between the Full-Team and Preplanning Team approaches. The preplanning meeting occurs every week with a core group of participants and the entire Scrum development team as optional participants. The entire Scrum development team is present only for the preplanning meeting of the last week of the current Sprint.

One of the benefits of using this approach is having a regular meeting with a core group of people while allowing anyone on the team to take part in the meeting. The benefit of making the meetings optional for the Scrum development team is that it allows them to manage the disruptions on their work for the Sprint.

Inviting the entire team for the preplanning meeting in the last week of the current Sprint allows everyone to start looking ahead to the next Sprint. It also contributes to creating a sense of team ownership and enables team members to ask their questions or voice their concerns.

Table 4.3 runs down the pros and cons of the Balanced Team approach.

Table 4.3   Pros and Cons of the Balanced Team Approach

Pros	Cons
• A smaller group of participants works better for distributed teams using teleconferences.	• There may be a loss of some communication or information because the full team is not always present.
• It allows the Product Owner to get information from stakeholders before the Sprint Planning meeting.	
• It provides a sense of team ownership.	
• All team members can ask questions or voice concerns.	
• It allows the optional team members to manage the disruptions on their work for the current Sprint.	

Considerations for Distributed Teams

The Preplanning Team and Balanced Team approaches are good for large distributed teams because they allow each Scrum Team to send only a few representatives to the preplanning meeting. These representatives will identify the concerns their team to the larger group and will bring back the information to their individual Scrum Teams.

In the Balanced Team approach, the preplanning meeting in the last week of the Sprint is a full team meeting. In the last week, each individual Scrum Team can schedule their own Full-Team preplanning meeting. This limits the number of participants to a single Scrum Team in each meeting, instead of trying to cram three or four Scrum Teams in the same one and making the team less productive for a portion of the audience.

Large distributed teams can also mix the different approaches depending on the needs of the different individual Scrum Teams. For example, the larger team may use the preplanning team approach, but some of the individual teams may be using the Full-Team approach in parallel to help their representatives be ready for distributed preplanning meeting.

Summary

There is no official Sprint preplanning meeting in Scrum, but teams typically engage in preplanning activities throughout the Sprint to ensure they are in a healthy position for their next Sprint Planning meeting. As part of preplanning, Scrum Teams clarify user stories, break down user stories, maintain the Product Backlog, and coordinate dependencies across Scrum Teams.

The benefit of discussing the user stories before the Sprint Planning meeting is that it gives the Product Owner more time to ask questions from stakeholders and get answers from them before the team needs them.

Another advantage of Sprint preplanning is that it also helps keep the momentum going between one Sprint and the next, which the Scrum Team could lose if they focus solely on the current Sprint. Focusing only on the current Sprint may cause them to discover too late there are some dependencies they did not manage or that some critical information is missing.

Preplanning is an investment a team makes that allows them to get early clarifications from the Product Owner and stakeholders and helps the Product Owner to prioritize the Product Backlog. The return on this investment is a more efficient Sprint Planning meeting.

References

Ambler, Scott. *Agile and Large Teams*, 2008. http://www.ddj.com/architect/208700162.

Deemer, P., G. Benefield, C. Larman, and B. Vodde. The Scrum Primer, from the Scrum Training Institute website, 2009. http://scrumtraininginstitute.com/home/stream_download/scrumprimer.

Schwaber, Ken. *The Enterprise and Scrum*. Redmond, WA: Microsoft Press, 2007.

Surdek, Steffan. *Agile Planning in Real Life*. DeveloperWorks, 2009. http://www.ibm.com/developerworks/linux/library/l-agile-plan/index.html?ca=drs-.

Sprint Planning

Plan for what it is difficult while it is easy, do what is great while it is small.

The Art of War, *Sun Tzu*

The purpose of the Sprint Planning meeting is for the Scrum Team to come to agreement on what work they will complete in the next Sprint and how they will complete that work. To plan the Sprint, the team needs to prepare for Sprint Planning. As discussed in Chapter 4, "Preparing for Sprint Planning," this involves grooming the Product Backlog and gaining an understanding of the velocity of the team. Using the information from Sprint preplanning, the whole Scrum Team takes part in the Sprint Planning meeting (see Figure 5.1).

The Sprint Planning meeting in a collocated environment typically consists of two back-to-back meetings (Schwaber 2009). In the first half of this meeting, the Scrum Team decides what they will do. The team does the following:

- Discusses the product vision
- Discusses and confirms the highest-priority user stories in the Product Backlog
- Identifies the user stories they will be able to complete during the Sprint
- Decides on a Sprint Goal

In the second half of the Sprint Planning meeting, the team decides how they are going to get the work done. They do the following:

- Design the work
- Identify and size the tasks (activities that take less than one day) needed to complete the work

- Confirm they will be able to complete the needed work
- Commit to the Sprint

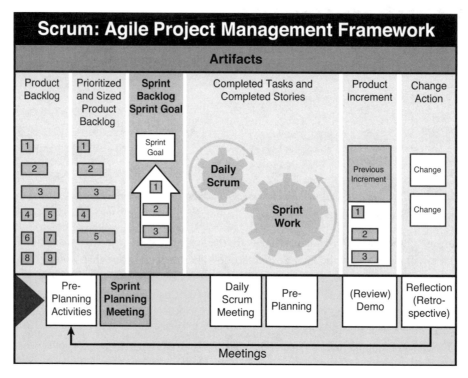

Figure 5.1   The Sprint Planning meeting

Distribution and scaling of Scrum Teams both have an impact on Sprint Planning. In enterprise Scrum where Scrum Team members are in different time zones, the two meetings do not typically happen back-to-back. Sprint Planning for scaled teams is different because there are more people contributing to developing the product. Scrum Teams must consider dependencies between them and look forward over more Sprints than a small-scale, collocated team. Scaled teams are more likely to coordinate sharing deep, specialized skills between teams. A hierarchy of Product Owners may need to coordinate the priorities between the Product Backlogs of different teams. And, teams must coordinate to create a releasable or nearly releasable product each Sprint.

This chapter discusses how scaled and distributed Scrum Teams engage in Sprint Planning. It highlights some areas to consider when setting up the Sprint Planning meetings, reviewing the Product Backlog, keeping the team focused on the vision, creating the Sprint Backlog, engaging stakeholders, and gaining commitment.

Adequately Preparing for the Sprint Planning Meeting

As discussed in Chapter 4, the Scrum Team should have the following information after the Sprint preplanning meetings:

- The Product Owner should have a prioritized list of requirements (user stories) in the Product Backlog for the team to use.

- Ideally, the user stories should already have the basic format of: "Who needs to do what and why?" The team should have a good understanding of the user stories as a result of discussing them and their acceptance conditions during the Sprint Preplanning meeting.

- The user stories should have accurate size estimates. If necessary, the team should have broken down user stories to fit within a Sprint.

Adequately preparing for the Sprint Planning meeting can mean the difference between a smooth, successful Sprint Planning meeting and a frustrating, lengthy event. Missing these key items is not the end of the world, but it can cause the planning meeting to be longer and more challenging for the team.

Sprint Planning Meeting Logistics

All members of the team must work together to commit to how much work they can complete, what work they will complete, and how they will work together to complete it. It is *not* reasonable for representatives of teams to commit to work for their teams. The teams should drive their own commitments.

KEY POINT   All members of the team commit to the Sprint Goal and user stories to complete during the Sprint.

Sprint Planning Meeting Logistics for Scaled Teams

For scaled teams coordinating to deliver a product, it is important to make sure all members who will be responsible for the work take part in Sprint Planning meetings. Chapter 2, "Challenges Faced by Distributed Teams," describes several models for working with scaled teams. Regardless of the model used, the team achieves team ownership, buy-in, and commitment when the people who are doing the work are the ones deciding what they can do during the Sprint. It's important that the whole team take part in Sprint Planning together, as a Scrum Team. If team members participate in Sprint Planning, but are not together, the team may not work together as well as they could (Cohn 2006).

Teams Using Representatives to Prepare for Sprint Planning

Although there are certain cases where distributed teams may provide representatives to help with Sprint preplanning, the whole team needs to take part in Sprint Planning. In Figure 4-2, there were three teams each, with nine people pulling highest-priority work from a common Product Backlog. The team had representatives who provided the initial estimates and then went back to their teams to determine if these were reasonable or if they needed to adjust them. The Sprint Planning meeting needs to involve all 27 team members.

Multiple Scrum Teams Working from a Common Product Backlog

All Scrum Team members working on a User Story in a combined Product Backlog should take part in Sprint Planning together. For example, in Figure 4-3, multiple teams were working on features identified in the Product Backlog. Each feature team of five to nine people estimated the stories their team would complete. Each of these teams could set up a separate Sprint Planning meeting and achieve the necessary commitments for the Sprint.

Independent Teams

For independent teams (refer to Figure 4-4), each team will meet for a separate Sprint Planning meeting.

Sprint Planning Meeting Logistics for Distributed Teams

Distributed teams need to find a time when the whole team can meet for Sprint Planning. For distributed teams without overlapping work hours, some team members will need to meet outside their regular working hours.

As discussed in Chapter 3, "Starting a Scrum Project," having access to a distributed Scrum planning tool can help with distributed communications. Everyone who is taking part in the Sprint Planning meeting should be able to see the product backlog, the user stories, the Sprint Backlog, tasks, and estimates. Besides having access to the distributed planning tool, the distributed team will want to have access to a desktop-sharing tool. One person can serve as the scribe and make updates to the Scrum planning tool based on the discussions and consensus of the team.

Because the Sprint Planning meeting is likely to include significant two-way conversation between participants, team members should carefully consider the guidelines provided in Chapter 2 for leading distributed meetings.

The First Half of Sprint Planning: Deciding What to Do

During the first half of Sprint Planning, the team decides what they will do within the Sprint. The Scrum Team reviews the vision, updates the Product Backlog if needed, and decides how they are going to engage stakeholders.

Reviewing Product Vision and Sprint Goal

At the beginning of the Sprint Planning meeting, the Product Owner will restate the high-level vision for the product. This helps the team consider the larger picture and think about their work in the context of the overall vision for the project. Scrum can be tactical, meaning the team can become focused on the immediate Sprint. By drawing attention back to the vision, the team and Product Owner can share an understanding of the value of the Sprint within the larger scheme of the project. If this is the first Sprint, the vision shared will match the early vision created before creation of the product roadmap. If this is a later Sprint, it is possible the Product Owner may have adjusted the vision based on new stakeholder information, changing business requirements, or new technical knowledge.

Scott Ambler, IBM Software Group Rational Chief Methodologist, takes the following approach:

> *I like to post the vision visibly so everyone remembers why we are working on the solution. For co-located teams, this means they will write it on the wall somewhere, typically on a piece of flip chart paper. For a distributed team, this will be on the home page of the project web site. The vision becomes a valuable reference that is accessible while you are discussing requirements or their solutions.*

After presenting the high-level vision, the Product Owner identifies the goal for the Sprint and discusses how the Sprint Goal will deliver value to the product as described in the vision.

Presenting both the high-level vision and the goal for the Sprint is valuable for helping distributed team members to have a common understanding of the result they are trying to achieve. Scaled teams coordinating to deliver a product also have a greater possibility of drifting out of alignment on goals if they do not often discuss them and any updates to them.

Reviewing the Product Backlog

Before the Sprint Planning meeting, the Product Owner will have prioritized the Product Backlog based on the latest information from the teams. There may be some changes that occurred between when the Product Owner last prioritized it and the Sprint Planning meeting, since these meetings are typically not back-to-back for enterprise teams:

- The previous Sprint review may have showed that not all stories completed as expected or the team needed to add more stories to the Product Backlog in response to feedback from stakeholders.

- In cases where team representatives help with preplanning, the team may have discovered they needed to adjust early estimates provided by their representatives.

- The Product Owner may have updated acceptance conditions for user stories because of the responses of stakeholders to the preplanning questions from the team.

- The quantity of work completed during the previous Sprint may have driven down the average velocity.

During Sprint Planning, the Product Owner presents the highest-priority user stories to the team. Usually, with distributed teams, the Product Owner or ScrumMaster will use a screen-sharing tool to display the user story, the estimates the team provided, and the acceptance conditions for the user story. Team members ask questions, discuss the story as a team, and clarify the user story. Thomas Starz, a ScrumMaster for IBM Tivoli® teams, writes:

> *In our case, the Product Owner has an hour to present the top user stories to the team to ensure that everybody has the same understanding. As ScrumMaster, I make sure the Product Owner is ready to describe in detail the user stories the team might be able tackle during the Sprint.*

Dealing with Incomplete Stories

When a Scrum Team did not complete all the user stories since the previous Sprint, they add those stories back to the Product Backlog for prioritization. However, in a scaled environment, there may be some dependencies that impact the different Scrum Teams that are coordinating for the Product Release. The fact that the team might not complete a story as expected should also have come up during the Scrum of Scrums meeting, especially when it involves dependencies. The Product Owner takes the impact of dependencies into consideration when reprioritizing the Product Backlog due to work the team did not complete during the Sprint.

Checking Estimates from Preplanning Teams

In scaled environments where teams send representatives to help with preplanning, it is important the teams who are going to be doing the work revisit the estimates. They should have the opportunity to discuss and change estimates as needed. As mentioned in the Chapter 4 discussion on using representatives, preplanning efforts are *not* a replacement for engaging the whole team.

Reviewing Changes Based on Stakeholder Feedback

Recall from Chapter 4 the Product Owner may leave the preplanning meeting with a list of questions to have answered by distributed stakeholders to clarify user stories and acceptance conditions. The responses to questions may have an impact on estimates of user stories and may cause reprioritization of the Product Backlog. For example, if clarifying the acceptance conditions for a user story causes the team to resize it from six to twelve points, the Product Owner may drop the user story in priority based on expected return on investment. The team should review changes made since the preplanning meeting, and the Product Owner should confirm the priorities of the Product Backlog.

Discussing Risks

The team is a trusted partner and technical consultant to the Product Owner. The team lets the Product Owner know if they see an opportunity to be more efficient by changing the priority of requirements. If the team believes there are higher-risk items that have a lower priority, the team, again, is responsible for discussing the priorities with the Product Owner.

Using Velocity to Estimate Work

The average velocity of the team may change between the Sprint preplanning and Planning meetings because of the results from the Sprint that completed after the preplanning meeting. The Scrum Team will take the latest information into account before committing to work for the Sprint.

Engaging Stakeholders

As the team is discussing acceptance conditions, test cases, and test data for stories, the team should also identify any needs for customer data for testing. Having real-world data as well as data created by the team can mean the difference between success and failure.

Elizabeth Woodward shares the following story:

In a past non-IBM project, we were responsible for delivering a UNIX® account management system for a university in the United States. Our test data at first consisted entirely of home addresses that matched the pattern for addresses in the United States. During an early round of testing, students provided home addresses in Malaysia, India and other countries that have a significantly different format of address fields than we had anticipated. Had we gathered sample data from our stakeholders in advance, we would have saved some development time.

In a large-scale environment with multiple customers, instead of a single customer, the Product Owner can help identify customers who are willing to share enough of their data to help the teams to test on real-world samples properly. The customer can adjust this data to pass any security or confidentiality requirements. To address the diversity of data by the Scrum team, the Product Owner can help identify which customers are representative of different markets. While the team is looking at needs for the current Sprint, they should look ahead just enough to give the Product Owner time to work through discussions with stakeholders to get the proper approvals to get the data. Depending on the case, the team may consider looking two or three Sprints ahead.

The Second Half of Sprint Planning: Deciding How to Get the Work Done

During the second half of Sprint Planning, the team decides how to get the work done. They create the Sprint Backlog, gain commitment, and update the release plan.

Creating the Sprint Backlog

The Product Owner reviews the highest-priority items in the Product Backlog with the team, and they will take a guess at how much work they can do within the Sprint. The team bases their early guess on their **velocity**—an average of how much work they have been able to do in each Sprint during the last few previous Sprints. Cohn recommends that teams on two-week Sprints look at the average of their last eight Sprints to get an idea of what they can complete. New teams that have not yet completed many Sprints will need to base their estimates off the last ones they completed. Cohn also recommends looking at an average of the worst three Sprints for a hint of the least amount of work the team might be able to carry out within the Sprint.

Each Sprint will have its own circumstances the team will consider when deciding how much work they can commit to. They will share any unusual tasks or meetings that might have an impact on the current Sprint, such as vacation, time-consuming overhead tasks, or special events.

It is possible the team may find that they are unable to pull off the next story on the Product Backlog because they do not have enough time left to finish it. In this case, the team may work with the Product Owner to select a lower-priority item with fewer points that it *can* complete within the Sprint.

The team can typically do this part of the Sprint Planning meeting within two hours for a two-week Sprint if the team prepared for meeting as discussed in Chapter 4 and the Product Owner provided all the needed information.

Identifying Tasks

Having a break between the first half and second half of Sprint Planning meeting gives the team time to think about the tasks needed to complete the work items. It also provides the Product Owner time to get any answers needed by the team.

It is common practice for team members to begin identifying tasks needed to get the work done before the Sprint Planning meeting. Although distributed teams can work together remotely to add tasks for each user story, having some tasks ready ahead of time can help reduce the time spent in the meeting. During the meeting, the team will be able to review, discuss, and achieve consensus more quickly.

It is important that team members not simply add their individual thoughts on the tasks to the Sprint Backlog. There is significant advantage to discussing the tasks and the approaches to find opportunities to work together more efficiently. The whole team needs a shared understanding of the steps involved with getting the work done, and only by working through the tasks together will they have a shared commitment to the Sprint.

During Sprint Planning, team members discuss tasks and the train of thought that went into finding out the tasks and try to make sure that they included most of the tasks necessary to complete the work item. The team also estimates how many hours each task will take. Identifying tasks and the time needed for tasks helps the team to decide if they can commit to completing all the stories their velocity suggested they might be able to complete.

Figure 5.2 shows a case where a four-person Scrum team expected to pull 34 story points worth of work after the first meeting. They based their decision on their velocity of the last Sprint. This team is working on a two-week Sprint, and based on the last few Sprints, they know each member can work on average 60 productive hours in a Sprint. This gives them roughly 240 productive hours the entire team can plan from in a single Sprint.

Four-person scrum team commits to completing 34 story points

Feature 1	Story 1	13 pts
	Story 2	8 pts
	Story 3	13 pts

Figure 5.2 The team pulls 34 story points from the backlog.

Figure 5.3 shows that after breaking down the tasks, they found out the tasks added up to more hours than they had available during the Sprint. The team felt comfortable committing to fewer story points than their velocity suggested.

Four-person Scrum breaks down tasks and adds up time estimates

Feature 1	Story 1	Task 1	24 h
		Task 2	16 h
		Task...	...
		Task n	...
		Total Hours	28 h
	Story 2	Task 1	8 h
		Task 2	20 h
		Task...	...
		Task n	...
		Total Hours	112 h
	Story 3	Task 1	12 h
		Task 2	20 h
		Task...	...
		Task n	...
		Total Hours	150 h
	Total Hours Committed to Sprint:		290 h

Figure 5.3 The four-person team identifies tasks and sums the time estimates.

Gaining Commitment

The ScrumMaster and team members will want to ensure everyone has come to a consensus on the commitment. When working with a distributed team, it is impossible to read the subtle body language that would let everyone know that members of the team are skeptical or not fully committed. With a distributed team, silences and verbal cues take on more significant meaning and because of this, the ScrumMaster needs to rely on the whole team to take responsibility for ensuring good communication. Team members who are sensing that other team members have unspoken issues need to take responsibility for drawing attention to the issues.

> **KEY POINT**   No one should interpret silence as agreement. Team members should phrase questions in a way that needs a verbal response to improve the understanding within the team.

By the end of the Sprint Planning meeting, the team will have a list of user stories and their associated tasks that they agree that they can complete within the Sprint.

Updating the Release Plan

Once the team has committed to stories, the Product Owners revisit the Release Plan mapping of user stories into Sprints. It is important for multiple Scrum teams working together to have more clarity on the next two to three Sprints. With the latest information, stories the team completed in the previous Sprint, stories taken off the Product Backlog for the current Sprint, and velocities of the teams, the Product Owner updates the release plan.

Jean-Louis Marcheaux provides the following tip:

I found it useful on many projects to draft the planning for the next Sprint also. Even if we know it can and will change, it helps predict the use of resources and gives the team a better vision of what they will carry out next, as well as better adherence to the release.

Summary

Enterprise Scrum Teams that prepare for Sprint Planning will have a much easier time during the Sprint Planning meeting. Allowing time between preparing for Sprint Planning and the Sprint Planning meeting provides the Scrum Team with time to gather information from distributed stakeholders and to coordinate between scaled teams. It is important that the whole team engage in Sprint Planning, so there is team buy-in and commitment for the Sprint. Each Scrum Team will review the high-priority stories in their Product Backlog and reprioritize as needed before creating the Sprint Backlog. Enterprise Scrum Teams often begin providing tasks for high-priority user stories before the Sprint Planning meeting. However, it is important that all team members discuss the tasks because it helps with communication for distributed and scaled teams and provides opportunities to find better ways of completing the user stories. The team should confirm that everyone commits to the Sprint Goal and Sprint Backlog. Silence on a teleconference is not a commitment. Once the team agrees to the Sprint Goal and Sprint Backlog, they are ready to begin collaborating to meet their commitments.

References

Beck, K., Beedle, M., van Bennekum, A., Cockburn, A., Cunningham, W., Fowler, M., et al. (February 2001). *Manifesto for Agile Software Development*. Retrieved November 30, 2008, from Manifesto for Agile Software Development. http://agilemanifesto.org/.

Cohn, M. (July 2006). *Sprint Planning: Better Together*. Retrieved November 30, 2008, from Mountain Goat Software. http://www.mountaingoatsoftware.com/article/28-Sprint-planning-better-together.

Schwaber, Ken. *Agile Software Development with Scrum*. Upper Saddle River, NJ: Prentice Hall, 2002.

CHAPTER 6

Distributed Daily Scrum Meetings

Many attempts to communicate are nullified by saying too much.

Servant Leadership, Robert Greenleaf

Once the Scrum Team has completed Sprint Planning, they will begin working together to complete user stories and meet the Sprint Goal. The Daily Scrum, shown in Figure 6.1, provides just-in-time planning and serves as a heartbeat for the Sprint. It is the time each day when the Scrum Team gets together for just 15 minutes and each team member responds to three simple questions (Schwaber 2002):

- What did you do yesterday?
- What are you going to do today?
- Do you have any blockers?

Although the idea is simple, keeping everyone focused on just the three questions can be a Distributed Daily Scrum Meetings significant challenge. Humorous videos on YouTube show just how bad a collocated Daily Scrum can be (ScrumMasters 2, 2006). Distributed communication makes the Daily Scrum even more challenging because communication through teleconference or some other channel is not as effective as being face-to-face. Many of subtleties of facial expression and body language are missing when holding meetings through teleconferences and to a lesser degree with video conferencing.

The combination of inefficient communication channels coupled with a meeting of team members located in different countries can cause the Daily Scrum heartbeat to become irregular and impact the health of the team.

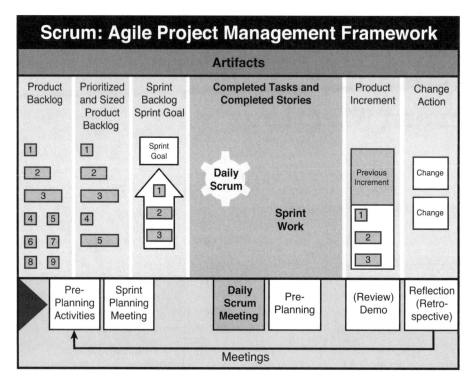

Figure 6.1   The Daily Scrum meeting

Ming Zhi Xie, an agile testing specialist with IBM Software Group's lab in Beijing, China, shared the early experience of his team with Scrum:

> *We would have liked to take part in the Daily Scrums, but with our teams 12 hours apart, it was difficult to schedule. It would have meant team members in China would be on the phone at 10 o'clock at night or team members in North Carolina would be on the phone at 3 o'clock in the morning. Neither was a good long-term solution. Separating into two local teams was unrealistic because of skills. We clearly needed an alternative.*

This chapter talks about how to answer the three questions and provides some tested techniques for conducting effective Daily Scrum meetings with distributed teams (Schwaber 2002).

Using the Three Questions Effectively

To make the Daily Scrum useful to everyone, it is important that team members understand the purpose behind the three questions they need to answer in the meeting. It is also important they provide responses that bring value to the rest of the team.

Answering the Three Questions

Here is an example where John, a fictional team member, answers the three questions of the Daily Scrum meeting:

Yesterday: I started writing the code to load information into the database.

Today: I'm going to handle some of the data issues that cropped up yesterday.

Blockers: I have no blockers.

On the surface, it appears John is answering the Daily Scrum questions, but how much value are these answers providing to the rest of the team. His responses are brief and resemble someone providing a status report, but the Daily Scrum meeting is not a status meeting. It is an opportunity for a team to get together to find ways to help one another and to make sure the team as a whole is able to continue making progress.

Before the Daily Scrum meeting, everyone needs to examine how their current work impacts other team members or identify who can help them resolve an issue. During the meeting, they need to communicate any relevant information to the rest of the team.

KEY POINT   Team members should communicate information that brings value to others on the team. They should also try to identify team members that can help them resolve their issues.

Here is a better response where John provides the same basic information but adds some more information to provide added value to the team:

Yesterday: I started writing the code to load user information into the database. I've discovered that some of the international addresses in the sample data provided by Company ABC do not meet the format we had expected. Mary, I think you are going to run into the same problem with the code to import the data into the label printing module. We can get together offline to discuss.

Today: I'm going to rewrite the module based on the sample data.

Blockers: It looks like there is a problem with the constraints we put on the tables, and we may need to update the design.

The greatest value of the Daily Scrum meeting is the communication between team members.

Coordinating the Team on a Daily Basis

The Daily Scrum meeting allows team members to communicate, coordinate their efforts, and possibly revise their plans daily based on the answers of the others. Using our preceding example, John clearly states Mary may run into the same problem that he faced when working with the sample data. This may change Mary's plans for the day, because now she needs to get with John to discuss this. The plans of another team member may also change to address the blocker that he identified.

> **KEY POINT**   Priorities can change daily. The Daily Scrum meeting provides a daily synchronization point for the team and allows them to revise their plans regularly.

Committing to the Team

The Daily Scrum meeting is where team members make a verbal commitment to the team. When they state what they are going to do today, they are making a verbal commitment to the rest of the team. The next day, when they state what they did yesterday, it is an opportunity for the rest of the team to confirm they met their commitments.

The Daily Scrum creates peer pressure on two fronts, as follows:

- To complete work that is blocking the progress of other team members.
- To create a sense of accountability within the team, in the case where team members do not deliver on the tasks they committed to the previous day.

The Daily Scrum keeps team members accountable as they will eventually need to justify themselves to the rest of the team if they continually do not deliver on their commitments.

> **KEY POINT**   Team members are making a verbal commitment to their team when they state what they are going to do today.

Verifying Progress

The two first questions allow the ScrumMaster to test the focus of the team. The team always needs to be working on stories coming out of the product backlog.

The ScrumMaster also wants to know if the team is completing the work they planned to complete during the Sprint. If estimates are expanding or new tasks come up, there will be an impact on the burndown chart. The ScrumMaster should question team members that are doing work that is not helping the team make progress toward the Sprint goals.

> **KEY POINT**   Tasks not opening and closing regularly are an early sign the team may be going off track.

When team members are not showing regular progress on their tasks for the Sprint, it can be a sign of outside distractions having an impact on their work for the Sprint. These may be meetings, task assignments for work outside the Sprint, or requests from others. It is important for team members to identify these distractions in the Daily Scrum so the ScrumMaster can help reduce or remove them. Steffan Surdek shares this story:

> *Once, I was working on a team with tight deadlines, and some of the team members that were on the critical path were regularly getting requests from another group to provide them with information. When I learned of these interruptions, I directed these team members to redirect the next question my way before taking any action on it. After they forwarded me the next question, I replied to the other team and let them know they were interfering with the deliverables of these team members. I also told them they should come through me in the future for such requests and I would redirect their queries to someone who would be available to help them.*

KEY POINT Team members not showing regular progress may be facing outside distractions the ScrumMaster should reduce or remove.

There is also the possibility that team tmembers who are new to Scrum are not used to depending on their team to help them resolve problems. Smart technical people can feel intense pressure to solve problems on their own and not to depend on others. Admitting any kind of difficulty can make them very uncomfortable. When the Scrum Team notices that a member is experiencing problems, they can encourage that person to work with others to get the help needed.

Resolving Blockers

The Daily Scrum allows team members to identify blockers they are facing that are preventing them from making progress on their work for the Sprint. Sutherland states there are different kinds of blockers a team may face (Sutherland 2006), as follows:

- *Software or technology not showing tup at the right time. These may be dependencies across teams or groups. The ScrumMaster or the team may not be able to resolve this. The management team may need to step in.*

- *Meetings irrelevant to the Scrum Team. Here again, the ScrumMaster may not be able to fix this, but it is the ScrumMaster's role to recognize it and bring it to the attention of the management team.*

- *Hard technical problems often slow things down. The team can often fix this, but at times, management must bring in other resources.*

Blockers may create new issues that may in turn become new tasks or user stories in the backlog. These may force the team to change the current plan.

Sutherland also states that it is important for the ScrumMaster to create a list of blockers and assign them to the team or to managers. A major responsibility of the ScrumMaster is to manage, prioritize, and assure this impediment backlog is burning down. The Scrum Team should expect management to help work the impediment backlog. Removing bottlenecks is the fastest way to improve productivity.

KEY POINT   The ScrumMaster should create a list of blockers and assign them to team members or managers. The ScrumMaster should also ensure the team is burning through the blocker list.

Daily Scrum Logistics

Scrum encourages collocated teams to meet in the same room at the same time every day for the Daily Scrum. To adapt this meeting to work in a distributed environment, the first step is for the team to decide how to best conduct it.

The distribution level will have an impact on how to conduct the Daily Scrum meeting. Conducting the Daily Scrums when team members are in the same time zone and speak the same language is much simpler than for a team with members spread in multiple countries and time zones, having many different languages and cultures.

Distributed teams with no overlapping work hours have the biggest challenge because they are scheduling a 15-minute meeting at a time outside the normal working hours of some team members.

Ways of Communicating During the Daily Scrum

Teams can use different ways to communicate during their Daily Scrum meetings, from face-to-face meetings to using an instant messaging tool. Teams need to select the methods that best suit their needs as well as their distribution level.

Face-to-Face Meeting

We recommend face-to-face Daily Scrum meetings for collocated teams. They foster stronger communication between team members, put pressure on team members to deliver on their commitments to their team, and encourage the Scrum Team to self-organize.

When a Scrum Team meets in the same location every day, it creates a routine for the team members as well as accountability for the meeting to start at the scheduled time. Manmohan Singh, a ScrumMaster in IBM, shares the following story about how the Daily Scrum meeting evolved in his Scrum Team:

> *In the early days of our Daily Scrum meetings, I often had to remind team members to come to the meeting. There was lot of inertia in the team because we were transitioning from traditional waterfall to agile. After a few months, the meeting became part of the daily routine of the team because team members found value in the meeting. I believe conducting the Daily Scrum meetings at a fixed time every day instilled the habit of attending the Scrum in the team, and today the team meets daily at the scheduled time*

in the conference room. When I am absent that day, a senior developer or QA member starts the meeting, takes the Scrum notes, and then communicates the blockers and issues to the entire distributed team. This is a clear signal of my team starting to turn into a self-organizing team.

I find the real value of the Daily Scrum meeting is the verbal communication that occurs between team members. Often, when a team member verbally updates the whole team on his tasks, dependencies, and issues, other participants have new information related to the tasks and everyone benefits from this. We also have cases where a team member has a dependency or an issue and someone else on the team immediately has the information on how to address the issue. This is a great way ffor us to unblock the team quickly.

Table 6.1 summarizes the pros and cons of the Face-to-Face Meeting approach.

Table 6.1   Summary of Pros and Cons for the Face-to-Face Meeting Approach

Pros	Cons
• Highest collaboration level. • Richest communication level. • No loss of nonverbal communication. • Promotes team self-organization. • Whole team takes part in each day.	• Requires a collocated team. A distributed team with several team members in one location can meet face-to-face and use a teleconference call to include others in the Daily Scrum.

KEY POINT   Having face-to-face Daily Scrum meetings gives the team the highest collaboration level possible.

Teleconference Meeting

When a face-to-face meeting is not possible for fthe entire Scrum Team, members can use a teleconference to call into the Daily Scrum. This method works well for distributed teams and for collocated part-time teams.

Distributed teams with overlapping work hours should find a time during the overlapping hours to meet every day at the same time and on the same teleconference number for the Daily Scrum. Collocated part-time teams may also find this approach useful as a backup to the face-to-face Daily Scrum. If a collocated team member is out of the office visiting a client site, at a conference, or working from home, he or she can dial into the Daily Scrum. It can be helpful to the Scrum Team to use the same teleconference number each day. This creates a routine for the team and makes it easier for team members to dial into the Daily Scrum. Sirsidynix shows teams can successfully combine the Daily Scrum of a collocated and a remote Scrum Team (Sutherland, Viktorov, Blount, and Puntikov 2007).

Daily Scrums can be harder to facilitate in a teleconference call format than a face-to-face format; the "Tips for Distributed Daily Scrums" section, later in this chapter, provides some additional guidance to help make the meeting run more smoothly.

KEY POINT   Distributed teams with overlapping work hours should use a teleconference call to the same phone number every day to hold their Daily Scrum meetings.

Table 6.2 shows the pros and cons of this approach.

Table 6.2   Summary of Pros and Cons for the Teleconference Meeting Approach

Pros	Cons
• Ideal for distributed teams with overlapping hours.	• Loss of nonverbal communication.
• Good backup for collocated teams when team members are working remotely.	• Hard to keep the people on the phone engaged.
• Allows team members to interact directly.	
• Whole team takes part in each day.	
• Team can discuss blockers and remove them immediately.	

Videoconference Meeting

An alternative to a teleconference is to do a videoconference instead. The main advantage of this approach is that team members get to see one another, so there is less nonverbal communication loss. The main challenge of this approach is how to be able to see everyone depending on the number of participants in the Daily Scrum.

This approach needs added hardware as each location joining the videoconference will need a webcam. To be able to conference multiple video streams at the same time, the team may also need extra software. There may be software and bandwidth limitations as well, which could cause problems with the video feed.

The other challenge is when there are multiple participants in one of the video streams—where should the focus of the webcam be? When only focusing on the current speaker, the remote participants will lose any nonverbal reactions of other participants at that location. When focusing on a larger group at a location, it may be difficult to see everyone.

Table 6.3 shows the pros and cons of this approach.

Table 6.3 Summary of Pros and Cons for the Videoconference Approach

Pros	Cons
• Potentially richer communication experience than a teleconference. • Allows team members to interact directly.	• Can be challenging to see everyone. • Needs added hardware and software. • Bandwidth or software limitations may affect the video streams.

Group Instant Messaging Approach

Another way to communicate during the Daily Scrum is to use an instant messaging tool with a group chat feature. At a regular time every day, the ScrumMaster invites all team members to a group chat to have them answer the three Daily Scrum questions.

This approach works with collocated or collocated part-time teams as well as distributed teams with overlapping work hours. The benefit is that by creating a transcript of the chat session, the ScrumMaster can send a set of notes to all team members by email or post on a wiki. These notes can help keep track of commitments individuals are making to the team and provide a way for members who are unavoidably absent from a Daily Scrum to review the tasks, commitments, and blockers of the Scrum Team.

Another benefit of using a group instant messaging session is that team members can type as much information as they want in the chat session. The approach allows team members not fluent in the language to prepare their text ahead of time and paste it into the group chat.

Doing the Daily Scrum this way can be chaotic depending on how the ScrumMaster conducts the meeting. There are two ways to approach it:

- All team members type in their answers to the three questions and post them in the chat whenever they are ready. The ScrumMaster sorts through stuff the answers each member provides and asks clarifying questions. This approach can make the discussions that happen in the chat difficult to follow because other team members may be posting their comments during a discussion.

- Conduct the chat session like a teleconference and have the ScrumMaster go around each participant in the chat and ask them for their answers to the Daily Scrum questions. When other team members have questions for the current participant, they can ask them right away or can wait until it is their own turn to speak. At the beginning of the meeting, the ScrumMaster should ask the people to queue up their answers to the three questions and wait for their turn before sending it out the team.

When using either of these methods, it is good practice for team members to prepare the answers to the questions five minutes before the Daily Scrum meeting. This allows team members to pay closer attention to what other team members are saying in the chat session.

Using a group instant messaging session to conduct the Daily Scrum also has some challenges. Because team members are not face-to-face in the same location, there is a loss of nonverbal communication as well as subtle verbal cues, such as tone of voice or inflections. It becomes more important for team members to ask for clarifications when there are doubts.

The Daily Scrum works best when it occurs at the same time every day as this helps create a routine the team can get into. One of the traps of the Group Instant Messaging approach is that it can fall solely on the shoulders of the ScrumMaster to launch the group chat session at the chosen time. To work around this problem, the team can name two or three people to serve as initiators for the instant messaging session and to coordinate among themselves to make sure the meeting always starts on time. Before taking part in a group chat, people typically wait for a meeting invitation to arrive before engaging; if it does not appear, they will focus on their work instead and forget about the meeting.

Table 6.4 summarizes the pros and cons of this approach.

Table 6.4   Summary of Pros and Cons for Group Instant Messaging Group Approach

Pros	Cons
• Whole team takes part in each day.	• The team loses both face-to-face and verbal communication. Unlike teleconference interaction, the Scrum Team cannot hear voice inflections.
• Team can discuss blockers and remove them immediately.	
• A transcript of the chat can easily become a set of notes for the meeting.	• No guarantee the Scrum Team is paying attention to the chat session.
• May be easier for non-language speakers to write their thoughts instead of speaking.	• Full accountability for the meeting occurring at the same time every day is fully on the ScrumMaster.
	• Can be chaotic depending on how the team conducts the meeting.

Approaches to Handling Time Zone Issues

Teams can use four different methods to deal with distributed Daily Scrums where the team has members with no overlap in their work hours, as follows:

- Daily Scrums through documentation
- Liaison approach
- Alternating meeting times
- Share the pain

Each solution has pros and cons the ScrumMaster and team should consider in deciding how to conduct their Daily Scrum meetings.

Daily Scrums Through Documentation

Perhaps the least effective way of handling distributed Daily Scrums with no overlap in the work-day is scheduling the Daily Scrum during a time when *most*—but not all—team members can meet. With this approach, team members who cannot meet as scheduled document their answers to the three questions in a wiki, through email, or in a document the team can access.

Figure 6.2 shows an extreme example of a team distributed in locations from San Jose, CA in the United States to Beijing, China. If the team adopts a single Daily Scrum meeting that is held at 9:00 AM in the morning in Toronto, Canada, the meeting will likely be outside standard working hours for the team members in San Jose, Bangalore, and Beijing. Such a team might try to compensate by having all team members document their answers to the three questions.

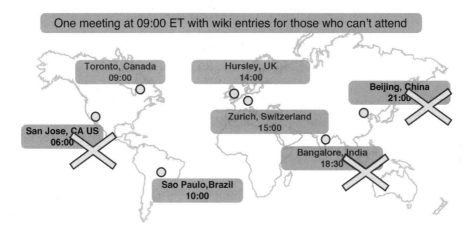

Figure 6.2 Single meeting time that works for both members

The primary advantage to this approach is that it can be better for sustainable pace. And it inconveniences no one since nobody is meeting outside their normal working hours.

However, because this approach is not interactive, those who cannot attend do not have the opportunity to hear directly from other team members or to get quick comments from them on their answers to the three questions. Also, this may cause members who do not take part in the Daily Scrum to feel less a part of the team or to feel the other members of the Scrum Team do not value their contribution as much. It is important that all members of the Scrum Team work together to make compromises to show they value everyone equally.

The lack of direct communication may also lead to some miscommunication when the documentation is not clear and the teams need some clarifications to understand. As an example, consider the statement: "We think we should meet biweekly." Does this mean the team would like to meet twice each week or once every two weeks? And consider the statement: "We should write the code in a way that is unlockable." Does this mean the programming language used should be unlockable or that the code should prevent locking?

Also, team members who do not verbally commit may not feel the same commitment to deliver. The Daily Scrum is a verbal commitment in front of peers that helps to put pressure on the team to meet their commitments.

Table 6.5 summarizes the pros and cons of the Single Meeting Time approach.

Table 6.5   Summary of Pros and Cons for Using a Single Meeting Time Approach

Pros	Cons
• Better for sustainable pace. • Nobody is inconvenienced by having to attend the Daily Scrum at a set time.	• Loss of information because of indirect communication. • This approach is not interactive and does not allow for questions. • Adversely impacts "whole team" experience since team members are not interacting. • Lessens accountability through peer pressure.

KEY POINT   When having Daily Scrums with some members typing in their responses to the questions, it is important to have the ScrumMaster express their written comments out loud. The team should address their issues quickly, just as the blockers of those attending the meeting in person.

The Liaison Approach

Another approach to conducting Daily Scrums with distributed teams with no overlapping work hours is to conduct two different Daily Scrums and to have a liaison attend both. Each meeting is at a time that is convenient for half of the members of the Scrum Team. The liaison, who is commonly the ScrumMaster, verbally shares the information from the other team with the team they are meeting with.

Figure 6.3 shows an example of a team that holds two different Daily Scrum meetings each day. The first meeting is at a time convenient for the half of the team in the more western time zones. The second meeting is at a time convenient for the other half of the team in the more eastern time zones. The ScrumMaster serves as a liaison, attending both meetings and verbally presenting the notes from the half of the team that is not present.

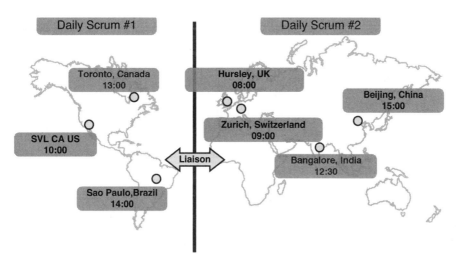

Figure 6.3 Liaison approach using two different Daily Scrum meetings

The advantage to this approach is that it helps with sustainable pace. No one other than the liaison is meeting outside their normal working hours. This can also help the whole team to have visibility into each others' efforts, though the team cannot address questions or blockers brought by team members who are not present immediately.

Pushpa Baskaran, a technical leader working at IBM, shares her experience using the Liaison approach:

> *I led a team of developers with subteams in China and the United States. It was impractical to expect all team members to be available for all meetings, and it was challenging to find a time slot that worked for everyone. So, I had two weekly scrum calls, one for the U.S. time zone, where Chinese developers were optional, and another for the Chinese time zone, where the American developers were optional. This approach allowed flexibility for team members and only the ScrumMaster (myself) needed to manage my work hours.*
>
> *When the China and North America team members were co-developing a task, one of them made the extra effort to work outside their regular hours. As the team gained more experience working in a globally distributed team environment, assigning and separating work modules, working outside regular hours reduced significantly.*

Possibly the worst side of this approach is that it is not the ideal method of communication. This can be a bit like a childhood game called "telephone," where one person tells a story to a second person, the second tells it to a third person, and so on. At the end of the chain, the story told is rarely the same as the story told by the original storyteller. The story told by the liaison will be similar, but not the same as the story told by the team member. To deal with this issue, some teams have each group record their Daily Scrum responses. The ScrumMaster can then play back the responses from one half of the team when meeting with the other half of the team.

The team can also splinter into two factions that would likely negatively impact the ability of the team to work together as a whole team.

Another consideration in taking this approach is that, unless there is a rotation in the role, there can be an impact to the work-life balance of the liaison.

Table 6.6 summarizes the pros and cons of the Liaison approach.

Table 6.6   Summary of Pros and Cons for the Liaison Approach

Pros	Cons
• Better for sustainable pace.	• Liaison might present the wrong information.
• Some degree of visibility into each of the tasks of each team member.	• Possible splintering of team into factions.
• Richer communication medium than through documentation. Allows for questions.	• Negative impact on work-life balance of the liaison.
	• Negative impact on "whole team" view.

Some teams improve the Liaison approach by having the whole team meet for the Daily Scrum at least occasionally. Gregg Gibson, of IBM System and Technology Group's Management Module Firmware organization, reports many teams within his organization tried both the Liaison approach and the Sharing the Pain approach described later in this chapter:

> *We are finding that even with the Liaison approach, it is helpful to get the entire team in a meeting at least occasionally. Otherwise, the team devolves into multiple teams that don't always work together effectively.*

KEY POINT   When using the Liaison approach, consider rotating the liaison responsibilities to reduce the burden on any one person.

Alternating Meeting Times

A third approach to scheduling Daily Scrums where members of the team have no overlap in work hours is to alternate meeting times. With this approach, the team holds one Daily Scrum during the normal workday for part of the Scrum Team and holds the other Daily Scrum during the normal work hours of the other part of the Scrum Team.

Ling, a Scrum Team member in Beijing, worked on a Scrum Team with members in Austin, TX and Raleigh, NC:

Our team was meeting daily at 12:00 PM Eastern Time. For me, in Beijing, it was after midnight. I often could not attend the Daily Scrums. The team later decided to switch to alternating meeting teams so I could attend at least part of the time in person.

Figure 6.4 shows a team that alternates their meetings between two different times. One meeting is most convenient for team members in Toronto, Sao Paulo, and Hursley. The other is more convenient for team members in Hursley, Zurich, Bangalore, and Beijing.

Figure 6.4   Alternating Meeting Times approach

The advantage of this approach is everyone has an opportunity to attend during their normal working hours at least every other day. Unlike the approach of having a fixed time always outside working hours for some team members, every team member has an opportunity to attend at least part of the time.

Figure 6.4 shows the given schedule of alternating meeting times that would possibly allow team members in Toronto, Zurich, and Hursley to meet daily comfortably, while other members may only join in every other day. Ideally, team members will be comfortable meeting outside traditional working hours. That can allow the whole team to meet daily, rather than every other day.

When the whole team does not meet daily, the team may not get the full benefit of the Daily Scrum.

KEY POINT   When meeting at alternating times, have teams members who cannot take part in the meeting log their responses to the three questions. At the meeting, have the ScrumMaster or a team member read the written responses from absent team members.

When using the Alternating Meeting Times approach, the team should check with everyone to make sure that they have the ability to call into the meeting outside their working hours.

Elizabeth Kumau, a test expert with IBM Test Services, gives this experience:

Some of my team members in India have to stay in the office or go to the office at night to attend meetings scheduled outside their normal working hours. Out of four team members, only one has home connection access.

In this example, some team members would not be able to attend some meetings when using the Alternating Meeting Times approach.

Table 6.7 summarizes the pros and cons of the Alternating Meeting Times approach.

Table 6.7   Summary of Pros and Cons for the Alternating Meeting Times Approach

Pros	Cons
• Everyone has a chance to attend the meeting. • Shares the pain across team members.	• Loss of information from team members who do not show up because the time is not good for them.

Sharing the Pain

A fourth approach—the one that most closely aligns with the spirit of co-located Scrum—is to have the team members *share the pain*. With this approach, the team works together to share the pain associated with being part of a distributed team. They select a time to meet that is best for the team as a whole.

Although sharing the pain may not sound like a great solution for the team, flexible work hours can be a benefit both to the employer and to the Scrum Team members. Matt, a ScrumMaster with IBM Sales and Distribution, describes the advantage of working flexible hours:

I had to be on a 15-minute Daily Scrum at 7:00 PM, after my normal workday. However, I also had the flexibility to attend my daughter's father-and-daughter lunch at school, which was on the other side of town. Working with a global team isn't always the most convenient, but I appreciate getting to be there for my kids' special events.

The best way to carry out this approach is to ask each member of the team the following questions:

- What times are best for you to meet?
- What times are you willing to meet?
- What times are off-limits?

Everyone considers the possibility of working outside their traditional work hours. The resulting Daily Scrum time is the time that works best for the entire team as a whole.

Elizabeth, a ScrumMaster with IBM Quality Software Engineering, talks about a case where asking the three questions would have been helpful:

I have learned to always ask the team what will work for them. Some of us are morning people, so a 5:00 AM meeting may not be a problem. Others are not available until 10:00 AM, but 9:00 PM is not a problem for them. I was working with a team that had members in Hyderabad, India and Saint John, Canada. I assumed—always a bad idea—the team I was working with in India was working on their local time. At the end of a 3:00 AM meeting to show my support for global teaming, they politely asked why I had called the meeting so early. Oops! They were working on Eastern Time! Now, I always ask the three questions: when is the best time, when are you available, and when is off-limits?

The advantage to the approach of sharing the pain is the whole team is taking part in the Daily Scrum each day, and the time selected for the meeting has the whole team sharing the pain. Everyone hears directly from the other team members, so there is less of a chance of confusion than the team might have with other methods.

However, not everyone may like working outside their normal working hours. When using this approach, the team should have the flexibility to take some time off from their normal working hours to compensate.

Table 6.8 summarizes the pros and cons of the Sharing the Pain approach.

Table 6.8   Summary of Pros and Cons for the Sharing the Pain Approach

Pros	Cons
• Aligns best with the interactive spirit of Scrum and Agile. • Whole team takes part in each day. • Everyone hears directly from team. • Team can discuss blockers and remove them immediately. • Team is better able to hold one another accountable. • Flexibility in work schedule.	• Some may not like working outside normal work hours. • Can be challenging for sustainable pace.

Tips for Distributed Daily Scrums

After the team decides on the times that they will meet for the Daily Scrum, they will start attending the Daily Scrums through a teleconference. And, while the general teleconference tips presented in Chapter 2 apply for the Daily Scrum meeting, the team will find there are some special nuances to the Daily Scrum.

The distributed Daily Scrum is unlike the other Scrum meetings in that the Daily Scrum is not a brainstorming, collaborative working session. Instead, it is a brief, intense 15 minutes with members' one-by-one answering questions. Although team members may ask quick questions for clarification, they should handle any in-depth discussion outside the Daily Scrum. This section offers tips to help teams to be more effective with the Daily Scrum.

Removing Side Conversations

Side conversations during the Daily Scrum are a distraction during a co-located Daily Scrum, but they are even more problematic during the *distributed* Daily Scrum. Side conversations introduce two main problems for the distributed team:

- **Increased distraction.** Background noise can be distracting on a teleconference. If the quality of the teleconference or phone lines is already making it difficult to hear everyone, background noise and other voices can make listening even more difficult.

- **Exclusion.** If the Scrum Team is a new team just beginning to learn to work together, and if there are issues between team members or new members on the team, background discussions can cause members on the phone to feel excluded.

Side conversations can be problematic where part of the team meets in one room and other members have dialed into the teleconference using separate phone lines, as shown in Figure 6.5.

One method to prevent side conversations is to have all members dial into the teleconference. Each person dialed in is immediately in an equal position to everyone else. Everyone is speaking directly into the phone, which can make it easier for everyone on the team to hear the conversation. And, verbal side conversations are less of a problem.

Of course, to promote teaming and to give everyone a chance to speak without disruptions, members of the team and the ScrumMaster should help to end any side conversations quickly.

Keeping the Team Engaged

Distributed team members who have teleconferenced into the Daily Scrum can become detached and distracted by other tasks.

Unfortunately, most of us have heard the clicking in the background as one person types away on an email message while another team member is diligently answering the three questions. Most of us who work as part of a distributed team have ourselves had distractions at one time or another by an email message, an instant message, or some other tasks in the middle of the Daily Scrum. Some of us have also heard the ever-popular excuse of "I was on mute" from a team member called on unexpectedly and scrambling to think of a response.

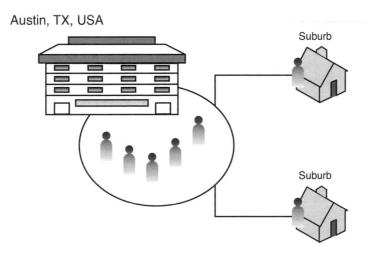

Figure 6.5   Scrum Team with collocated and remote team members

Because the Daily Scrum is an intense 15 minutes, it is especially important for team members to remain actively engaged during the call. If necessary, close down applications, step away from the machine, turn on a screen saver, or just commit to stay focused.

Possibly the best way to stay engaged and to make sure that others on the team stay engaged is to make the time as valuable as possible for the team. Bill Krebs, a coach with IBM Quality Software Engineering, suggests:

> *To help your team members to find value in your responses, focus on the three A's of the Scrum meeting:*
>
> * ***Awareness.*** *Build awareness of what the team is working on.*
>
> * ***Advertising.*** *Advertise for collaboration.*
>
> * ***Attack blockers.*** *The team and ScrumMaster should strive to fix all blockers within one hour of the Daily Scrum.*

Facilitating the Meeting

Facilitating a Daily Scrum meeting can be more challenging for the ScrumMaster working with a distributed team. On collocated teams, members are able to read body language and use body language to show a speaker they are taking the meeting off track. The distributed ScrumMaster and team members have to rely on other techniques.

As an example, the ScrumMaster with a co-located team starts with the person on his or her left and goes around the room asking for responses to the three questions. In a distributed environment, as individuals come into the call, they will identify who they are. The ScrumMaster then calls each person and asks for their response. They may respond in the order they arrived at the tele-conference or the ScrumMaster may choose to call on each person. One team member reported:

Early on, we experimented with having the team members go in alphabetical order by name, so the ScrumMaster wouldn't have to call on individuals. We found it to be distracting and much less efficient than just having the ScrumMaster call on people.

Another example is a case where the ScrumMaster is trying to move on from one team member to the next. In a co-located environment, the ScrumMaster can turn his or her body to the next team member when someone is being too verbose or elaborating beyond the responses to the three questions. By teleconference, this technique is not available. Instead, the ScrumMaster is likely to have to interrupt the speaker verbally. Although this would be rude in other cases, verbally interrupting can help the team to more efficiently use the Daily Scrum time.

Using a technique for getting people to focus on just the three questions and to streamline their responses can help to prevent having to interrupt. One technique presented by Bill Krebs of IBM Quality Software Engineering is to focus on the "top two":

I like to ask teams to give two headlines of what they did yesterday, two headlines of what they are going to do today, and any blockers. This helps to keep them from getting into too much detail about how they did the work.

Jean-Louis Marecheaux has used a countdown timer to streamline responses:

I have used a countdown timer in the past, visually displayed on a web conference like NetMeeting or ST Unyte. It helped speakers keep track of the time left within the allowed time slot.

Taking Daily Scrum Notes

Notes are typically not taken during the Daily Scrum; the team must only log the blockers. However, when working with a distributed team, it can be helpful to have the notes available in a common location. Wikis that allow multiple users to write at the same time can be a good repository for Daily Scrum notes. Regardless of the archiving tool used, it is easier for the team to use a single, common archive.

Having the notes available in a common location allows those not able to attend the Daily Scrum to share their tasks with others and provides them with a way to learn about the tasks of other team members.

Taking notes for the Daily Scrum can also help distributed teams that are dealing with language difficulties. For those who are using their second language on the teleconference, having the text prepared earlier can help them to state their responses. And, it can help others who are using the primary language of the meeting to understand what they are saying.

Daily Scrum notes are especially important for teams working in a regulatory compliance environment (such as the FDA, HIPPA, or others), which one-third of agile teams claim to do (Ambler 2009).

Dealing with Language Barriers

The Daily Scrum is an intense meeting with rapid communication. When a distributed team uses a language that is not the first language of all participants, communication becomes more difficult. Although one-on-one meetings and interactive meetings provide opportunities for those members using their second language to ask questions, translation on the Daily Scrum call can create significant delays.

There are two ways teams can use to deal with language barriers:

- **Use a chat session.** The person who is having difficulty can ping one of the team members who is not speaking to get clarification.

- **Set a longer time-box for the Daily Scrum.** Scrum is about the team working together effectively. If the team is consistently unable to complete the Daily Scrum in 15 minutes because of language issues, set a time-box that works for the team and stick to it. This is not an excuse to poorly manage the Daily Scrum, but instead is a way of handling a language barrier. Matt Ganis shared the following story:

    > One of our Scrum Teams had a daily 15-minute Scrum scheduled between team members in India and the U.S. We quickly found that 15 minutes was not enough time to resolve issues or come to a common understanding on what we were discussing. We decided that since the Daily Scrum was the one time the team was sure to talk during the day (because of time zone issues) that it would make sense to expand the duration to 45–60 minutes. The first part of the meeting, we did a traditional standup meeting, followed by a more detailed discussion of issues and plans to address the "blockers."

Tools to Help with Distributed Daily Scrum

Because the Daily Scrum is such a short meeting and focuses on verbal responses to three questions, there is little need for tools. However, a chat tool, wiki or other repository, and a full-duplex phone can be helpful.

Chat tools can be a distraction for some team members, but they can also be valuable in cases where a team is having language issues. The person who is having difficulty understanding someone else's responses can ask questions through chat without disrupting the Daily Scrum. The team may want to cut and paste or save the chat transcript to a wiki for future reference.

A wiki or other repository can be helpful for sharing Daily Scrum notes. Notes can be helpful in communicating with team members who are unable to attend a given Daily Scrum as discussed earlier in this chapter.

If part of the team is calling in from a conference room and using a speakerphone, it should be a full-duplex phone. With half-duplex phones, participants can only hear only one speaker at a time, either the team members in the room or an individual dialed into the teleconference separately. If someone goes on and on without pausing, it can be impossible to interrupt their monologue. With only 1–2 minutes granted for each person, this can be a major obstacle to hearing every team member within 15 minutes. Fortunately, the telephone buttons will still work while the person is speaking, so the ScrumMaster or a team member can push a button to get the attention of the other person. But, this is not ideal. Invest in a full-duplex phone if possible.

Videoconferencing tools offer mixed results. From performance issues to setting the camera so everyone is visible to the time needed to set up the Daily Scrum, videoconferencing today may be more of a headache than it is worth. There are, however, teams that have had success with using a wide-angle web camera for the Daily Scrums.

Scrum of Scrums

Besides the Daily Scrum, scaled Scrum Teams will want to engage in a Scrum of Scrums, where representatives from the different teams answer the following four questions:

- What has your team done since the last meeting?
- What will your team do before the next meeting?
- What blockers does your team have?
- What blockers are you about to cause for another team?

The Scrum of Scrums should include five to nine people. Each Scrum Team sends one or two representatives, depending on how many teams are working together. Representatives may be the ScrumMaster or development team members who are knowledgeable about the code of interest to the teams engaging in the Scrum of Scrums. The Product Owner (or Product Owners in an environment with a hierarchy of Product Owners) may also take part in identifying dependencies or issues that might impact the priorities in the Product Backlog.

During the Scrum of Scrums, teams discuss future dependencies, commitments to other team members, issues with integration, and other points that impact one another.

The frequency and duration of the Scrum of Scrums meetings should be enough to allow the Scrum Teams to coordinate their work. Projects with higher dependencies or greater collaboration between teams should engage in Scrum of Scrums more often.

Summary

The first step to running effective Daily Scrums is to decide the meeting days and times for the team. The distribution level has an impact on how challenging the Daily Scrums will be for the team. Collocated teams with members that telecommute part-time can successfully engage in the Daily Scrum by calling into the meeting. Geographically distributed teams with an overlap in workdays can set up a time to meet daily during their standard workday. Teams with no overlap in their workdays are the most challenging to schedule.

There are four different approaches that teams can take to dealing with no overlap in their workdays. The Sharing the Pain model more closely aligns with providing the same benefit as co-located teams.

The following sections will discuss how to conduct the Daily Scrum meeting first for teams with and without any overlapping work hours. Table 6.9 shows the different approaches with which collocated and distributed teams can decide to perform their Daily Scrum meetings and the method we recommend these teams use.

Table 6.9 Summary of Different Daily Scrum Approaches with Recommendations

Team Type	Possible Approaches	Recommendations
Collocated Team	• Face-to-Face Meeting • Teleconference • Videoconference • Instant Messaging	Face-to-face meeting; it increases the communication, commitment, and collaboration between team members.
Collocated Part-Time	• Face-to-Face Meeting • Teleconference • Videoconference • Instant Messaging	Face-to-face meeting for the collocated team members with a teleconference line open for remote team members.
Distributed with Overlapping Work Hours	• Face-to-Face Meeting • Teleconference • Videoconference • Instant Messaging	Team members should find a time where the work hours overlap and members in the same location meet face-to-face with a teleconference line open to talk with remote team members. If members in the different locations are unable to hear each other, they should consider having everyone dial in. When verbal language is a problem, you can use an instant messaging session at the same time for clarity.
Distributed without Overlapping Work Hours	• Share the Pain • Alternating Meeting Times • Using a Liaison • Documentation	Share the pain by selecting a standard meeting time when everyone will attend because it respects the spirit of Scrum and agile the best. Alternating meeting times also works well by allowing the team to switch off on times that are most comfortable.

Regardless of the approach the team selects for their Daily Scrums, the team has an opportunity to reevaluate the decision at the end of each Sprint. During the retrospective, the team can discuss whether they should consider adopting a different model to improve their performance.

Once the team begins conducting distributed Daily Scrums, they will discover some issues related to the unique points of the Daily Scrum (for example: brevity, intensity, and one-way communication pattern). To be productive, the team and ScrumMaster will need to remove side conversations, effectively facilitate the Daily Scrum, use notes where necessary, overcome language barriers, and recognize local schedules and holidays.

Tools are less of an issue with the Daily Scrum. A chat tool can help to overcome language barriers, the team can use a wiki or another repository to store notes, and a full-duplex phone can help when some of the team members meet in the same conference room.

Scaled teams will engage in Scrum of Scrums meetings as well as Daily Scrums to help with coordination and integration between teams.

References

Ambler, Scott. *Agile Practices Survey Results* (Ambysoft, July 2009). Retrieved December 16, 2009, from Scott Ambler's website: http://www.ambysoft.com/surveys/practices2009.html#Figure7.

Schwaber, K. *Agile Software Development with Scrum*. Upper Saddle River, NJ: Prentice Hall, 2002.

ScrumMasters 2 (December 4, 2006). Retrieved November 10, 2008, from YouTube: http://www.youtube.com/watch?v=B3htbxIkzzM.

Sutherland, J., A. Viktorov, J. Blount, and N. Puntikov (2007). *Fully Distributed Scrum: The Secret Sauce for Hyperproductive Outsourced Development Teams*. HICSS'40, Hawaii International Conference on Software Systems. Waikoloa: University of Hawai'i at Manoa.

Sutherland, Jeff (June 3, 2006). *Why the Three Questions in the Daily Scrum Meeting*. Retrieved July 2, 2009, from Jeff Sutherland's website: http://jeffsutherland.com/Scrum/2006/06/why-three-questions-in-daily-Scrum.html.

Effective Collaboration During a Sprint

No one can whistle a symphony. It takes a whole orchestra to play it.

H.E. Luccock

Combine inefficient communication channels with conducting a meeting with members who are in different countries and the inherent difficulties can cause the Daily Scrum heartbeat to become irregular and impact the health of the team.

In a large-scale distributed enterprise environment, delivering valuable solutions early and often is one of the most significant changes for new Scrum Teams. Development team members who previously worked months before delivering value now find they are working to deliver functioning software every two weeks.

Product managers who become Product Owners discover they must actively bridge between stakeholders and the development team *daily* to deliver valuable software every Sprint (see Figure 7.1). The team, Product Owner, ScrumMaster, and other stakeholders need to consider business value carefully throughout development, rather than just at the beginning and end of a project.

A manager who may have previously been able to let blockers stand for days or weeks can no longer afford to do that when the team is delivering software every two weeks. Managers may find that ScrumMasters are raising issues and asking managers to address them within a 24-hour period.

All of these are significant changes that will enable the team to deliver valuable software that meets stakeholders' needs with minimized risk of failure. This first part of this chapter focuses on tips for helping teams, Product Owners, and ScrumMasters to collaborate effectively during a Sprint.

Although Scrum provides a framework that does not mandate underlying practices, IBM Scrum Teams have found three practices to be particularly valuable to fostering distributed collaboration during the Sprint and helping teams complete user stories within a Sprint: continuous integration, test automation, and test-driven development. The second part of this chapter discusses these practices and how they can help distributed teams to identify and correct issues more quickly, improve collaboration between team members, and improve their effectiveness.

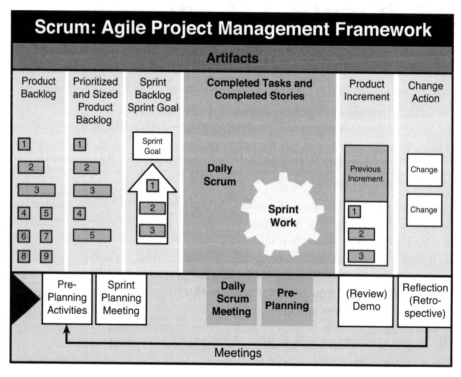

Figure 7.1   The Sprint

Communicating During the Sprint

Chapter 2, "Challenges Faced by Distributed Teams," provided many tips for handling distributed meetings, and Chapter 6, "Distributed Daily Scrum Meetings," provided tips for Daily Scrums. During a Sprint, the distributed Scrum Team is likely to engage in many informal distributed meetings. This section provides more guidance on communicating during the Sprint.

Remember that agile teams value working software over comprehensive documentation. Being a distributed team is *not* a good reason to invest significant cycles in comprehensive documentation throughout the Sprint. For collocated and distributed teams, the best way to transfer information to a new member is software code and team discussions; however, distributed teams are likely to need to rely more on documentation to communicate.

Documentation to Overcome Distance

Distributed teams with little or no overlapping work hours may need more email and other written documentation to communicate effectively between team members. Documentation allows the team to build and preserve a common understanding.

When the language of the team meetings is not the native language of all team members, written language may be a more reliable and accurate method of communication. It is usually easier for non-native speakers to understand written language than spoken language, which is why teams should consider supplementing verbal discussions with text-based alternatives, such as a chat tool or informal documentation.

KEY POINT   Because of language barriers, distributed teams often need more written documentation than collocated teams.

Many teams will incorporate an online chat system to record the main discussion points of a meeting or Daily Scrum, or they use a screen-sharing tool to display notes. This has the advantage of not only keeping a record of what they discussed (when they save the text), but also allowing those that may not speak the language fluently to read the main points to gain a better understanding. As the meetings continue, the ScrumMaster should record important points in text and follow up with questions such as the following:

- Did I record your concern accurately?
- Did I capture the actions accurately?

Using the Right Tools

Scrum places value on individuals and interactions over processes and tools. Although tools can help the team to perform, they cannot create an effective team. In a distributed environment, tools and good practices can help team members communicate more effectively, but it is more important to make sure the tools the team introduces will help them get the job done.

As an example, a distributed team considering various distributed collaboration tools for their Daily Scrums should first examine the value it will bring against the cost of using it. A 3D virtual world meeting room may be intriguing for Daily Scrums, but if everyone needs five minutes to get into the virtual team room and ready for the Scrum, it may not be helpful or practical. The Daily Scrum is a 15-minute meeting, so a simple teleconference can just as easily allow each person to answer the standard three questions.

KEY POINT   Focus on meeting the core principles of Scrum rather than adopting tools for the sake of having them.

Valuing the Whole Team

Scrum Teams coordinating to deliver a product should each be a whole cross-functional team and should work on independent features as much as possible, rather than components, to minimize dependencies that will slow down development.

In a globally distributed development environment, there are more delays in communications and fewer opportunities to work together throughout the normal workday. As a result, teams must work harder to prevent an "us" versus "them" attitude in the team. Questions that members can ask themselves include the following:

- Are you reaching out to your team members in the other country or time zone?

- Have you made an effort to pick up the phone or chat, rather than relying on slower email communication?

- If you are part of a collocated group with one or more distributed members, have you made an effort to include remote team members when an impromptu meeting comes up?

- Are you following the recommendations for distributed communications in Chapter 2 in working with distributed members?

- Are you providing a quick update of information helpful to other team members before you leave for the day?

- Are you always making the same team members stay late due to time zone issues?

- Are impromptu discussions around coffee breaks communicated to the rest of the team?

- What actions are you taking to double-check team members receive communication of key items as intended (for example, asking for a summary of understanding or a quick interim review of progress to check if the team is heading in the right direction)?

- Does your team fall into the habit of using language that refers to the team members who are in different locations as "the team in the other country" or "the other team"?

- Are you labeling team members or stereotyping? (For example, "Those people in Austin are always late. They never get it right.")

- Are the dependencies between team members in different locations so high they need to communicate multiple times a day?

Transparency

Individuals and interactions also refer to interactions between the development team, managers, Product Owners, and others. Transparency in Scrum is important, and ensuring everyone is aware of how much work remains is part of this.

As pictured in Figure 7.2, teams can use a task board set up in a conference room with the stories on paper cards. An alternative to this, as mentioned in Chapter 2, is using an agile project management tool. In such cases, team members need to take responsibility for identifying tasks that are open, in progress, and completed so everyone is aware of the current status.

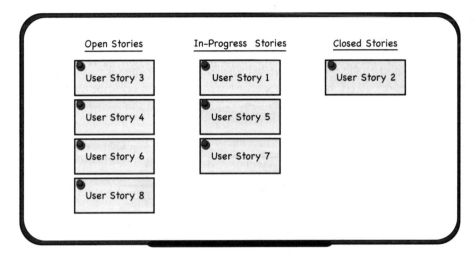

Figure 7.2   Simple task board with paper cards

Interacting with others to keep everyone informed is important. Tools are just a way of helping the team communicate the status of the project with one another and with people outside the team. Daily Scrums and the Scrum of Scrums meetings, as discussed in Chapter 6, are important for preserving transparency

Handling New Requests in the Middle of a Sprint

Scrum Teams may also find that stakeholders are asking for changes in the middle of a Sprint. The beauty of Scrum is that it provides a simple framework for embracing change in a controlled way. Throughout the Sprint, the Sprint Backlog does not change; however, the requirements for a project can change and stakeholders can add or remove items from the Product Backlog. Additionally, defect reports may be coming in from production and the team needs to add defect work items to the Product Backlog. Regardless of the number of changes in the Product Backlog, the business can be confident that their teams have uninterrupted time to work on the highest-priority requirements to deliver value at the end of every Sprint.

Single Point of Entry

Occasionally, teams may find that stakeholders still expect them to drop whatever they are doing and start working on new requests immediately and will not take "no" for an answer. These stakeholders have a much greater opportunity to get someone to take on their request in a distributed environment because when one team member refuses, they just move on and ask someone else.

In a collocated environment, the team is more likely to recognize several team members are getting outside requests, but it is less obvious in a distributed environment that someone approached different team members with the same request.

It can be disruptive when several team members are receiving requests from different stakeholders. It can be tempting for someone to just accept the added work, especially when talking to someone in a position of authority. One team member working on something else may not have a big impact on the overall Sprint, but when many others start taking on extra work (see Figure 7.3), the team will be much less productive overall. This can cause the team to start working at a pace that is not sustainable.

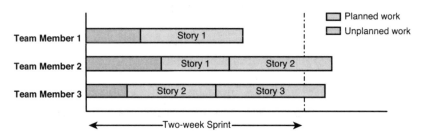

Figure 7.3   Effect of unplanned work on the team

When the team is dealing with disruptions by people in a position of authority or other stakeholders, the ScrumMaster can remind them the proper response is to ask the stakeholder to work with the Product Owner, who will decide the priority of the new requirement.

KEY POINT   In Scrum, the team commits to sending requests through the Product Owner(s), who will decide the priority of the request in the Product Backlog.

The Daily Scrum is the place where the ScrumMaster can uncover people who are working on user stories other than the ones in the Sprint Plan. Questioning work outside the tasks needed to complete the user stories selected for the Sprint is how the team can help prevent new work from coming in the middle of the Sprint.

Elizabeth Woodward, an IBM Agile Consultant, shares the following story:

We had a team that consistently worked on tasks that were outside what they had committed to do during the Sprint. As a result, they were not completing the stories they needed to meet their commitments. To address this problem, we adjusted the questions asked during the Daily Scrum. Each person had to identify which story they were talking about before they answered the three Daily Scrum questions. This helped the team to recognize when they were working on other tasks and to address the problem as a team.

Value of the Well-Groomed Backlog

A well-groomed product backlog allows the Product Owner to see the impact on the schedule or features of the product of any changes requested by stakeholders. The team provides a relative cost of the new requirement to the Product Owner, who will decide the relative value of it compared to the rest of the work in the Backlog. The Product Owner, stakeholders, and team are able to embrace the change and address the highest-priority work.

When the team is working with a fixed release date, it may not be able to complete lower-priority work. When working with fixed content in the release, the addition will impact the target date. Arming everyone with real information helps to ensure the team is delivering the highest value in each Sprint.

Shortening the Sprint

When a stakeholder continually pushes back strongly and interrupts the team often, one solution may be to consider a shorter Sprint length. If the team is on a four-week Sprint, the stakeholder only has to wait two weeks on average before the team can address their request (if it's a high-enough priority). If they are on a two-week Sprint, the stakeholder only has to wait one week on average.

Communication delays may tempt the distributed Scrum Team to work in longer Sprints, but this is counterproductive. Having a shorter development cycle creates a greater sense of urgency when team members communicate with one another throughout the Sprint.

The shorter the development cycle, the more opportunity there is for the team to reflect, identify ways to improve their development processes, and adapt quickly. A shorter cycle also means there is less time between when the stakeholders add requests to the Product Backlog and when the team is able to address them.

KEY POINT   Shorter Sprint lengths make the team more responsive to stakeholders. They also allow the team to adapt to change more rapidly.

Teams should strive to find the Sprint length that is right for them. When they are too long, they will impede discussing new high-priority items, and when they are too short, the only work will be clarifications between team members.

Dealing with Defects

Some Scrum Teams may be responsible for developing the next version of a product while handling maintenance for the current version. When urgent defects, critical situations, or high-priority customer calls are disrupting development work continually, the team may want to consider creating a user story with a certain number of story points in the Sprint to deal with the problems.

Within the story, they can set a priority for the maintenance tasks. When a customer reports a higher-priority maintenance problem in the middle of the Sprint, the team will drop a lower-priority maintenance task off the bottom of the list.

Another approach alternative is to create a subteam to focus only on handling these issues during the Sprint. When using this approach, it is important to rotate team members in and out of this subteam, so everyone has the opportunity to engage in development and not label some people as maintenance staff. One benefit of this approach is that everyone directly feels the pain caused by poor product quality.

Another approach, depending on the skill set of the technical support team answering the customer calls, is to enable that team to make the necessary code changes and have these changes reviewed by developers.

Disruptions at the Team Member Level

Some teams also use creative approaches to help control interruptions at the individual team member level. Andy Pittaway, a Global Business Services Executive Project Manager, shares how his team limits interruptions:

> *A simple technique that worked well in the past for us was buying a red baseball cap for every member of the team. The rule was that if someone wanted to focus on a specific task for awhile, they would either put the cap on their head or on top of their monitor. This sent a message to the other team members that said they were only available if needed urgently and otherwise, they should come back later.*
>
> *Sometimes when the team was busy, they would put a red hat on the team room door, and it would stop unnecessary distractions from entering the room and to signal they were focusing on a particular priority. Clearly, team members should not abuse the use of the red hat and cannot use it all day and every day. My experience is that people would often use it well, and I have not yet come across an abuse of it where I had to intervene; usually the team sorts out any issues of this type for themselves.*

Handling Stories the Team Cannot Complete During the Sprint

Teams commit to delivering a set of stories at the start of each Sprint, but during the Sprint, teams may realize they are not able to deliver on their commitments. Misunderstandings about user stories may cause the team to identify the wrong tasks or to estimate the time they need to complete the work wrongly. Whenever these happen in the middle of a Sprint, the team (ScrumMaster, Product Owner, development team, and stakeholders) needs to decide on the best course of action.

There are multiple reasons that may explain why it happened. Maybe the acceptance conditions were weak or the team did not spend enough time discussing the user story before committing to complete it. When estimates go from hours to days or from days to weeks, another possible cause is that maybe the user story is just too big to fit in the Sprint. Whatever the reason, the team needs to identify how it can prevent this from happening in the future.

Before working toward the solution, the team first needs to identify the work they need to do to complete the story through meetings between team members or with the Product Owner. Once team members identify the work, the next step is to see if they can contain the extra work in the current Sprint plan. If that fails, the next step is to see if there are team members who have some available time as well as the right skills to help complete the work in the Sprint.

Assuming this also fails and the development team cannot contain the work, the team needs to talk with the Product Owner to explain its findings and decide what to do next. One choice may be to split the story into two parts: one the team can complete within the Sprint, and a second one the team will add to the backlog. An alternative may be to move a lower-priority story assigned to the same team members back to the Backlog to allow them to contain other work.

The team should discuss the choices that will allow them to meet the Sprint goal successfully, and should consider ending the Sprint only if there is no possibility of meeting its goal.

When teams make decisions that impact the project, it is a recommended practice to preserve a decision log that is always available to the team. This allows the team to keep track of the decisions they made and not reverse one without understanding the reason behind it. Andy Pittaway shares how his team used a log to keep track of the effects of reversing one of the decisions they made during the project:

> *The team made key decisions but sometimes reversed them later in the project, and this was a real issue that affected projects. To resolve this issue, we created a simple decision log. We used it for key decisions only and it contained the key decisions made, with some information about who decided and when. One key piece of information logged, however, was the impact if the team reversed the decision. We printed this log and placed it on the team room wall!*

When the estimates are consistently wrong and the team continually needs to move stories to the next Sprint, that behavior is usually a red flag and points to a larger problem. Is the team over-committing in the Sprint Planning meeting? Does the team understand the work it needs to do to complete a story? The team needs to have this discussion as part of its retrospective (see Chapter 9, "Retrospectives").

Handling Blockers During the Sprint

Chapter 6 on Daily Scrums provided tips on how to handle distributed Daily Scrums. In the large-scale enterprise transitioning to agile, the ScrumMaster is likely to hear from Scrum Team members who are facing blockers preventing them from working in an agile way.

The first teams within the enterprise that take an agile approach will be the most affected by legacy or traditional processes. The ScrumMaster and management team will need to work together to address the inhibitors. The team may not be able to complete as much during early Sprints due to the inhibitors. However, dealing directly with inhibitors will help increase the velocity of the team over time, as well as the velocity of other teams as they transition to Scrum.

Within IBM, the Integrated Product Development (IPD) process is a governance process that helps manage investment in product development projects. It does not mandate that teams identify fine-grained requirements and a delivery date at the start of a project. However, various interpretations over time led to the investment review boards expecting to see detailed requirements and a delivery date 18 months before delivery. An executive workgroup within IBM reworked the process to help agile teams overcome their blockers related to IPD. Much of the work involved changing the mind-set and expectations of what teams needed to present to the review board.

As a second example, the process for protecting intellectual property was too long for teams to review their work with external stakeholders after a two-week or four-week Sprint. Previously, a team might not have shown an invention to a customer until the end of a longer development process. Agile teams need to be able to get feedback from customers on their product—which includes the invention—within the Sprint. The executive team worked with IBM Legal to change processes for a more rapid turnaround.

As the team is working through the Sprint, it is important for the team to raise the issues and for the ScrumMaster to engage the executive team to remove blockers. Although some changes may not happen immediately, over time the invested effort will help to increase productivity.

Having a team of executives with the passion and the power to remove corporate-level blockers can help teams to improve their productivity.

Responding to Questions During the Sprint

The Product Owner for enterprise and distributed teams may have to work harder to uphold relationships and connections between the representative stakeholders (including customers) and the teams. Throughout the Sprint, if the team has a question for a stakeholder or needs to have a stakeholder expert interact directly with the team, the Product Owner helps the team and ScrumMaster as needed to get the question answered. Delays in getting feedback from stakeholders can impact whether the team successfully completes stories within the Sprint. When the Product Owner is in a time zone that differs significantly from the development team members and ScrumMaster, there may be more times when the team will have to wait on a response to a question or wait on an expert stakeholder to provide direct help to the Scrum Team.

One of the issues often faced by teams starting to use agile in an organization is slow decision making. The speed to make decisions needs to be very different in an agile project than in traditional projects. Andy Pittaway, an IBM Global Services Executive Project Manager, discusses an approach his team used to reduce the number of stakeholders while still getting the necessary information:

> On one particular project, we discovered that we needed to consult with more than 50 stakeholders on key decisions as we moved forward. We viewed this as an issue, so to resolve it, we introduced a funneling technique where we named a representative for each group of stakeholders who was responsible (and empowered) to represent many stakeholders. In this manner, the project needed to deal with less than 10 stakeholders.

It is also possible the Product Owner, customers, and other stakeholders are all in different time zones. In an enterprise product development environment, the Product Owner has the opportunity to select representative stakeholders and may decide to select stakeholders from a time zone that matches the team. But, having enough global stakeholder representation on the product will help the team to deliver the right product.

For enterprise product development, the Product Owner should look for ways to match representative stakeholders with the teams' working hours and to be available during that time as well. For applications the team is developing for a specific client, the Product Owner may not have the flexibility to choose stakeholder representatives available during the full working day of the client.

Some Product Owners work with Product Owner assistants who are available during the hours when the Product Owner is unavailable. This gives the team members who work when the Product Owner is off-duty the ability to get answers to their questions during the Sprint.

Aslam Hirani talks about his experience with his team:

We have a client subject matter expert (SME) located offshore on rotation basis to help answer queries from teams. Team members can walk up to the SME and get the issues resolved. As the Sprint durations are small, it is important to save time in getting the queries about the user stories answered. We had a domain specialist (proxy customer) as part of the offshore team. The domain specialist team member used to understand the user stories one or two Sprints in advance and then explain to the team during the Sprint. The domain specialist also helped the Product Owner team in preparing use cases; it worked well with our team.

Sustainable Pace

Most developers have been through at least one "death march" software development project in their careers (Yourdon 2003). The project is at risk and everyone is working 16-hour or longer days to try to complete an unrealistic amount of work by an unrealistic due date. Some development team members have to take pride in stories of how they managed to "successfully" deliver on the target release date under difficult circumstances. Stories of existing on three hours of sleep, no showers, and little time for families and friends are not uncommon at the end of some projects. In Scrum, this scenario is not a success—it is a failure.

Agile teams value people. The goal is for team members to be able to deliver significant value each Sprint while also being able to uphold a healthy balance. Scrum Teams should be able to spend time with families, take care of their health, contribute back to their communities, and engage in a healthy, balanced life. The Scrum Team focuses on committing only to the work it expects it can complete within the Sprint and knows it is working on the highest-value work items.

Almost every team that adopts Scrum overestimates the work it can complete for each of the first two Sprints. This is particularly true for enterprise product development projects where teams deliver tangible results later in the project. By having short Sprints, the team improves on its ability to estimate how much work it can complete within a Sprint. The team achieves a sustainable pace without burning out the team.

Sharing Time Zone Challenges

Distributed teams spread across time zones may have more challenges related to sustainable pace. In deciding how to handle Daily Scrums and other meetings, the teams are likely to "share the pain" by adjusting their hours to provide a greater overlap in working hours. Team members in one time zone may have to adjust their hours to match the working hours of other team members. If some team members are morning people who are regularly staying awake for meetings until 10:00 PM, a sustainable pace problem may arise. If parents are calling in to a Daily Scrum every day while they are trying to prepare their children for school, they may have a long-term problem sustaining this pace. The Scrum Team should adjust the schedule as needed, so conflicts are not persistent over time.

Some collocated team members may feel their decision only need to best suit the majority when there is only a small distributed minority. They may wonder why the majority should change because of one or two people, or senior team members may question why they need to adjust as much as the newest members of team. Being a team means everyone has equal participation and shares the challenges and rewards.

Sharing the pain by adjusting work hours to provide a greater overlap is not the best solution to this problem, as teams do not always share it equally. Sometimes, the reality is the same team or members are feeling most of the pain. One approach to help manage such cases is to make sure that teams in different time zones are fully self-sufficient and the team spreads the work to minimize dependencies.

Avoiding Double Workdays

Another problem for sustainable pace in the distributed environment is that teams sometimes adjust their hours to work with team members in another time zone, but work their own normal hours in addition. It is important the team sets up boundaries and that team members understand that coming in early leads to leaving early and that staying late means arriving late too. How each team member completes their work is up to the team member, and the team member must be responsible for working to complete the work to which they committed.

Peer pressure can also contribute to development team members working double days. It is not uncommon for a Scrum development team member who is working a sane workweek to feel the contempt of non-Scrum development team members in the same office area who are working a death march. Also, in an environment where people view death march survivors as heroes, the whole team may need to adjust its thinking and become used to members working "only" a regular workday.

Although every team will face times where it needs to push a bit harder to achieve a goal, consistently long days are a problem that can impact morale, productivity, and quality. When team members notice someone arriving or staying late, they should inquire and discuss during the reflection to see if there is a problem with the commitment the team made?

Distributed teams can look for opportunities to increase velocity by using a "follow the sun" model and carrying out key practices. Team members distributed across time zones should avoid the double workday that includes their normal working hours *and* the working hours of team members in a different time zone.

Continuous Integration

Continuous integration is a set of software development practices, behaviors, and principles for automating and improving how to integrate and certify software continuously, so engineers can detect and fix problems early and deliver quality software (Duvall 2008). Continuous integration is the key to delivering stable, high-quality code consistently and quickly, which results in reducing time to market.

Reports Any Build Failures to the Team

One of the benefits of continuous integration is that it allows the team to know the current state of the code in the integration branch of the source control system. At the end of the build, the server generates an email notice to say whether a build completed successfully or failed.

The challenge that sending all these email notices presents is that team members may stop paying attention to them when they receive too many of them; if the build is regularly successful, they may not even realize one of their check-ins introduced the problem. To address this issue, some teams only send a notice email to developers when the build fails. Others send the email to only the developers who delivered changes since the last successful build. Jyoti Jalvi discusses how her team uses this approach:

> *In my organization, we use hourly builds and send out a cumulative report. For the sake of this example, let's assume the 9:00 AM build was the last successful build and a test failed in the 10:00 AM build. The server will send an email to the developers who delivered changes since the 9:00 AM build. If the 11:00 AM build still fails a message goes to everyone who delivered code between 9:00 AM and 11:00 AM. This sometimes causes the developers who delivered changes after the original build break to complain, but overall this works for us.*

Teams need to find the balance that works best for them because sending email to everyone will flood the entire team with information. The flip side is that sending the notice to too few team members may miss someone who would be able to help fix the problem.

An alternative to using email is to have a web-based console that displays the status of the last few builds that all team members can access. A variation of this is to have a notification icon in the system tray of every developer's machine to show them the status of the latest build. Some teams use different icons to show if the build was successful, failed, or is in progress.

Reduces the Risk of Integrating Code

In a traditional model, development teams typically integrate their code later in the development process, after many people on the team have made many changes. At that point, it becomes more difficult to find the source of any build errors. Integrating code early and often allows teams to focus on smaller change sets, which allows them to identify errors quickly and address them while they are still fresh in the minds of the developers that made the changes.

Figure 7.4 shows three build profiles that can apply to many systems or applications. An individual developer manually starts private builds in their own workspaces as they are developing and testing new functionality. Integrators manually start an integration build when merging new code with the latest version of the code base in the source code repository. The release engineer will do a release build manually in yet another environment.

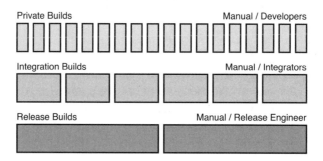

Figure 7.4   Three types of system builds

Julio Sanchez, a team lead at IBM, talks about the practice his team uses during private builds:

> *One of the key practices when developing new or maintaining code is to avoid checking-in code to the repository without someone else looking at it first. In our team, all the features and defects go through a certification process before completing the change records. Some other developer on the team will always receive and verify the changes made and make sure it is the right design and implementation.*
>
> *This practice helped the team to identify design problems and avoid introducing defects in scenarios we did not cover.*

The integration build is where teams get the most benefit from continuous integration. Developers typically integrate their changes to the integration branch manually or using a merge tool but do not always run a manual build to confirm their changes did not break the build for others. For large teams, they may build one subsystem at a time and later integrate it into the build of the entire system. In cases such as these, it may take a couple of days for the team to realize something is wrong. Continuous integration ensures a build runs regularly and allows the team to identify integration issues earlier when they are less costly to fix.

Pushpa Baskaran is a technical leader working for IBM's Web Application Development group. Her organization is responsible for 45–50 applications. They have also found significant value with continuous integration:

Continuous integration has helped my teams. We started by using continuous integra-
tion and unit testing. During the build when there is a problem with the unit tests, an
email goes out to the entire team of developers, so someone can pounce on it right
away. Because we do the build several times a day, it is a small delta of code we are
looking at, and it helps us to be efficient and focus on a small change. We do not want to
build up all the changes over a long time and end with huge problems that we spend
hours or even days examining. I see that as a major plus for our team. Our system also
shows the number of unit tests for our team and our test problem logs. We have different
types of testing that we have also automated, including release verification and user
testing. We see fewer issues in our tests and better quality in production.

Another benefit of integrating code regularly is that it forces developers to break down their work into smaller chunks they can deliver incrementally instead of delivering code only once they complete their work. These smaller testable deliverables allow the team members testing the feature to start their work in parallel with the development.

Establishes Greater Confidence in the Product

When developers are doing the unit testing of their code, they should also create automated unit tests the team can incorporate in the build. Assuming the tests have good code coverage, they can serve as documentation for the source code and help teams identify broken code faster. Some teams also create unit tests to certify critical defect fixes that they can use as built-in regression testing for the product.

Disciplined agile teams will include static code analysis tools, such as Rational Software Analyzer, which scan the source code looking for bugs or deviance from coding conventions. This can be particularly important on distributed development teams, where it can be difficult to ensure conformance to common coding conventions among subteams, or when outsourcing some of the system to another organization.

Because continuous integration certifies every build, developers can make changes with more confidence and the entire team can remain in sync with the latest build.

Reduces the Time to Find Integration Issues

Jyoti Jalvi, an IBM Software Group Information Management developer, is responsible for continuous integration infrastructure for more than 100 engineers spread across the globe. The main labs are in Lenexa, Kansas and San Jose, California. She is responsible for at least five active code lines, and each one has many platforms they build every night. They have about 12–15 platforms for each code line for Informix® products. So, they perform about 100+ builds each night. Jyoti offers the following view of the value of continuous integration:

With continuous integration, we receive many benefits. The build server certifies devel-
oper fixes within four hours and automatically tests the fixes after validating the builds,
and that takes about six hours. When there are integration issues, we find out about

them within six hours instead of the twenty-four hours it used to take us. Developers receive the build status by email, so they can see and fix problems. The next time the build runs, the build status changes from fail to pass automatically. That is huge. It does not need any intervention from our team. Our organization is enjoying great benefit from CI, and we are continuing to improve our practices.

Improves the Efficiency of the Team

Continuous integration helps improve the efficiency of a team by automating once and then reusing as much as possible. This removes human error, provides consistency, and frees up people to do higher-value work.

Automating compiling and packaging the build allows anyone on the team to start a build on-demand without human intervention just by connecting to the build server. Using a separate dedicated server provides a clean environment for the build and provides a centralized location for the team to collect the latest build.

Automating the unit tests that developers write and including them into the build process helps provide built-in testing for the product. Their tests also improve efficiency by providing documentation for others on the team who may need to use their code in the future. The team can also run other tools such as static analysis to run as part of the build.

Automating the build notices allows the team to learn about broken builds quickly and fix them as soon as possible. This helps other team members avoid getting broken code that will then cause them headaches with their private builds.

Julio Sanchez shares some comments from one of the developers on his team about continuous integration:

I had never used continuous integration in this way before and it impressed me how the use of this practice helps avoid problem injection. In a project like ours, where there are thousands of lines of code, it is easy to change code that can impact some other functionality. With continuous integration, we know on a daily basis when something goes wrong because of the build notification we receive via email. Personally, I wholeheartedly recommend the use of this good practice of unit testing; I would even say it is a must!

Builds Can Run at Different Frequencies

Running builds many times a day in a repeatable way is what provides the key benefits of continuous integration, but how often is enough to reap the rewards? Teams approach this question in a couple of different ways.

One approach is to schedule an automatic hourly build. Every hour the build server wakes up, begins a new build, and sends out a notice email with the status. Team can also consider fine-tuning this approach by first having the build server check if someone delivered a change since the last build. If there are no changes, it does not start a new build. The benefit of an hourly build is the team knows about a failure closer to the time of the code integration, and team members can take action on it earlier.

Jyoti Jalvi discusses how her organization uses this approach:

Our teams work in similar time zones, with a few people in the U.S., a few in Germany, and a few more working at the India Lab. A build will automatically run at the top of the hour after someone checks-in code. The build engineer will receive an email only for successful builds, but when there is a build failure, the developers who delivered the latest changes will receive the notice email. After receiving the message, they fix the problem and send out a note identifying the problem and how they solved it.

Some distributed teams working together on the same code base, while chasing the sun, schedule integration builds at specific times of the day. This creates checkpoints during the day where the team makes sure the code base is compiling successfully before the next team starts working on it. Pushpa Baskaran shares how her teams in China and the United States use scheduled builds to help their distributed teams continue one another's work:

We have spaced the build windows with one in the China time zone and two in the U.S. time zones. The Chinese team runs their build at the end of their workday and their developers leave an hour later. This allows them to resolve issues before leaving for the day, but when problems remain, the U.S. team members come online and are able to work immediately on it. Different email messages going out to specific recipients help. For example, for a disk space problem or some permission problem within the build server, the build engineers will receive a build failure email, but for unit-test failures, the larger group of developers will receive a unit test failure email.

Test Automation

Test automation is the use of software to set up preconditions for tests, control the execution of tests, compare test results to the expected results, and report on the results (Kolawa and Huizinga 2007). To streamline the testing and help the team to get as much done as possible within a two-week Sprint, teams will want to automate time-consuming manual processes where possible. For most of the teams within IBM, automating the installation and configuration of the operating system is the first step and provides a high return on investment.

This section discusses how test automation helps improve team collaboration during a Sprint.

Dedicated Automation Teams

It is easy to forget test automation is similar to a development project. The main difference is that testers are writing the code instead of developers. Some projects have separate test teams responsible for creating the automated test cases, and in other projects, individuals from the test teams specialize in test automation.

Separate test automation teams may be working with multiple Scrum Teams on a project, which makes their stakeholders the developers and testers working on the project. They have their own Product Backlog specifically for automation stories, which they use to plan their Sprints.

Monica Luke talks about her team and their stakeholders:

> *By taking our test team agile, we gave ourselves flexibility on how we define stakehold-ers and how we get the right input. The development team is one of our primary stake-holders; they tell us what is ready for us to automate to allow us to stay more closely coupled with the product. Our other stakeholders are the test teams doing manual exe-cutions that tell us their highest-priority items for automation as well.*

Test automation is not something team members should be doing in their spare time. To see the benefits, there needs to be at least some team members dedicated to creating automated test cases.

Identify High-Value Automated Tests

Teams should not aim for 100% test coverage, as that is neither practical nor cost-effective. Teams improve their effectiveness during a Sprint by identifying the test cases that will give them the biggest return on their time investment. Testing installation and configuration of the operating system, regression tests, as well as acceptance into testing tests all have a high rate of return because the team will repeat these often and in different environments.

When teams begin their test automation journey, they need to balance the cost of spending time developing the test against the value it will bring to the team. Automating the wrong or the easiest thing is a waste of both time and money, and brings a false sense of security when many of these bad automated test cases are passing. Steffan Surdek shares a story about a team testing the wrong things:

> *One of the teams I worked with had a subteam that was the gold standard to follow. They had it all—continuous integration as well as a large test suite that reported a high success rate for the API. The team decided they should start using the API supplied by the gold standard team to support the developing of a new browser-based tool for the product. When the team started using the API in real-life cases, they started realizing that it was not as stable as they originally thought. There were many unit tests, but they did not cover simple scenarios the API did not handle well, such as bad parameters for the API calls. The team opened many defects against something they had originally expected to be solid because they were misled by the success rate of the tests.*

Automate What Is Stable

Creating automated test cases for parts of the project that are stable will help teams improve their effectiveness and avoid rework. Good communication between the developers and the team members creating the tests is important because it is not cost-effective to automate testing for parts of the project that are still volatile or in development. Change is part of the game in software development, but there needs to be a base that is stable enough to test before considering automating the testing. Monica Luke talks about stability and change:

> *Test automation depends a lot on how committed the team is to stabilizing parts of the product and how often you have to rework the automation. Stable and not making changes are two different issues. You need to expect change and build the automation for change. When the development team is agile, we can work with them to encourage sufficient stabilization in product code in one iteration, so we can build the GUI automation for it in the next iteration. This requires a real commitment by both development and the test automation team to communicate honestly about what is stable.*

Automated Tests Can Run at Any Time

One of the benefits of test automation is the team can schedule automated tests to run. The testers and development teams will identify different scenarios to automate. Some of these may complete in a short period of time, such as a couple of hours. Others may complete in a longer period of time. Once there is automation for tests, they can run repeatedly without human intervention, whenever the team needs them.

Does the team have a scenario that needs a couple of days to complete? They can run it over the weekend and look at the test results Monday morning. Is there a case that needs to run every day? The team can schedule it to run overnight or even during the day if they have dedicated machines for testing.

Automation Helps Improve Software Quality

Automated test tools run fast, much faster than a human tester, but the team needs to keep in mind it will see most of the benefits of automation in the next release of the product. To see benefits earlier, the focus should be on automating lengthy repetitive tests, as this will free testers to spend time manually testing new features.

Test-Driven Development

Test-driven development (TDD) is a third practice that can help distributed teams to complete their work within a Sprint (see Figure 7.5). TDD is a programming practice where developers create just enough code to pass a failing test (Koskela 2008). First, the developer writes a test. Then, the developer writes the code that will make the test pass. The developer then **refactors** the code—evolves it to a better design—knowing there are other tests that will keep the code from breaking. TDD is a way of designing code, as well as a way of testing code. Developers write **unit tests**, the small tests that fail first. Testers work with developers to ensure that any later tests do not repeat the work the developers have already done.

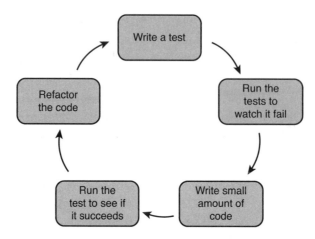

Figure 7.5   Test-driven development

Provides Documentation and Working Examples of Code

One of the benefits of TDD is that as developers are writing their unit tests, they are providing documentation and working samples for the code they are testing. This allows other team members to gain a quick understanding of the code when they need to work with it. To understand how the system works, developers just need to become familiar with the unit tests.

For distributed teams, if someone is working on code written by a developer in another geographical location, having the built-in documentation in the code helps reduce their dependency on the author and enables them to work with the code faster. Working directly with the source code provides a common language for the developers and removes languages barriers.

Helps Reduce the Time to Fix Defects

For developers, TDD can also help reduce the time it takes to fix new defects. After analyzing the defect and isolating the cause, a developer may be able to create a unit test specific to the case that is causing the problem. By using such tests and fixing the area where the problem is occurring, the developer can save the time needed to create a full build, start the application, get to the right place, and test the fix manually.

Justin Gordon, a TDD coach and trainer within IBM, talks about how using TDD to help resolve defects is a good way to introduce developers to the practice:

> *One area where it is almost easy to do some TDD is when you get a bug. If the developer writes a test for the bug, they will not have to think about how they are going to be testing because the test case does it all. With an existing testing infrastructure, the idea is to write a test case that reproduces the bug and fails until the developer resolves the defect. This is a good way to start with TDD.*

Helps Improve Code Quality and Provides a Safety Net for Changes

One of the benefits of TDD is better quality of code because the team writes the unit tests first, providing test coverage for all or most of the code. This provides an early defect detection process where developers can improve the code knowing the existing set of tests will detect any problems. TDD also helps developers to think of code in small units that they write, test independently, and integrate together later. This leads to smaller, more-focused classes, looser coupling, and cleaner interfaces.

Julio Sanchez, a team lead at IBM, talks about how TDD helped improve the code quality on his team:

> *On the team I am on, there were some developers in different countries, and TDD helped us a lot in the quality of the product because of all the unit tests. No matter who develops the next piece of code, the whole team knows they should run the tests, so we do a lot of testing before we check in the code.*

> *One developer on our team said the following about TDD:*

> *My impression at the first moment that I began to use this practice was: "This is going to be a waste of time." After some time, I realized it is a powerful tool, and if I learn how to use it, the code is going to be more consistent and almost error free.*

TDD can help team members feel a greater sense of completion in their work at the end of a Sprint. Mike Thompson, a software developer with IBM Software Group Application and Integration Middleware, talks about how having a suite of unit tests helps meet the "done, done, done" criteria of a user story and helps improve the confidence when refactoring code:

> *TDD is best for the done, done, done criteria. The fact you are building up a history of tests and a bucket of tests you can run helps you make code changes and refactor with such a high confidence level that nothing else can compare to. It reinforces the "done, done, done" feeling at the end of a Sprint.*

To help promote the practice of creating unit tests, some teams define a minimum percentage of test coverage in their build tool to ensure team members cannot check in code without any unit tests.

Helps Team Members Work Together and Collaborate

When teams are evolving from a traditional development model to agile, it is a huge attitude shift to adopt TDD. In every team, there are believers and nonbelievers. A challenge of TDD is that many team members may continue to write code first and develop their unit tests later, and there is no real way to know this is happening.

One common approach teams use to help reluctant team members adopt TDD is to identify some agile missionaries and pair them with others on the team to help spread the practice.

Another approach to get familiar with TDD is to start by using it to help fix defects or to use a throwaway project to help get comfortable with the practice. This is how Mike Thompson, an agile and TDD instructor in IBM, started learning about the practice:

> *When I started with TDD, I created a throwaway project that helped me to get more comfortable with JUnit. Trying to do TDD inside a big project when you never did it before can be intimidating, so it is good to try it as a throwaway project for a day or two, until you get the basic flow and logic.*

Another approach that teams use is to set up lunchtime sessions where team members can learn TDD by learning from one of the gurus on the team and by creating cases that are relevant to their work.

Helps Teams Move Away from Big Upfront Designs

TDD can also help teams move away from doing a big design upfront. Agile modeling helps the team to think through the big issues, and TDD allows you to address the detailed issues (Astels 2003). With TDD, you break down a feature into smaller testable chunks and create small teams to start working on some code right away. This code can be small prototypes that act as tracer bullets through slices of functionality. Mike Thompson discusses how using this approach helped his team deliver results quicker:

> *We are just starting now on a new project, and instead of doing an upfront design, we are tackling it via TDD and a more agile "broken-down" approach. If we had decided to do an upfront design, we would probably still be working on it and it would not be testable. Instead, we already have sample code projects that help prove our thoughts were correct, and we have production and sample code that will help us move along. Instead of creating a document, we created living code, and I think that is the most powerful effect that TDD has. If you start with TDD and let your design evolve from that, anything you come up with will inherently be testable because you are doing TDD.*

Unit Tests and Continuous Integration

Many teams within IBM have set up unit tests with continuous integration. Whenever a developer checks-in code, they run unit tests to ensure that new changes have not broken the larger body of code. Justin Gordon explains how TDD helps his team to be more agile:

> *TDD helps the team be more agile because you can go and look at the code and look at a particular build number of the code and know if there is a serious problem. It is much easier to track when someone introduces some sort of problem. That helps our team with members in India, the U.S., and the UK. Each member knows if the code is stable or broken, which is important when working with a large and complicated body of code.*

Pushpa Baskaran describes how her team uses unit tests with continuous integration and the value that her team experienced:

> *We started the agile journey about two years ago—at the end of 2007. When we did this transformation, we put our heads together to decide how we could become more agile and saw unit tests and test-driven development as key to helping us with this journey. We took a major application with no unit tests and started creating some. We did not get there overnight; we worked on it over several months and now we have 80–90% of that application—legacy code—covered by unit tests. We use test-driven development now for any new work on this application.*
>
> *We also took our unit tests and developed scripts to include them in our daily builds. We build three times a day for testing and have several environments, so automating this part helped our team. We see the benefits every day through the number of problem logs we get in to test, and the testers are also able to see them in the reduction in the number of defects and improved product quality.*

Handling Infrastructure Projects

It is likely the team will not have fully set up continuous integration or test automation at the start of a project, reflections will identify whether starting or improving these abilities might be of value. After each Sprint, the team should look at what is working and what is not working, decide on how to improve, and try the changes in the next Sprint (Crispin and Gregory 2009).

We recommend adding infrastructure work to the Product Backlog and discussing it with the Product Owner to give the work visibility. Teams that try to fit infrastructure development into their spare time may experience problems with sustainable pace. Additionally, the Product Owner and managers should be aware of the business value of providing the team with the tools and infrastructure they believe they need to increase their productivity.

An alternative approach in the enterprise where there are large numbers of teams who need automation is to provide a test automation development team. Monica Luke describes the approach of her organization of having a test automation development team supporting product development teams:

> *We develop our test automation in an agile way, but we are on four-week iterations. At the end of every four weeks, we deliver working automation on the latest build of the product under test. So, we put working automation in Rational Asset Manager (RAM), and it is in one place where all the test execution teams can find the current best version of the test automation. RAM provides versioning, so as you get more automation and more versions of the product under test, they can get the snapshots that match the version they are trying to use. So, when you patch, you can go back and get the right set of automation.*

Identifying user stories for infrastructure through the Product Backlog and having a team dedicated to infrastructure are two ways to help teams to complete their Sprints more efficiently.

Summary

There are many considerations for distributed teams working together during a Sprint. By taking these considerations into account and addressing them, Distributed Scrum Teams will become high-performing Scrum Teams.

Documentation can help distributed teams overcome the challenges of distance by providing a common language for communications. Teams should create just enough documentation to ensure they have a common understanding. Valuing the whole team and having transparency into what is happening helps build stronger, more effective teams.

Team members should defer any outside requests to the Product Owner to keep a single point of entry to their work. This also allows the Product Owner to set the priority of each request by comparing it with what is in the backlog. When interruptions become too frequent, the team should consider shortening the Sprint to allow it to focus on the work of the Sprint and reduce the wait time of new requests from stakeholders.

Teams may misunderstand a user story they committed to completing during a Sprint and need to work out how they will recover with the Product Owner. One method to address work the team cannot contain in a Sprint is to separate the story in two parts: one it will complete this Sprint, and one it will add to the backlog.

Teams can use three key practices to collaborate more effectively. The first one is continuous integration, which allows teams to reduce the risks integrating code by merging changes to the main branch early and often. The build server sends a notice to the team after any build failure gives them the opportunity to detect and fix problems early, while the impact is minimal.

The second practice is test automation, which helps teams automate some of the repetitive test tasks and helps reduce human intervention and error when running the same test over and over. Teams should not aim for full test coverage immediately but should initially focus on automating what will provide them with the greatest return on their time investment. Creating automated test cases is a full-time activity, and the team needs to dedicate members to doing the work.

The third key practice is test-driven development, where developers write a unit test before writing just enough code to make the unit test pass a failing test. TDD provides many benefits, such as better quality of code and test coverage for all or most of the code. This provides an early defect detection process, as well as a safety net for developers to improve the code, knowing the existing set of tests will detect problems they introduce.

References

Astels, David. *Test Driven Development: A Practical Guide*. Boston: Pearson Education, Inc., 2003.

Crispin, Lisa and J. Gregory. *Agile Testing: A Practical Guide for Testers and Agile Teams*. Boston: Pearson Education, Inc., 2009.

Duvall, Paul M., Steve Matyas, and Andrew Glover. *Continuous Integration: Improving Software Quality and Reducing Risk*. Boston: Pearson Education, Inc., 2008.

Kaner, Cern, Avoiding Shelfware: A Manager's View of Automated GUI Testing, 1998. http://www.kaner.com/pdfs/shelfwar.pdf.

Kolawa, Adam and D. Huizinga. *Automated Defect Prevention: Best Practices in Software Management*. Wiley-IEEE Computer Society Press. p. 74, 2007.

Koskela, Lasse. Test Driven: *Practical TDD and Acceptance TDD for Java Developers*. Greenwich, CT: Manning Publications Co., 2008.

Lee, Kevin A. *Realizing Continuous Integration*, 2005. http://www.ibm.com/developerworks/rational/library/sep05/lee/.

Yourdon, Ed. *Death March* (2nd Edition). Boston: Prentice Hall, 2003.

CHAPTER 8

End of Sprint Reviews

Tell me and I'll forget; show me and I'll remember; involve me and I'll understand.

Chinese quote

The primary purpose of the **Sprint Review** meeting—also referred to as the demo meeting—is to assess whether the Scrum Team achieved the Sprint Goal (see Figure 8.1). The development team, Product Owner, ScrumMaster, and stakeholders take part in the Sprint Review to assess whether the Scrum Team met the Sprint Goal. They also discuss the work done during the Sprint to ensure that everyone is still in alignment with the overall goals for the project. Participants review working code and sometimes evidence that a suite of automated test cases passed or failed. The automated test cases show the software meets one or many of the acceptance conditions. Proof of concept prototypes can also be valuable for getting early feedback. The Sprint Review provides valuable information for the next Sprint Planning meeting.

Enterprise Scrum Teams have special considerations for reviews that small-scale, collocated, application development teams are less likely to experience.

This chapter discusses how enterprise teams prepare their stakeholders for the meeting and engage in reviews. It includes approaches for scheduling Sprint Reviews in a distributed environment and tips for demonstrating results during the meeting.

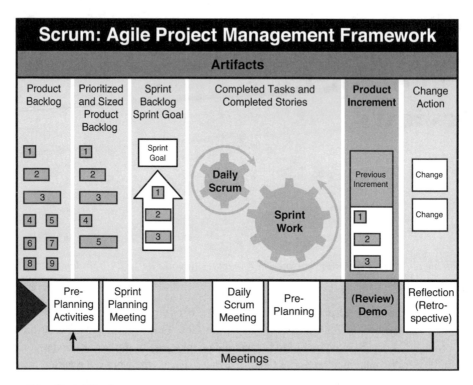

Figure 8.1   Sprint Review

Who Participates in the Reviews

Ideally, the Scrum Team—Product Owner, ScrumMaster, and development team—demonstrates the results of the Sprint to stakeholders at the end of every Sprint. Recall from Chapter 3, "Starting a Scrum Project," that stakeholders include principles, partners, end users, and insiders.

Enterprise Stakeholders

Given the purpose of the Sprint Review is to get information from stakeholders on the Sprint Goal and to discuss the completed work, Scrum Teams need to make sure that they include stakeholders in the meeting. Although this sounds intuitive, teams that are transitioning to agile often use the Sprint Review meeting to show the Sprint to the Scrum Team. If the Scrum Team needs to review their functioning code, they can automate using a static code analysis tool such as IBM Rational Software Analyzer as part of their continuous integration practice. If they need to review completed user stories with each other to confirm that they have completed the work, they should consider getting together to engage in that communication before the end of the Sprint. The Sprint Review meeting has a different purpose. Not engaging stakeholders during the Sprint Review increases the project's risks over time because the Scrum Team may drift farther out of alignment with stakeholders' expectations.

New Scrum Teams in the enterprise will need to establish new routines with stakeholder representatives to engage them in Scrum. As discussed in Chapter 3 during Release Planning, the Product Owner creates relationships with stakeholders, who will provide feedback throughout the project. During Sprint Planning, as discussed in Chapter 4, "Preparing for Sprint Planning," the Product Owner will confirm attendance of key stakeholders at the next Sprint Reviews.

Not every representative stakeholder will take part in a review at the end of every Sprint. If the Scrum Team is on a two-week Sprint, for example, the likelihood of having principals attend every two weeks is unlikely. Still, the Scrum Team should strive for frequent feedback from all categories of stakeholders.

One caution for new enterprise Scrum Teams is that new teams inevitably over-commit for their first Sprint. Shifting from 18-months to 2-weeks to deliver value is a major shift for teams. Working together to finish a user story completely with a Sprint—coding, testing, information development, and more—can be a challenge. New teams often spend the first Sprint or two learning how to break down work, so they can complete it within a Sprint. If the Product Owner gets commitment from a principal to attend the first Sprint or two, there is a risk the team ends the Sprint with no completed stories. This could be a detractor for stakeholders who are new to agile development, so teams may want to consider waiting a Sprint or two before engaging stakeholders, particularly principals.

Who Should Present

Some Scrum Teams will have the team members who worked together on a particular user story explain it to the stakeholders in the meeting. This is a good practice because it puts the spotlight, in front of stakeholders and management, on the development team. It also puts some extra pressure on them to meet their commitments.

Andy Pittaway, an IBM Global Services Executive Project Manager, shares a story about his team showing a project to the general public and the impact it had on the team.

> *I was responsible for an agile project that delivered a web site to sell a product on the Internet which had never been previously available online. Early in the project, the Product Owner told the team they were going to be the people hosting an "internet-café" at a launch show and they would be showing the site to members of the public. This had an excellent impact on building team commitment, and I am sure it affected the quality of the solution positively.*

The negative side of having those who worked on the user story present is that they may avoid softer areas of the feature or may only step through the "golden path" in the software. A good, healthy relationship requires honesty and openness between the participants in the Sprint Review.

KEY POINT Having team members show their own work allows them to avoid softer areas and follow the golden path through their code. There are multiple ways of avoiding this: Have someone else present, have a script that goes through the acceptance conditions, or make sure you identify and cover the alternative paths in use cases.

For large hierarchical distributed teams using an integration Scrum Team or integration team as described by Scott Ambler the question of who should do the presentation can become a sensitive issue because of the purpose of those teams (Ambler 2008). They are responsible for bringing the work that other Scrum Teams produce into the main branch. For the Scrum Teams to maintain a sense of ownership and commitment, they should also take part in the Sprint Review meeting.

A good Sprint Review meeting needs good communication. Distributed teams of different first languages must find a way to communicate effectively among themselves and with stakeholders.

Though we recommend the development team conduct the demo, with distributed teams there may be language barriers. Some team members may be difficult for a customer to understand because of accents or poor knowledge of the language. In such cases, the development team should pick another member that can represent the team in front of the customer. Team members who are most able to communicate effectively with the team, Product Owner, ScrumMaster, and stakeholders should present.

One approach that teams use on occasion is to have a fluent speaker present what the team has completed and serve as a translator between stakeholders, team members, Product Owners, and the ScrumMaster.

Another approach is to record the demonstration before the meeting to allow the developers to create the recording at their own pace in the language of the meeting or to have a fluent speaker speak over the recorded demonstration.

Preparing Stakeholders

In a large-scale distributed environment, teams need to schedule demonstration meetings well in advance. When the team is working on an enterprise product reaching many customers, the product owner will need to identify the right stakeholders to attend the demo and get their commitment to attend. Occasionally, the team can work with the same set of representative stakeholders throughout development, but in other cases, different representatives might be able to provide more detailed comments on specific features during different Sprints.

At different times throughout the project, comments from specific groups of stakeholders may be of more value. The team should include all groups—principals, insiders, partners, and end users, as discussed in Chapter 3.

The Product Owner should also work to set expectations before the demonstration. For many stakeholders, having an opportunity to provide comments on an enterprise product at the end of Sprints will be a significant departure from providing comments during a beta near the end of the development cycle. For teams where external customers attend the Sprint Review meetings, it is important to manage their expectations about what they will see during the meeting. Customers need to understand the team may need to complete more stories before they consider certain feature as done. They also need to know their comments are important, but there is no guarantee the team will incorporate all of them in the current release if at all. The Product Owner will consider their requests alongside all the remaining stories in the Product Backlog.

Where multiple teams are developing features for a given product, the product owner may need to coordinate one review of the integrated work, rather than conducting separate reviews with the same stakeholders for each Scrum Team. Although they may value an opportunity to provide comments, they may be less happy with multiple teams asking them to attend their demonstrations. Teams need to value the time of their stakeholders. When working with a hierarchy of distributed product owners on a large-scale project, the product owners will need to work together to schedule effective demos for key stakeholders and work with the teams to decide what they will show.

Paul Sims, an IBM agile coach, discusses how he handles invitations of internal stakeholders in Sprint Review meetings:

> *What I like to do is group stories by role, and coordinate the review that way. For example, we will invite Marketing Managers or Catalog Managers to demos of stories relevant to them. In our case, this needs coordination among Product Owners across the IBM® WebSphere® Commerce solutions.*

The team should engage project sponsors—those responsible for deciding whether to fund an enterprise project—for each Sprint. In a large-scale, distributed environment, development teams may become distanced from those who decided on the funding for the project. Keeping the connection between those making the business decisions and the technical development team is important to ensuring the team continues to deliver content with the highest business value.

Reviewing the Strategic Vision of the Product

At the beginning of the demonstration, the Product Owner should summarize the shared vision of the product, initially created during Release Planning as discussed in Chapter 3. This is important in a scaled environment where multiple, distributed Scrum Teams are working together to deliver a product. Having the Product Owner review the shared vision of the product gives everyone working on the project an understanding of the context of the work that they are reviewing.

After reviewing the strategic vision, the Product Owner should review the objectives for the Sprint. To be a "successful" Sprint, the Sprint must meet the objectives for the Sprint. When working with multiple features teams, each team will likely have a different Sprint goal. It can be helpful for the different teams to review the goals of their peer teams, so they understand how their work fits into the context of the overall project.

Approaches to Help Focus the Review

The focus of the Sprint Review should not be on a series of tasks completed during the Sprint. If the team is using user stories, which we recommend, each story should identify a requirement from the view of the stakeholder and the acceptance conditions. The whole team is responsible for delivering the story.

This section presents two approaches teams can use to improve the value and the focus of the meeting, as follows:

- Use themes and a script
- Have the Product Owner introduce each presentation

Using Themes and a Script

When teams plan their work based on themes for each Sprint, this allows them to group related stories. In turn, this opens the door to the Product Owner creating a script the team can follow during the Sprint Review meeting to tell a story.

Steffan Surdek shares the following story:

On one of the teams I worked on, at the start of the last week of the Sprint, the Product Owner gave the team the script they would be following for the demo day. This script tied together all the stories the team developed during the Sprint. Our first few demos seemed artificial and forced, but with each successive Sprint, the scripts progressively got better and the demos were better as well. The main benefit the team found in doing demos this way was the storytelling.

The script can help the team cover all facets of the acceptance conditions for a story. For example, during the demonstration script, the user may go from trying a feature to the related online help to better understand how to use it. Doing the demonstration this way helps show the real state of completion of a feature or user story versus presenting all features first and then all the online help changes second.

One other benefit of using a script is that it can help manage the case where the people presenting are avoiding soft areas of the code. If the script has good coverage for the work the team completed, it will force them to go through every area thoroughly.

Having the Product Owner Introduce Each Presentation

Another approach that adds value and focus to the demonstration meeting is for the Product Owner or ScrumMaster to introduce each presenter and provide some context on what they will present. This context may include the target user, as well as what this user is trying to do in the user story. This approach is helpful for teams that go through the completed user stories and have the team members present their work.

Doing this helps everyone in the meeting to better consume what the presenter will show them and get into the right mind-set to provide their comments.

Ryan Shillington discusses this approach on his team where a member of the development team, rather than the Product Owner, provides context for the demonstration:

The biggest piece of advice that I've learned is that although you can coach people to try to give context, there's a role of "Demo Master" in the same vein as ScrumMaster. One person needs to understand and be able to explain at a high level what people are seeing during the meeting. Ideally the person that gives the 1000-foot view is not the same person who has the view from ground level. Once you have this low-level perspective, it becomes challenging to talk at the high-level view.

Scheduling for Teams with Overlapping Work Hours

Depending on the time difference between the locations of the different team members, finding the right time to schedule the meeting can be a challenge. For distributed teams with overlapping work hours, it is typically easier to schedule the Sprint Review meeting so everyone can attend but this can also create some quirks because this meeting marks the end of the Sprint.

To explain this, Table 8.1 shows the case of two teams working with a three-hour time difference between them. Assume the teams decide to use the time of Scrum Team 1 to schedule the meeting, and they schedule a two-hour meeting for two o'clock in the afternoon. This places Scrum Team 2 in a position where team members must complete their work for the Sprint in the morning.

Table 8.1 Two Teams Working with Overlapping Working Hours

Team	Review Meeting Time
Scrum Team 1	02:00 PM
Scrum Team 2	11:00 AM

In this case, the Scrum Team 2 members should aim to complete their work by the end of the second to last day of the Sprint and plan their tasks and hours for the Sprint to make this possible. Sprints do not have to start on Monday and end on Fridays, as long as the start and end days are always the same. In the morning of the last day of the Sprint, the team members can start preparing for the next Sprint or fix last-minute defects to help secure the quality of their work for the Sprint.

KEY POINT Make sure all team members, regardless of the time zone, can complete their work and prepare for the demo.

Scheduling for Teams with No Overlapping Work Hours

Chapter 6, "Distributed Daily Scrum Meetings," identified different approaches distributed teams can use for daily Scrum meetings. In this section, we will discuss some approaches that can also work for the Sprint Review meeting, as follows:

- Alternating meeting times
- Multiple demonstration meetings
- Sharing the pain
- Feeling the pain
- Recording the meeting

When using any approach that forces some team members to work outside their working hours, the team should check with everyone to make sure that they are able to call into the meeting.

Alternating Meeting Times

One approach to scheduling demonstrations where members of the team have no overlap in work hours is to alternate meeting times. With this approach, the team holds one Sprint Review meeting during the normal workday for part of the Scrum Team and holds the other Sprint Review meeting during the normal work hours of the other part of the Scrum Team.

Figure 8.2 shows a team that alternates their meetings between two different times. One meeting is most convenient for team members in Toronto, Sao Paulo, and Hursley. The other is more convenient for team members in Hursley, Zurich, Bangalore, and Beijing.

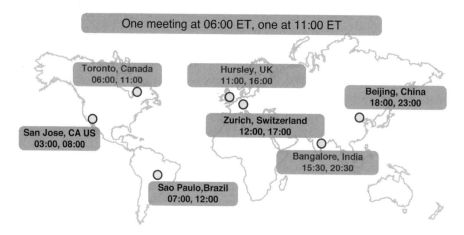

Figure 8.2   Alternating Meeting Times approach

The advantage of this approach is everyone has an opportunity to attend during their normal working hours, unlike the approach of having a fixed time always outside working hours for the same team members.

The major disadvantage of this approach is the team will have to coordinate to demonstrate all stories—even those done by team members who are in the "off" time zone that Sprint. This may mean that someone from the time zone of the demonstration meeting will connect with the "off" time zone members for a preparation session to learn how to demo the work, respond to questions, and discuss progress.

If it would take too much time for another team member to be able to show and explain, the team can consider recording demonstrations by the "off" time zone team members. Members can record their part of the presentation ahead of time and the person leading the meeting can play the recording during the meeting. The team can capture any comments stakeholders provide for the recorded presentation and post it on a wiki so all can see the team members' replies to the comments.

Unfortunately, stakeholders, the Product Owner, team members, and the ScrumMaster will not be able to discuss interactively the completed work with the "off" time zone team members. The team may need extra time to follow up with the team members who were unable to take part in the meeting.

Multiple Sprint Review Meetings

An alternative to the Alternating Meeting Times approach is to schedule multiple demonstration meetings, each meeting being at a time that different parts of the team can attend. This approach can be suitable for Scrum Teams with a Product Backlog separated by feature sets and for Scrum Teams that work off their own individual Product Backlogs.

The advantage of this approach is everyone has an opportunity to attend during their normal working hours. Unlike the approach of having a fixed time always outside working hours for some team members, every team member has an opportunity to attend the demonstration meeting of their Scrum Team.

One of the disadvantages of this approach depends on whether the individual Scrum Teams each have a local Product Owner and stakeholders. If these key participants are not available at the time the demonstration meeting occurs, there is no real purpose to holding the meeting besides doing an internal demonstration to the Scrum Team.

Another disadvantage of this approach is that team members will only see a demonstration of the stories the Scrum Teams taking part in that specific meeting worked on during the Sprint.

KEY POINT When having multiple demonstration meetings, team members may only be able to see the work completed by the teams taking part in the demonstration meeting.

To get the full picture of the work the team completed during the Sprint, team members will need to combine this approach with the approach of recording the Sprint Review meeting, which we will discuss later in this chapter. You might also want to have a demo environment where the team deploys the current working build of the system. That way, anyone can play with the latest version whenever they want. If you adopt a continuous deployment strategy as part of continuous integration, you can use your continuous integration tool, such as IBM Rational Build Forge, to deploy your working builds automatically into this demo environment.

Sharing the Pain

Teams can use the approach of sharing the pain. With this approach, the team works together to share the pain associated with being part of a distributed team. They select a time to meet that is best for the team, stakeholders, Product Owner, and ScrumMaster. Everyone considers the possibility of working outside their traditional work hours. The resulting Sprint Review meeting time is the time that works best for the entire team as a whole.

The advantage to the approach of sharing the pain is the whole team is taking part in the Sprint Review meeting, and the time selected for the meeting has the whole team sharing the pain. Everyone hears straight from the other team members, so there is less of a chance of confusion than the team might have with other methods.

However, unlike the daily Scrum meeting, the Sprint Review meeting is not a 15-minute meeting, and not everyone may like working outside their normal working hours for a meeting lasting multiple hours. When using this approach, the team should have the flexibility to take some time off from their normal working hours to compensate or shift the working hours on the day when entire team needs to meet.

Feeling the Pain

This approach is not one that we recommend, but it is one that does occur with some teams. In this case, one team will always feel the pain of doing demonstrations of their work at a fixed time, outside their work hours. This case often occurs on teams where the Product Owner and stakeholders are not in the same location as the Scrum Team carrying out the work.

The major disadvantage is the team members doing the demonstration are always doing it outside their working hours. Teams can manage this in several different ways, as follows:

- Rotate the people doing the demonstrations. Developers who complete the work do not always need to be the ones that show it. Testers or technical writers that worked on the same user story can also present the work. The alternative to this is for the team to pick someone who will do the presentation and make sure they train that person to be able to present on their behalf.

- Schedule the demonstration meeting at the time that is less inconvenient to them. This tries to incorporate the Sharing the Pain approach we discussed earlier.

- Individual members of the distributed team can prepare a recording of their parts of the demonstration meeting the host of the meeting can play back during the meeting. Using this approach limits the number of team members forced to attend the meeting outside their regular office hours.

As in the Sharing the Pain approach, when using this approach, the team should have the flexibility to take some time off from their normal working hours to compensate.

Recording the Entire Sprint Review Meeting

One of the goals of the Sprint Review meeting is to allow team members and other stakeholders to provide comments on the work the team completed during the Sprint. One of the main challenges of distributed teams is that not everyone can attend the meeting, so if some team members cannot attend the meeting, how can the team, stakeholders, Product Owner, and ScrumMaster discuss the deliverable?

One of the ways to resolve this is for the team to record the meeting, both the slides team members are presenting, the demonstrations they are doing, as well as the audio of the Sprint Review meeting. Teams can then make these recordings available to everyone through a wiki or a shared network storage location.

KEY POINT Recording the Sprint Review meeting provides a way for all team members to see the work the team did during the Sprint and to provide their comments. It also provides proof that you held the review for teams that find themselves in regulatory compliance situations.

Challenges Teams Face

There are many challenges that teams face in the review meeting that applies to both collocated and distributed teams. This section discusses some of them and suggests ways that teams can work around these issues.

Not Keeping Track of the Stakeholder Comments

One of the main purposes of doing the end of Sprint demonstration is to allow key stakeholders and the Product Owner to provide early comments to the team. During the meeting, the team needs to capture these comments so the Product Owner and the development team can decide which ones they will act on. You may want to have at least two people take detailed notes during the meeting. One person will probably not be enough if the conversation becomes too active. Also, transcribing a recording can add significant work for the team. It generally takes three to six hours to transcribe each hour of recording.

The team needs to consider how they will handle each piece of stakeholder feedback. Some comments may turn into user stories for new requests and others may turn into extra acceptance conditions for a user story.

Before teams can decide how to handle the comments, they first need to make sure they are capturing the comments during the demonstration meeting. There are many ways of doing this; teams can gather them in a single location like a spreadsheet or a wiki page, or they can add them to the project-tracking tool as issues or user stories.

One approach teams use is to capture the feedback without worrying about the format of the comments (point form, raw text); what is important is the team understands what they need to do. After the meeting, they review the comments with the Product Owner and decide which ones to act on. The next step is to work with the Product Owner to create new user stories, decide their relative priority, and add them to the Product Backlog.

A better approach would be to teach stakeholders how to write user stories and ask them to express their comments as user stories including information about their business value. This allows the Product Owner to compare new requirements in the same format as the existing ones in the Product Backlog. And, it also removes any interpretation errors the team could make by interpreting comments.

Both approaches result in having a user story added to the Product Backlog; the risk when doing this is that will crowd the Product Backlog with user stories the team should not be considering. This is why the Product Owner must maintain the Backlog regularly to remove clutter.

Demos May Provide a False Sense of Completion

Another challenge that teams face is the demo may provide a false sense of completion to the stakeholders. For example, a web application needs the team to display a web page with information it pulls from a database. If the user story in the current Sprint is to create a placeholder for that page and the team uses mock data that looks too real, a stakeholder looking at the demo may think the team is further ahead than they are.

One way to help avoid this is to add a DRAFT watermark on any screenshots or to use data that is clearly not real. Steffan Surdek shares this story about screenshots looking a little bit too real for a stakeholder during a presentation he did in a Sprint Review meeting:

> As the User Experience lead on my team, I often show presentations to walk the team through screen mock-ups of a feature to give everyone a sense of the work coming up in the next Sprint. I usually create high-fidelity screenshots that look real as this helps me make sure the screen is doable for the developers. During one meeting, an external stakeholder suddenly asked me when we were going to fix the bug with showing some debug buttons in one of the property editor screens I showed in my presentation. This was a flaw with the base backgrounds I use in my mock-ups, but the stakeholder forgot he was not looking at a real screen.

The Team Has Nothing to Present

What should happen when the team has such a nightmare of a Sprint they have nothing that works they can show at the end of the Sprint? The last alternative the team should consider is canceling the demonstration meeting, because if they do, they will give the message to the entire team and the stakeholders that it is not important. Canceling it that first time also makes it much easier to cancel again the next time it is not convenient for the team to present.

What the team should do is still hold the meeting at the originally scheduled time, and they should still go over the list of stories the team committed to for the Sprint. They should discuss the stories the team did and did not complete.

After the Sprint Review meeting, the team should probably hold a longer reflection using the time scheduled for the demonstration meeting to discuss what went wrong and identify the issues they must address for the next Sprint to be successful.

Should the team schedule a demonstration meeting early the following week to make up for the one they missed? This can be a slippery slope to get on because the team may lose their sense of commitment, and doing so removes the time boxing a Sprint provides. For the sake of argument, let's assume that an extra day or two gives the team something interesting to show; another meeting date will impact the work the team is doing in the following Sprint. If the team decides to schedule one anyway, they need to be sure they will not have to cancel it again. The best approach is to wait until the following Sprint.

When a team regularly has nothing to show at the end of a Sprint, it is a red flag, and the team needs to work at finding the reasons behind this and address them. Perhaps team members are over-committing themselves at each Sprint because their user stories are too big to complete.

KEY POINT   The show must go on. When the team has nothing to show at the end of the Sprint, they should still hold the meeting and admit the stories they did not complete to the Product Owner and stakeholders.

Added Challenges of Distributed Teams

Large-scale distributed Scrum Teams face additional challenges related to demonstrating all stories implemented by a large team and coordination of reviews when Scrum Teams are using different Sprint lengths.

Neglecting to Demo the Work of Part of the Team

One of the challenges of distributed teams is not demonstrating stories that part of the distributed team completed during the Sprint. This can happen on teams with no overlapping hours when the time of the meeting would be outside the regular hours of the part of the team that worked on the story.

Using a recording is a good way to provide team members that cannot attend the Sprint Review meeting with a way to participate. Team members can record demonstrations ahead of time, and the person leading the Sprint Review meeting can play the recording at the right time in the Sprint Review meeting. The team can capture any comments stakeholders provide for the recorded presentation and discuss with the members who missed the Review.

The team can also use short (two minutes or less), high-quality recordings as tutorials or as extra information for the documentation.

Coordinate with Teams on Different Sprint Lengths

In Chapter 3, we discussed a team that uses three-week iterations instead of the six-week iterations the rest of their product family uses. How does the team with the shorter iterations handle their demonstration meetings? They simply change their target audience for the Sprint Review meeting every second meeting.

In the first mini-iteration, they still do a Sprint Review meeting, but only with the Scrum Team, the Product Owner, and a limited set of stakeholders. At the end of the product family's iteration, they include stakeholders from the larger product family in the meeting as well. During the demonstration meeting, they will show some of the key user stories from the first mini-iteration and then they will show the user stories the team completed in the second mini-iteration.

Remote Demonstrations

For distributed Sprint Review meetings, network delays and poor network performance can impact the effectiveness of demonstrations. Additionally, every site where distributed Scrum Team members work may not have the same type of equipment, office configuration, and software. Knowing the differences and limitations can affect the success of the Sprint Review meeting.

Network Delays and Poor Performance

For distributed demonstrations, network delays and poor performance of distributed screen-sharing tools can be painful. Screen refreshes that do not adequately capture mouse movements to allow a realistic demonstration of completed software can transform a demonstration into a review of the tools used for the remote meeting instead of the work completed.

As discussed in Chapter 2, "Challenges Faced by Distributed Teams," the team should test their tools ahead of time to be sure the distributed meeting will run smoothly. If network performance becomes a stumbling block, the team can consider making the recordings available for download before the demonstration meeting and discussing them through a teleconference.

Ming Xie Zhi, an agile coach for IBM China Development Lab, explains how one member of his team used recordings in Sprint Review meetings:

> We usually had an engineer who was familiar with the system environment set one up for the Sprint Review. Because of Internet bandwidth issues, the demo was slow, and we kept hearing people on the conference complain about the speed of the screen refresh. After one of those meetings, someone introduced a tool for recording the demonstration. The team could access the tool and download the demo file before the Sprint Review meeting and play it during the review or even a planning meeting. This turned out to be an effective solution.
>
> Since the test team had complete user stories and end-to-end testing scenarios, it proved be interesting when a tester was giving the demo. They would show the stakeholder an accurate picture of the Sprint achievements and in proper sequence and logic. The tester had prepared a checklist of "features" based on the Sprint backlog, to confirm stakeholder acceptance when going through the recorded demo.

Services May Vary by Location

The services available in the locations of each distributed team may vary. The team needs to understand the different environments in which their remote members are working. Teams have a tendency to assume automatically all teams have the same environment as they do, but that is not always the case. Using a checklist with the basic requirements for taking part in the demonstration meeting is a good way for the team to ensure all sites meet a minimum set of conditions.

Matt Ganis shares the following story:

> *I was working with a development team in India for the Second Life project, and we would have regular Sprint Review meetings where the team could show their progress they made. During a Sprint Review meeting, on our side, we would ask: "Show us that house." There would be a delay and then, the house would pop up, then another delay, and they would ask me what I thought about it. So I would then ask: "Great, can you spin it to the left?" Again, you'd hear them run to the other room and then it would spin as we asked. It turned out that in that location, there was no Internet access in the conference rooms where the phones were, so the team members would run from the conference room to a lab where they had Internet access. They would do what I asked and run back to the conference room to continue the conversation with us. In this case, because I was not local, I had no way of knowing they had this problem. It came out over a series of phone calls, as we were doing deeper and deeper reviews.*

What items should be on such a checklist? The basics such as phone, network connectivity, and minimum bandwidth are a good start. There may be other items on the checklist, such as downloads for conferencing or presentation software or if showing recordings, the team may need to install video and audio codecs on the machine they will use for the demonstration. In reality, the checklists may never be complete, but they will provide a good starting point for discussions.

Another approach is for one site to set up a single machine with a standard configuration that everyone uses during the demonstration meeting. Before the start of the meeting, team members can access the machine (remotely or locally) to bookmark links, set up scripts, and do a quick dry run of their presentation. One of the added benefits of this approach is that it removes some of the complexities of the demonstration.

Availability of resources can also be a challenge in different distributed locations. For example, if multiple team members are sharing a single phone, it can make it difficult to schedule meetings with them all at the same time.

Demos Outside of Office Hours

Distributed team members attending meetings outside their working hours face a different set of challenges. Should they go back home or stay late at the office to attend the meeting? If their Internet access at home is much slower than at work, or if they cannot dial a toll-free number to attend the call, they may have no choice but to remain late at the office. Depending on what time they leave from work, they may also face other difficulties, such as peak traffic times or lack of availability of public transport.

Matt Ganis shares a story about meeting with some team members in his India team and the traffic challenges they faced:

There were times where we would want to schedule a meeting and would schedule it around 2:00 PM my time. Around that time, traffic in India is horrendous, and they would never get home on time, so they would sometimes have to wait until 5:00 PM or 6:00 PM my time to get in the local van that brought them back home. When that happened, they would typically get back home after midnight their time.

Summary

Reviews are a way for the Product Owner and the stakeholders to determine if the outcome of the Sprint met the Sprint Goal. It allows the development team to regularly show the work they completed and get comments early in the release when they still have time to consider them. Product Owners need to identify the right stakeholders to invite to the meeting and consider hosting a separate demonstration meeting for external customers.

At the start of the demonstration meeting, teams should identify the stories they committed to completing during the Sprint, the ones they completed, and the ones they did not complete.

Using a script to guide the demonstration meeting is a good way to allow the meeting to tell a compelling story to the stakeholders. To simplify creating the demonstration script, the Product Owner and development team need to also consider identifying themes for the work they will tackle at each Sprint.

There are multiple approaches distributed teams can take to manage the pain of the demonstration meeting. Teams need to consider these and identify the ones that will work best for them.

It is important for the team to keep track of the comments provided during the demonstration meeting and to identify the ones on which they will act. It is only when the team decides to carry out work related to one of the comments that they should either create a user story for it or add it to the acceptance conditions of an existing user story.

References

Ambler, Scott. "How system integration actually occurs on large teams." *Dr. Dobbs Agile Newsletter*, June 2008. http://www.ddj.com/architect/208800147?cid=Ambysoft.

Retrospectives

In the business world, the rearview mirror is always clearer than the windshield.

Warren Buffett

Enterprise Scrum Teams have special considerations for reviews that small-scale, collocated, application development teams are less likely to experience.

At certain points during the development cycle, teams need to stop, look at what they are doing, and make subtle mid-course changes if the need arises. Teams refer to the way of performing this "self-analysis" as a "**reflection**" or "**retrospective**" (Kerth 2001). Scrum Teams manage change and risk by adapting. But to adapt, they must identify opportunities for change and decide if they should undertake them.

In essence, a **Sprint Retrospective** is a meeting where the Scrum Team "looks back" on the previous Sprint in an attempt to analyze or assess how well they performed. This meeting takes place after the Sprint Review meeting, and its purpose is to allow the team to learn from the previous Sprint and to apply the lessons they learned to the next one (see Figure 9.1).

Sprint Retrospectives

Traditional reviews, typically called project post-mortems, usually happen at the end of a project. By doing a retrospective at the end of each Sprint instead, it allows the team to identify pain points throughout the project and identify ways to address them midstream, while there is still time in the project.

During the Sprint Retrospective, the Scrum Team needs to identify what they did that helped them be successful or practices individual team members tried that worked well for them during the Sprint. Talking about their successes, no matter how small, helps the team get something positive out of the meeting and identify what they need to keep doing in future Sprints or projects. When the team completes a Sprint where things didn't go as well as expected, this helps the team members to see that not everything went wrong during the Sprint. The retrospective allows them to "take away" the "good" things and identify the "bad."

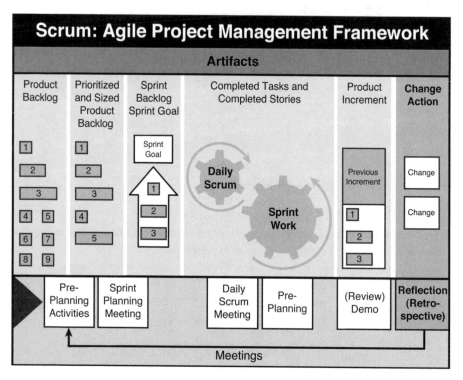

Figure 9.1   Sprint Retrospectives

After talking about what went well, it is critical for the Scrum Team to discuss what did not go well during the Sprint. The Scrum Team needs to discuss these issues more closely and identify what they can do in the next Sprint to lessen their impact or resolve them. Identifying these issues also helps prevent the team from repeating these same mistakes in the future. This retrospective meeting is all about getting the team to communicate about what they need to do to be a more effective, better-performing team on the next Sprint or project. Team members should view this meeting as a positive experience, even when the Sprint or project they are discussing had issues.

This is not a meeting to place blame on an individual or a group of individuals; it is the time the team takes to think about how they performed during the last Sprint. The Scrum Team participates in the Sprint Retrospective.

What Should Come Out of a Retrospective?

It is important to make sure the retrospective does not turn into a complaint session. At the end of the retrospective, the team should be turning issues into actionable items the team can walk away with. These can be areas of improvement, changes to the procedures the team follows, or other specific work items. Creating action items allows the team to look back and keep track to see if they acted on the items they said they were going to do in the last reflection.

It may be tempting for new teams to address a long list of action items immediately. However, they are more likely to be successful if they identify one or two action items to address. What matters is not how long the list is, but how committed the team is to following through with them. A new Agile team is more likely to improve when they follow through on addressing one or two action items identified from each Sprint, rather than identifying a long list and following through on none of them during the Sprint.

When there are multiple teams, the teams can have a joint retrospective about what they can change to more effectively coordinate their delivery of the product and the delivery process. However, each team should focus on what *they* can do differently, rather than focus on what they think *the other Scrum Teams* should do differently. As Paul Sims, a software engineer and Agile coach on the IBM Software Group WebSphere Commerce team, points out, his team likes to share improvement items coming out of the retrospectives to enable shared learning among the team members:

> *To spark retrospective discussion, we use a lightweight, customized version of IBM Rational Self Check administered through a Web survey to identify areas of agility and issues teams need to address. We consult project management, ScrumMasters, and our quality champion to select the survey questions. We ask each Scrum team to hold its own retrospective discussion based on the Self Check results and identify one or two actions team members can take in the next sprint to improve their development process. It's important to focus on a small number of team-valued actions. Scrum teams record their improvement tasks in their next sprint backlog and estimate these tasks alongside their feature development tasks. These improvement tasks are a part of the Sprint goal and the team commits to completing them. In the first week of the following Sprint, we encourage ScrumMasters to briefly share their learning with each other in a one-hour "retrospective of retrospectives" meeting. ScrumMasters summarize the issues their team is working to resolve and the actions the team is taking. This allows Scrum Teams to learn from each other and fosters a continuous improvement culture throughout the development organization.*

No matter what these action items are, teams should keep track of them and follow-up on them at the end of the next Sprint. One approach Scrum Teams use to track them is to add them as tasks or retrospective items in the tracking tool used on the project. Others teams simply use spreadsheets or wiki with the list of items on which to follow up. In either case, this allows the identified items to remain visible on the Sprint backlog in future Sprints to account for effort spent on continuous improvement of the team.

Retrospective Timing

In a distributed environment when multiple Scrum Teams are contributing to the same project, there may be a need for the teams to conduct a joint retrospective meeting. The need for, and the timing or frequency of, these meetings depends a lot on how closely the teams work together.

To be effective and timely, teams should call joint retrospectives as soon as possible after having their own team meeting. Depending on the number of teams involved in a joint retrospective, teams may want to limit the number of participants from each Scrum Team to keep the meeting productive.

Hold Joint Retrospective as Needed

This approach works well for totally isolated Scrum Teams with limited dependencies working together, and it may also work for teams with more dependencies. In this approach, each Scrum Team first holds their individual Sprint Retrospective meetings at the end of each Sprint. When team members from either team identify issues in the way the teams work together, the teams will have a joint retrospective to identify how and where they can address these issues.

The benefit of this approach is that it limits the number of joint meetings and brings added importance to the meetings when they do occur.

The negative side of this approach is that because the teams are not meeting regularly, they may not be identifying other areas on which they could improve. Additionally, Sprint Retrospectives are an opportunity for team building. Each time the team skips a joint meeting, they lose an opportunity to learn to work together more effectively.

Hold Regular Joint Retrospectives

This approach works for Scrum Teams that are working on the same Sprint length and are synchronizing their Sprints. In this approach, the Scrum Teams working together will conduct their individual Sprint retrospectives at the end of each Sprint and then will conduct a joint retrospective.

The benefit of this approach is that it promotes communication between the Scrum Teams involved in a project. Because of the regular opportunity to talk, they can find ways to improve their working relationship throughout the duration of the project. Some teams will hold joint "retrospective of retrospectives" at the end of each Sprint. In this exercise, each Scrum Team has up to five minutes to share their observations and improvement actions with the other.

The cons of this approach are that it may take away from time team members will be able to spend on the Sprint.

Joint Retrospectives for Teams on Different Sprint Lengths

In Chapter 3, "Starting a Scrum Project," we talked about multiple teams that coordinate but do not follow the same Sprint duration. These teams will not be able to have a joint coordinated reflection at the end of each Scrum Team's Sprint. Figure 9.2 shows how scaled teams may decide to conduct their reflections.

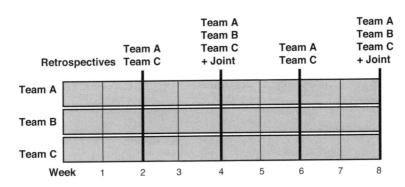

Figure 9.2   Retrospectives for coordinating teams

In an enterprise environment, Scrum Teams conduct their own Sprint reflection at the end of each Sprint. When multiple Scrum Teams are contributing to the same project, the scaled Scrum Teams may also conduct joint retrospectives, the frequency of which depends on the interdependency of the teams and their Sprint durations.

Retrospectives for Teams in the Same Product Family

Teams working together on a suite of related products may also want to hold joint retrospective meetings. How closely the product teams are working together drives how often they need to get together. It may be necessary for certain product teams to meet more often than the entire product family.

One of the approaches these related teams take is to each hold their Sprint Retrospectives, and teams with regular dependencies between each meet for a joint retrospective as they need to. At the end of the release, each product team does a retrospective for the release and then they have a joint retrospective at the product team level.

Conducting Retrospectives After Reviews

For teams with a collocated Scrum Team and other stakeholders, retrospectives commonly take place immediately after the Sprint review.

Collocated part-time teams should strongly consider coming together face-to-face for the Sprint Retrospective because these meetings often focus on difficulties the team experienced and the feelings of team members.

For distributed teams with overlapping work hours, the team may need to postpone the Sprint retrospective until the next overlap in work hours, possibly the next working day. This gives the entire team the opportunity to meet during normal working hours. Teams should conduct the retrospective as quickly as possible after the review and before the start of the next Sprint, so they can carry out their action items that should help lead to improvement.

For distributed teams with no overlapping work hours, having the Sprint retrospective immediately after the Sprint review may cause some members to work even further outside their normal working hours. Teams should poll remote team members to decide the best time that works for the whole team.

Larger Retrospectives

Some teams decide to carry out additional retrospectives at the end of the project. During these retrospectives, team members can reflect and comment on release quality and capability. The team talks about the project, and then defines and records the various milestones within the project to improve on or continue in future releases. Although these meetings can provide value, teams should also engage in Sprint Retrospectives to allow them to improve from Sprint to Sprint.

Building Trust

To have a successful Sprint retrospective, the participants must view the meeting environment as "safe" to feel open enough to be honest and share their views. As participants enter a retrospective, they need to develop a sense of trust and honesty with one another, which in turn will lead to a wider degree of openness.

This sense of trust allows teammates to learn to take comments from other team members positively instead of misinterpreting them and feeling under attack. They realize others are not making comments to criticize them personally, but to help the entire team improve. It's important to remember how to give feedback during the retrospective. It's better to say, "When this happens, I feel...," instead of "You always [some behavior]." To build a trust environment, team members should adopt a guideline of "no blaming." Team members can mention the name of another team member or another part of the organization in appreciation for what they have done, but it is not acceptable to name for the purpose of placing blame. Team members can discuss problems and issues but not mention names.

As team members begin to trust each other, they are more likely to feel comfortable telling other members their true feelings. Figure 9.3 shows the relationships between trust, honesty, and openness.

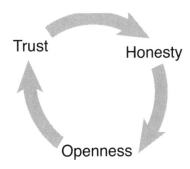

Figure 9.3   Getting comments for retrospectives

Effects of Distance

As a Scrum Team, we assume everyone goes into the phases or releases of agile development with the same base assumptions and knowledge, but this is not always the case. The key purpose of a retrospective is to talk about what the team can improve on and how to get to where the team wants to be.

The challenge in a distributed environment is developing a rich set of communication channels within the team using tools and methods that inherently deliver less-than-perfect communication paths between people or groups. It is the tacit knowledge, the things that the team cannot write down, that comes out during conversation and collaboration.

The facilitator of a distributed retrospective needs to understand the cultural differences on the team. Understanding how different cultures interact when they want to change something or have issues they want to talk about can help the facilitator encourage participation from all team members. In a retrospective, issues will come up that are either uncomfortable or confrontational, and without being in the same room, it is not possible to read everyone's body language. It is easy for team members on the phone to claim they have nothing to say on a controversial topic without anyone realizing they are squirming in their chair because something upset them.

Preparing for the Retrospective

The facilitator for the retrospective can help the retrospective to be more productive by preparing the team and working with the team to identify a process that will work best for them. The facilitator will want to set expectations, understand the personalities and cultural differences of team members and offer anonymity if necessary.

Setting Expectations

The facilitator, especially for distributed teams, should talk to the team ahead of the first retrospective and explain the expectations for the retrospective. These meetings can be difficult because the team is dealing with problems and issues that need to improve, but these may not be obvious to everyone on the team. Different people react to criticisms and comments about their work in different ways, so the facilitator needs to go out of his or her way to lay the groundwork for this meeting before it begins.

The facilitator should also ensure that everyone understands what Norm Kerth calls the "Retrospective Prime Directive":

> *Regardless of what we discover [during the Retrospective], we understand and believe that everyone did the best job they could, given what they knew at the time, their skills and abilities, the resources available, and the situation at hand (Kerth 2001).*

Experienced teams might have a set of rules and expectations posted on the wall or on a wiki page to remind them and to provide a resource for new team members.

Understanding the Team Members' Personalities

Team have a different combination of personalities, and the facilitator of the retrospective needs to understand the personalities of team members to lead the meeting effectively. Some will be introverts and some will be extroverts. Some people are quieter than others or may want to avoid confrontation. Some may have stronger ties with certain team members. Others may come from different cultures.

Although it is always important to understand the personalities of participants in the retrospective, it is even more important when conducting a retrospective with a distributed team. As discussed in Chapter 2, "Challenges Faced by Distributed Teams," visual cues are unavailable, and the meeting facilitator will rely on what he hears to help the team to discuss some potentially difficult topics.

Before the retrospective, the person leading the meeting should talk to participants about their comfort level in sharing their thoughts with the team during a retrospective. They can also get valuable insight about the personality of a team member from the manager, other team members, colleagues, and friends. Or, they can learn through observation, which may be the hard way for the first retrospectives. Learning about the personalities of individual team members will help the facilitator guide the retrospective and provide a comfortable, safe environment for all participants.

One technique often used is to take the temperature of the room by anonymously querying the attendees of a retrospective to see how they would feel about speaking freely during the meeting. Because of the anonymity, they do not know how *individuals* are feeling, but it can give a sense of the feelings of the team. For example, some members may feel confident enough to speak their mind freely during the meeting, while others may be reluctant to speak up. In a distributed retrospective, having the knowledge of the collective mind-set or "feelings" of the team is important. Because of the lack of visual cues, knowing the temperature of the room may help the facilitator of the meeting get a feeling for times where something someone said is making another participant uncomfortable or keeping them quiet.

Respecting Cultural Differences

The impact of different cultures is not something to take lightly. Some cultures view speaking out openly against colleagues as disrespectful. With the IBM China Lab, Leslie Ekas, a U.S.-based ScrumMaster, had a difficult time getting team members to speak up. Because of this, she relied on written comments for the retrospective, which they provided in a large quantity, but were they were always quiet on the phone.

There are some clear advantages to getting comments to a retrospective in written form. As Ming Zhi (a software engineer in the IBM China lab) points out, in the Chinese culture, developers that disagree with a specific statement will at times still say "yes" in global meetings, confusing their western teammates. Having the comments in written form removes some of this ambiguity.

Offering Anonymity

In general, offering a way to provide information to the retrospective through anonymous, nonverbal comments can improve the success of the retrospective. This enables those who are less comfortable speaking in front of others to contribute. Team can collect feedback before the meeting to give everyone time to think about what they want to share.

Norm Kerth suggests that teams engage in an exercise to measure how safe they feel about talking openly and determining if the team needs additional steps to feel safe engaging in a retrospective (2001). Without a safe environment, the team will not be able to deal with the issues they need to discuss.

Asking for Comments Before the Retrospective Meeting

Many IBM ScrumMasters remarked participation in retrospectives varies from person to person, and one good way of getting participation is asking for comments before the meeting and then working off those comments during the meeting.

Many ask the team for comments about issues or problems they noticed since the previous Sprint Retrospective and summarize them for team discussion. The result is still an action plan and a list of behaviors the team needs to change or continue in the period until the next Retrospective.

What Went Well and What Can We Improve?

Some teams within IBM use the questions: "What went well?," "What did we learn?," "What would you like to see done differently?," and "What still puzzles us?" (Kerth 2001). The organizer of the Retrospective sends an email to each participant or provides a central repository where participants can enter their responses. In one case, Matt Ganis, a ScrumMaster in IBM's Sales and Distribution division, had his Scrum Team supply comments in a word-processing file. These files were then sent by the individual team members to his secretary, who extracted the attachment, renamed it (to preserve anonymity), and passed it to the facilitator for summarization.

In some cases, the team may know who raised an issue, and in other cases, the team may prefer to be able to provide comments anonymously.

Providing Questions to Focus the Discussion

Many teams use IBM Rational Self Check or a variation on the approach (Kroll and Krebs 2008). With this approach, team members respond to a set of questions developed or selected by the team. The questions represent items the team believes are important to using Scrum. The following is an example used to help the team evaluate their use of daily Scrums: Do you conduct daily 15-minute meetings covering what you did, what you are going to do, and to identify any obstacles? Although the team can identify any number of questions, IBM coaches recommend that teams use fewer than 15 to keep it quick and to target specific areas where the team will find the highest value from providing responses. The purpose is to focus on a few issues and address them *effectively* instead of trying to address a lot of issues and address them *poorly.*

The team words the questions so team members can answer them on a scale of one to ten, with ten being the best response. A one suggests the person responding believes the team never does the practice. A five suggests the person responding believes the team does the practice half the time or feels they do the practice poorly. A ten suggests the person responding feels the team masters the practice. Team members can provide any number from one to ten.

Once each team member provides their answers, the retrospective facilitator consolidates the results, calculating an average and standard deviation for each question. The responses that received a low average or a high standard deviation are marked for discussion during the retrospective meeting. A low average indicates the team believes they are carrying out a practice poorly and a high standard deviation means different members of the team have a different understanding of how well the team is doing. Both cases are good opportunities for a focused discussion.

Having a consistent set of questions helps teams to track their progress over time, increasing their overall process improvement efforts.

Consolidating Comments Is Extra Work

Be aware that techniques that involve getting comments from team members before the retrospective can involve extra work for the person asking for them. Leslie Ekas, an Agile and Lean coach for IBM's Software group, comments on this approach:

> It adds time for the person doing it, there's no question. It took me an hour or two for a recent reflection I did with comments from 30–35 people. It does take time, but it did get comments from people that I would not have heard from. So, I felt it was worth the time in that case. I would not do it all the time for a big-enough crowd. When I worried I would not hear from certain people and I wanted to make sure everyone had a voice, this approach worked for me.

Ming Zhi Xie, an agile coach for IBM China Development Lab, suggested a lower-effort approach to this method. His approach is to have the team identify issues they would like to discuss during the reflection in an online database. This keeps the issues anonymous and non-confrontational at the start.

Conducting the Retrospective

As previously outlined, distributed teams typically have the meeting facilitator or ScrumMaster collect comments from team members for the retrospective ahead of time. The entire team then openly discusses the comments during the meeting. Andy Pittaway, an IBM Executive Project Manager, reports that his teams often find it helpful to have a facilitator who is not part of the team run their retrospectives. By doing this, the facilitator of the retrospective can focus on the job of facilitating and remain impartial. Pittaway further comments "that it is often useful for the external facilitator (from an observation perspective) to gather ideas for their own team—in a way allowing for cross-organizational continuous improvement."

Discussing Reported Issues

During their retrospective, the team reviews the reported issues and, if others feel strongly enough, the team addresses them, creates their action plans, and logs them as actions they will revisit in follow-on Sprint retrospectives to evaluate their success.

Corville Allen, a Technical Lead for IBM's WebSphere Process Server, takes the following approach when leading his team's retrospectives:

> *I keep it anonymous. But as I talk about the comments, I give the opportunity to the person who provided the comment to speak up if they wanted to add something. So I will say: "Someone did not like how we did code coverage in this release. Does that person want to clarify?" and if they speak up, then that is fine and they usually do.*

This is an important idea; remember, as we stated earlier, it is much easier for participants on a conference call to keep quiet rather than speak up. Because of this, having a set of talking points prepared ahead of time can help drive the meeting. One approach to achieve this is asking all team members to provide two issues they think the team needs to fix and to propose solutions on how to fix them.

As Elizabeth Woodward remembers:

> *In the beginning, one team I worked with had retrospectives where people just wanted to get through it as fast as possible, not necessarily taking full advantage of the meeting they were having. Having those talking points helped to better focus discussions on how the team could improve instead of coming in with a blank slate.*

When using this approach, the person consolidating the issues may see patterns emerge in what team members are identifying. The issues may also turn out to be a mixed set of results, but the issues people identified will still help create some conversation. One method to complete this approach is to list all issues team members identified in a spreadsheet, a wiki, or an electronic agile project management tool such as IBM Rational Team Concert without identifying the people who sent the comments. In the retrospective, the meeting facilitator can then show the results to the team and identify the top issues the participants want to discuss during the retrospective.

Giving Everyone a Chance to Engage

The meeting facilitator needs to balance speaking opportunity during the retrospective teleconference and keep the people on the call aware of who is speaking—the facilitator or members of the team. The team members should be speaking most of the time, and the facilitator should be identifying who is making which points to open them up for response and discussion by others on the team. Teams may want to adopt a meeting protocol where the person speaking identifies themselves before speaking—for example, "This is Paul, and I think ...." This can be invaluable to new teams where they need to "learn" their teammate's voice on a conference call.

Elizabeth Woodward, an IBM Transformation Consultant, uses the following technique when leading distributed retrospectives:

> Sometimes larger personalities can drown out certain team members on the teleconference. It is important to keep track of who is speaking and who has not had a chance to respond. By calling on those individuals, the facilitator may be giving the person an opportunity to respond by waiting for a good break in the conversation. "Bob, thanks. Mary.... On Bob's point about not finding any value in the burndown chart, we haven't had a chance to hear from you yet. Did you have anything to add to this topic?" This politely ends Bob's longer dialog and opens the door for Mary to provide comments.

Extroverts like to think aloud, whereas introverts prefer to listen first, consider what others are sharing, and talk when they are confident in their thoughts. Meeting facilitators can help balance discussions by letting the extroverts speak first and then calling on introverts to share their conclusions.

Some team members may go on and on and on. Often they are restating a point, thinking the team does not understand because they do not have the visual confirmation they would receive during a face-to-face meeting. One technique the meeting facilitator can use is to repeat what team members have said and ask if that captures the concern, or they can let the speaker know they captured it in the meeting notes.

Another way that distributed teams prevent this issue is by displaying the notes using a screen-sharing tool. This enables everyone to see someone captured their concerns and comments and allows them to make corrections as needed. To make it easier on the facilitator to focus on the meeting, some teams pick a scribe to take notes during the meeting.

Using Common Terminology

During the distributed retrospective, the meeting facilitator can promote understanding by making sure that everyone is using common terminology during the meeting. Language differences can obviously cause misunderstandings, but members of a team who all speak the same language may also find that they are interpreting words differently. John Sutcliffe, a Senior Manager with IBM Software Group Information Management's Performance Management organization, provides the following story:

> When IBM bought Cognos, the development team had discussions with the IBM build engineering team. They said they wanted to take over our installs, and we thought installs meant when you are done, the software runs. They meant, "We'll drop the files onto the machine, and then you can take over and do the configuration to make it run."

State the Obvious

One technique to use on a teleconference is to paraphrase the speaker or state the obvious. Paraphrasing the speaker can help identify miscommunication and help the speaker clarify what they meant to say.

Keep the Conversation on Track

Most people who have attended a retrospective have experienced the case where someone on the team, perhaps themselves, has taken the conversation off track. It can be difficult to interrupt without the visual cues, but the facilitator of the retrospective can help to bring the conversation back on course by asking the following questions:

- How does this fit in with the topic the team is discussing? This question helps the team to consider the current topic and whether they are on track or need to adjust.
- This is an important discussion, but not necessarily retrospective. Should we table this discussion for another meeting? (Schedule the meeting if the team believes there is value.)
- How do you want to capture that topic in the notes? This question forces the speaker to consider how their points fit in with the topic and to capture their concerns succinctly.

Managing Time Effectively

Besides making sure team members stay on topic, the meeting facilitator needs to manage the time spent on discussing the different issues effectively. Because of the more emotional nature of a retrospective meeting, it is good practice to try to ensure the meeting starts and ends at the scheduled time. When team members see retrospectives continually running longer than originally planned, they may find less value in taking part in or even attending the meeting.

One reason behind the approach of identifying topics before the meeting by polling team members is to allow more focused discussions on a limited range of topics. Once the team identifies the top two or three issues, the team should timebox the time spent discussing each of them.

When the team reaches the final minutes of the allotted time, the meeting facilitator starts working with the team to identify if they want to try to work on this issue in the next Sprint. If this is the case, the next step is to start identifying the action items the team needs to take and the goal they want to achieve in the Sprint. At the end of the allotted time, the team moves on to the next topic.

When limiting the discussions to a limited set of issues, it is important for the team to agree this is the right set to be talking about in the meeting. The meeting facilitator may want to keep a window of time open for unplanned issues that come up during the retrospective.

Release Retrospectives

Norman Kerth describes one method typically used for retrospectives that cover longer periods of a Scrum project or an entire Scrum project in his book, *Project Retrospectives: A Handbook for Team Reviews* (Kerth 2001). In Kerth's method, when asking a team to take part in a retrospective, the entire team meets to pick apart a particular time span of a project.

The team talks about the project, and then defines and records the milestones in the project. The milestones are specific points in time during the project that were memorable or important in the minds of team members. Teams do this so when people begin discussing their involvements, they can think back on the project and perhaps remember their feelings or thoughts during that particular moment.

There is no rule about the number of milestones the team can place on their timeline. Obviously, the more milestones, the harder it becomes for everyone on the team to make comments about that specific time frame, and it may become harder to manage.

For their first retrospective, Matt Ganis provided the sample of the timeline shown in Figure 9.4 that his team came up with to describe their project.

In this project, the team was a newly formed agile team. One of the first thoughts that came to the collective team's memory when asked about their experience was the early training they all went through together. The first few milestones were about the team formation, training, and early results at some new practices like Daily Scrum meetings. The next set of milestones simply referred to the start of the project, a midpoint in the release where a major product demonstration occurred, and the product's use into production.

It does not matter what the specific milestones are. What matters is the various members on the team can use those milestones to talk about their feelings about the team's performance and the way they functioned at specific points in the project.

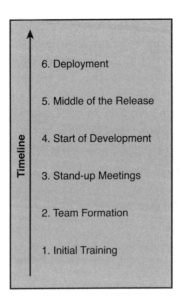

Figure 9.4   Project milestones

Once the team creates their timeline, the work begins. The participants of the retrospective need to think about each milestone on the timeline and comment about their feelings during the project. Specifically, they need to think about the answers to the following four questions:

- What did we do well at this milestone?
- Given what we did at this milestone, how could we do it better?
- What did we learn (about ourselves, our process, or our project) at this milestone?
- Looking back at this milestone, what is still puzzling or what open questions remain?

Summary

Each distributed Scrum Team in a scaled environment engages in a Sprint Retrospective at the end of each Sprint. Where multiple teams work on a project together, they conduct another joint retrospective that provides them with an opportunity to improve in their cross-team collaboration and ability to work together to deliver a project. How often scaled teams will meet depends on how much interaction they have between them.

Trust is at the heart of openness and is important to a successful retrospective. Meeting facilitators can use distributed techniques and good preparation skills to get to know the team and to provide a comfortable, open environment. Facilitators of distributed retrospectives rely on effective facilitation skills to balance communication on the teleconference.

To complement their Sprint Retrospectives, some teams may also benefit from Release Retrospectives that allow the team to discuss key milestones during the previous project.

Each retrospective should result in action items the team commits to address at the next opportunity. Retrospectives help teams to adapt and fine-tune their performance to deliver greater business value.

Jean Tabaka's book, *Collaboration Explained*, provides a wealth of additional tips on how to facilitate meetings. Esther Derby's and Diana Larsen's book, *Agile Retrospectives*, and Norman Kerth's book, *Project Retrospectives*, both provide helpful tips for conducting retrospectives.

References

Derby, Esther and D. Larsen. *Agile Retrospectives: Making Good Teams Great*. Dallas, ST: Pragmatic Bookshelf, 2006.

Kerth, Norman L. *Project Retrospectives: A Handbook for Team Reviews*. New York: Dorset House Publishing Co., Inc., 2001.

Kroll, P. and B. Krebs. *Survey Introducing IBM Rational Self-Check for Software Teams*. June 3, 2008. http://www.ibm.com/developerworks/rational/library/edge/08/may08/kroll_krebs/index.html.

Tabaka, Jean. *Collaboration Explained: Facilitation Skills for Software Project Leaders*. Boston: Addison-Wesley Professional, 2006.

CHAPTER 10

Closing Thoughts

"Action is the foundational key to all success."

Pablo Picasso

At certain points during the development cycle, teams need to stop, look at what they are doing, and make subtle mid-course changes if the need arises. Teams refer to the way of performing this "self-analysis" as a **"reflection"** or **"retrospective"** (Kerth 2001). Scrum Teams manage change and risk by adapting. But to adapt, they must identify opportunities for change and decide if they should undertake them.

The reality is that working with distributed teams can be very challenging whether you are using Scrum or not. The challenges increase as the type of distribution increases from Collocated, to Distributed Part-Time, to Distributed with Overlapping Work Hours to Distributed with No Overlap in Work Hours. If possible, large-scale distributed teams should look for ways to reduce their level of distribution and organize as cross-functional, collocated Scrum Teams.

Our goal throughout the process of writing this book was to identify the following:

- The challenges that teams encounter
- Solutions for dealing with the challenges
- The impact of different approaches

Having a strong understanding of the core principles, roles, meetings, and artifacts of Scrum is essential. Before making changes to Scrum, distributed teams need to understand the potential impact of making the change. They need to get to their root problems to determine if they need to improve in their understanding and adherence to Scrum, rather than immediately thinking that Scrum needs to be changed. As an example, we have encountered some teams that have decided to skip the Daily Scrum because members of their distributed team skip the meetings. Asking *why* will help the team to get to the root problem. Why are they skipping meetings? Are they not getting the value that they should out of them? Does the Daily Scrum fall outside of normal working hours so that it is impossible for some members to attend? Rather than changing Scrum by cancelling the Scrum meetings, ask the questions that will allow your team to deal with the root issue.

We strongly recommend that teams have the final say in the approaches they will use because they are the ones who are responsible for delivering on their commitments. One important key to having success as a distributed team is to have a high commitment level from all team members, and the best way to get that is to give them ownership over how they will work.

Another key to success is valuing the entire team and not having an "us versus them" atmosphere between different Scrum Teams on the project. When teams working together do not have overlapping working hours, it can be challenging to build relationships. The best ways to do this is to find ways to share the pain of being a distributed team, to get to know each other as people, and to foster frequent, quality communications between team members.

Teams should also use their Sprint Retrospectives to see what they are doing and how they are communicating is working for them; when they need to adjust, they should do so as fast as possible. Retrospectives are powerful tools that help teams be responsive to their stakeholder needs as well as their own.

Teams should feel free to adjust any of the approaches and solutions that we present to help them better suit their needs. Our hope is that you will share what you learn with the global Scrum community, so that everyone can continue to improve.

We wish you luck in your adventure as a distributed Scrum Team!

Index

Addison Wesley

REGISTER

THIS PRODUCT

informit.com/register

Register the Addison-Wesley, Exam Cram, Prentice Hall, Que, and Sams products you own to unlock great benefits.

To begin the registration process, simply go to **informit.com/register** to sign in or create an account. You will then be prompted to enter the 10- or 13-digit ISBN that appears on the back cover of your product.

Registering your products can unlock the following benefits:

- Access to supplemental content, including bonus chapters, source code, or project files.
- A coupon to be used on your next purchase.

Registration benefits vary by product. Benefits will be listed on your Account page under Registered Products.

**informIT.com**

THE TRUSTED TECHNOLOGY LEARNING SOURCE

Addison-Wesley | Cisco Press | Exam Cram
IBM Press | Que | Prentice Hall | Sams

SAFARI BOOKS ONLINE

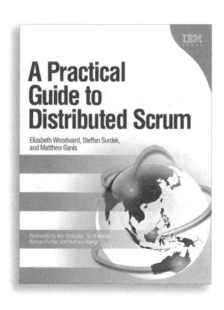